The Ultralight Angler

The Ultralight Angler

How to Catch Big Fish on Light Tackle

Mark Feldman

ILLUSTRATED BY TOM MCFARLAND

Ragged Mountain Press
Camden, Maine

Published by Ragged Mountain Press
10 9 8 7 6 5 4 3 2 1

Library of Congress Cataloging-in-Publication Data
Feldman, Mark L.
The ultralight angler : big fish on light tackle / Mark Feldman ;
illustrated by Tom McFarland
p. cm.
Includes index.
ISBN 0-07-020475-6 (alk. paper)
1. Fishing. 2. Fishing tackle. I. Title.
SH441.F44 1995
799.1'2—dc20 95-10777
CIP

Questions regarding the content of this book should be addressed to:
Ragged Mountain Press
P.O. Box 220
Camden, ME 04843
207-236-4837

Questions regarding the ordering of this book should be addressed to:
The McGraw • Hill Companies
Customer Service Department
P.O. Box 547
Blacklick, OH 43004
Retail customers: 1-800-822-8158
Bookstores: 1-800-722-4726

A portion of the profits from the sale of each Ragged Mountain Press book is donated to an environmental cause.

The Ultralight Angler is printed on recycled paper containing a minimum of 50% total recycled paper with 10% postconsumer de-inked fiber. ♻

Printed by Quebecor Printing, Fairfield, PA
Design by Eugenie S. Delaney
Production and page layout by Janet Robbins
Edited by James R. Babb, Ellen Egan, Ann Greenleaf, and Pamela Benner

With thanks to S. Paul Natoli

and David Brickman for showing

a boy how to fish.

Contents

Acknowledgments

WHEN I WAS A YOUNG, arrogant university student, a professor took me aside one day to set the record straight—she explained that whatever knowledge I had acquired derived from the intelligence and insight, the effort and experience of those who came before me.

Fishing is no exception. This book is a collection of lessons I learned mostly from others, occasionally the hard way. I am grateful to all those who have taught me about the art of ultralight fishing.

My thanks to Bill Kirk at *New Zealand Fisherman* for giving me the opportunity to write about fishing. And thanks also to the librarians at the Summit Public Library for their help in gathering material. Gail M. Morchower at the IGFA library was especially helpful.

Special thanks to Tony Goodman for teaching me the ways of the sea and to my wife, Elizabeth, for putting up with the life of a "fishing widow."

And, of course, a debt of gratitude to my Dad for having the wisdom to let me go when I was ready.

INTRODUCTION

The Magic River

BACK IN THE 1950S THE RIVER FLOWED quietly through the countryside of northern New Jersey, past a few scattered farms, on through the oak and hickory forests and the freshwater bogs, and out across the open meadows. Fish, turtles, newts, and frogs filled its waters. Squirrels, deer, fox, muskrats, raccoons, and woodchucks lived along its banks.

On a cool, fall evening an eight-year-old boy bicycling across a bridge paused to look down at the river and saw something that would change his life: in an upstream backwater, an enormous snapping turtle had caught a carp in its powerful jaws. The boy watched in fascination as the two creatures struggled in the water below. To him, the pool below the bridge was a savage place where wild creatures struggled for existence in an endless cycle of life and death. The child was enthralled; he longed to draw closer.

But it was late, and he was far from home. He pedaled on toward the first of the many housing developments that would soon scar the landscape. Darkness was approaching, and his parents were worried. The neighbors had already reported his wide-ranging journeys on the bicycle. When he returned unharmed, his parents greeted him with the anger born of relief. The boy was grounded for a month, and his bicycle locked up until the spring.

But the boy could not forget the great turtle or the dying carp, and he repeated the story to anyone who would listen. His parents were city

folk and didn't really understand this, but they recognized the need to wander—a desire they could not contain, one they should perhaps encourage.

His birthday came in April, as winter slowly gave way to spring and life began to reappear in the forests around the house. It was the perfect occasion for the return of his bicycle; and with it, he got permission to ride to the river.

There was another gift. It came in three packages—two small boxes and a long cylinder. From the first little box came an ancient bait-casting reel donated by a fisherman uncle. The second box held a child's book on fishing. The long cylinder contained a brand-new, solid-fiberglass fishing rod. Obsession quickly replaced excitement as the boy endlessly practiced casting on the quiet street. After weeks of work he could throw a one-ounce weight across the road without creating a backlash in the old baitcaster. He read and reread the fishing book until he could tie knots, make bait, and figure out where fish might live.

By the end of April the river had warmed. Armed with his new fishing rod, the boy returned at last to the bridge, the snapping turtle, and the carp.

Beneath the busy bridge lay a different world. Under thick concrete, the songs of birds and the splashes of fish were easily heard above the river's quiet flow and the din of New York commuters. The current had washed a deep hole in the river bottom where the water swirled around a concrete piling. Close upstream was an eddy. He'd seen a picture of one just like it in his fishing book, and he knew that its swirling motion dispersed food to the fish swimming in the waters around the piling. Here he would find his prey.

The boy was shaking with excitement. He was Tribal Hunter, alone in the wilderness, fearlessly seeking food for his people. Trembling hands kneaded a piece of bread into a doughball and buried the hook inside. The first few casts flew wide of the mark, but persistence paid off—a cast landed just inches from the eddy.

Within seconds the heavy glass rod arced, and the boy felt himself locked in mortal combat with the unknown. As the great fish fought against the line, the great hunter became a child again, heart beating wildly within frail chest. The fish—many years older than the boy and far closer to the heart of life—hurled his weight against the heavy rod. The boy's arms began to weaken; gradually he was drawn toward the water.

The boy now knew he was just another element in the wild world he had sought, where the hunter can suddenly become the hunted.

With desperate energy he locked battered fingers around the reel and began to struggle back up the beach, slowly dragging the flailing fish onto the sandbar, its great tail flapping against the hard sand.

But some things are not meant to be. The carp gave one last great heave, flipped free of the hook, and slipped back into the protective waters of the Magic River.

As years passed, the boy spent more and more time by the river, hoping to recapture the thrill of that first fishing adventure. His skills improved, and he discovered he could hook more fish by using lighter tackle. And with the light lines, the fish always had a chance to escape, preserving the excitement of the struggle.

Since no one at home wanted to clean fish, he usually released his catch to fight another day. He took great satisfaction in his ability to pluck the fish from the river at will and great pleasure in his power to restore their freedom.

Later the river provided a refuge from the trials of a painful adolescence in the crowded and complex life of suburban New Jersey. He escaped to the river from a harshly competitive society, and the river engulfed him in harmony.

As his fishing skills matured and the lines became lighter, the young man concentrated on fish to the exclusion of all else, learning to fuse intellect and instinct in a contest against the fish and their river. The struggle satisfied his drive to hunt, to conquer adversity, and to participate in something greater than himself.

Today, anglers everywhere are discovering what that young man learned on the river. In a world with too many people and too few fish, ultralight tackle can evoke the exhilaration of that first fishing trip without threatening the fish populations that provide such pleasure to us all.

CHAPTER ONE

A Little Bit About Ultralight

BEGINNING ANGLERS FIND just catching fish a challenge. Then, with time and experience an angler acquires the proficiency to find and hook fish relatively easily. What chance does a big bluefish or jack have against 8-pound (4-kilogram) line in the hands of an experienced angler? Where's the excitement, where's the challenge if the angler *knows* the fish will be landed barring divine intervention?

On the other hand, there's plenty of excitement when you're playing a big fish with a 2-kg line—one false move and the fish will be gone, dragging your terminal tackle behind him. And the challenge of landing a big fish *against* the odds is far more interesting than simply filling the boat with the carcasses of your victims. Ultralight fishing can be difficult and frustrating, though, unless you master the techniques and the gear.

As a beginner, you can expect to lose most fish heavier than the strength of your line, but with practice you can routinely land 10- to 20-pound (5- to 9-kg) fish on 2-kg line—*if* you pick your times and your spots well. Landing big bass in heavy weed with ultralight gear is just not possible. Neither is landing sharks on the flats after dark. (Yes, the sharks are there and feeding, but without enough light you won't be able to follow your fish and boat it safely.)

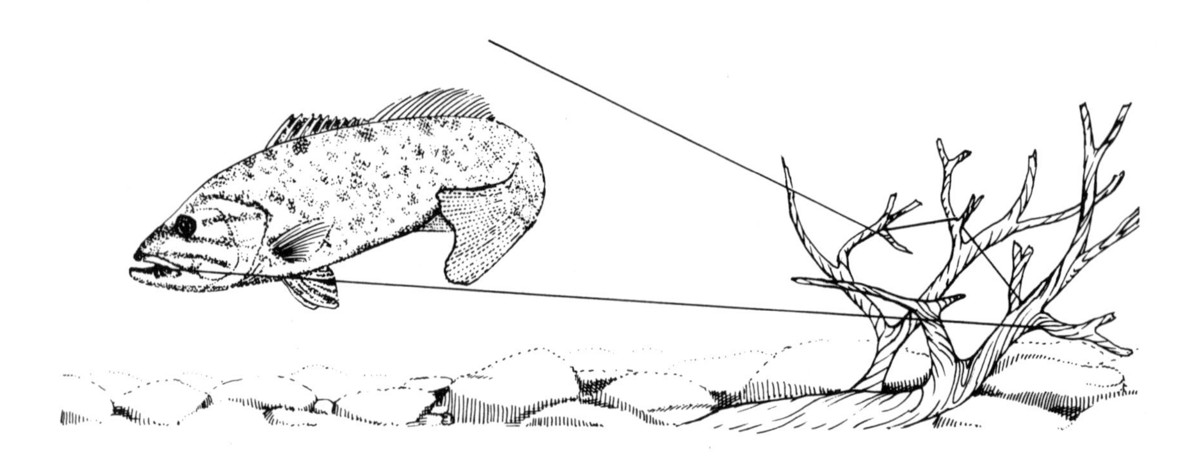

Don't try to fish ultralight around snags or heavy cover. It will ruin your day.

To catch big fish on ultralight line, you'll need high-tech tackle. You've got to know enough about it to make an informed choice at the store and to care for it afterward, or it will fail when you need it most.

To understand ultralight tackle it's helpful to know something about its history.

The breaking strength of ultralight line is designated in metric units of 1 or 2 kilograms (kg). One-kg line is a little stronger than 2-pound line, and 2-kg line is a little stronger than 4-pound. Hereafter, all references to ultralight-line strength will be in kilograms. You will find the exact conversion factors in Chapter Two.

A Short History of Ultralight

While Americans were busy exploiting their seemingly limitless supplies of wildlife, the Europeans had already discovered that there were only so many fish to be caught. They had also learned that, in a competitive environment, it's the person with the most skill and the lightest tackle who brings home the fish.

The English were the first to develop the modern spinning reel. In 1905 Alfred Holden Illingworth found a way to cast light lines without using heavy weights and patented a reel design based on the spindles used in the booming textile industry. Its 3:1 gear ratio made it possible to both cast and retrieve lures without performing acrobatics.

Some of these "thread-line" reels made it to the United States, but they were expensive and not really necessary then. Most Americans still lived in the countryside, where there were plenty of fish and not too many people trying to catch them.

But things began to change after World War II. A French company called Mitchell developed a relatively compact and inexpensive spinning reel that was artfully marketed to American buyers. The impact of the new spinning reels remained modest until nylon fishing lines began to appear in the 1950s. By today's standards those lines were hopelessly stiff and tangle-prone, but they were far superior to the soggy linen or silk lines of the day. The Mitchell spinning reel and the monofilament nylon line were an unbeatable combination and a big step toward making ultralight fishing possible.

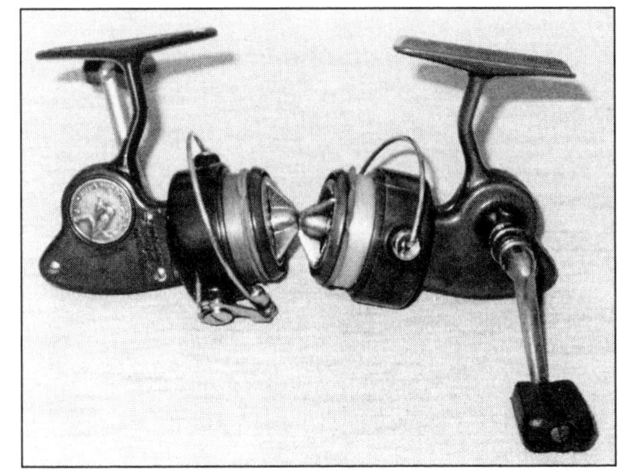

The Italians get the prize for producing the first true ultralight spinning reel. It was called the Alcedo Micron and, by any standard, it was a great reel; it's avidly sought by collectors and tackle connoisseurs even today. It features a compact body but a reasonably large spool, which minimizes the spinning reel's greatest fault: Dreaded Line Twist. It's hard to believe these reels were made nearly 40 years ago; I have two of them and still find them useful.

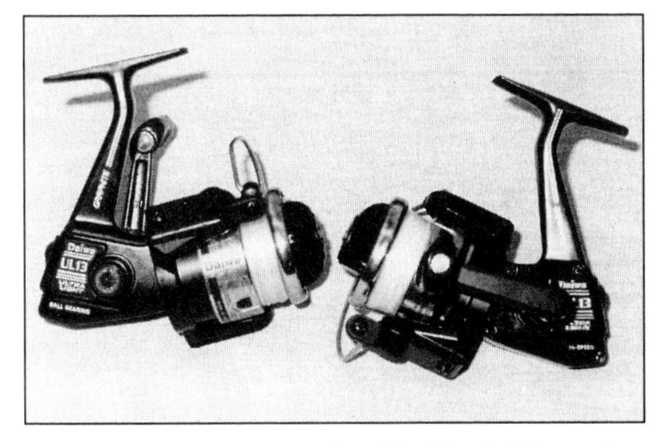

Top: The Alcedo Micron, the world's first ultralight spinning reel.

Bottom: The Daiwa UL13, a modern spinning reel designed specifically for ultralight lines; only the details have changed since the Alcedo Micron was designed 40 years ago.

Labeling confusion set in after the Alcedo Micron was introduced. The designation "ultralight" was applied to a wide variety of seemingly unrelated equipment. Bass anglers using 8-pound (4-kg) line, medium-size spinning reels, and fast-action 6-foot rods considered their tackle ultralight. Trout anglers using 1-kg line, miniature spinning reels, and slow-action 7-foot rods considered their tackle ultralight. Steelhead anglers using 2-kg line, any reel, and 12-foot noodle rods considered *their* tackle ultralight. European coarse anglers using ½-kg line, single-action reels, and 15-foot rods considered *their* tackle ultralight.

So what is "ultralight"? It's a relative term and can mean whatever you want it to. In this book the term relates to the use of 1- and 2-kg line to catch hard-fighting fish weighing more than 4 pounds. We'll focus on the techniques you need to master for open-water lake fishing as well as for harbor and bay fishing. You'll also find information on picking sites you can fish with 2-kg line from the shorelines of large rivers and estuaries.

My goal is for you to know how, when, and where to use ultralight for maximum enjoyment. I don't want to see you wasting your time trying to pull pike out of thick weed with 1-kg line, and I don't want you to be hopelessly outgunned trying to pull a yellowtail out of 60 feet of water with a noodle rod. Ultralight fishing is about meeting the challenge of catching powerful fish in a fair fight. It's about having fun and maybe—just maybe—catching a world record.

A Brief Look at the Gear

Once you decide to start fishing ultralight, you'll have to make a basic choice between spinning and bait-casting tackle. To make that choice you will need to understand the differences between spinning and bait-casting reels and the effect of these differences on the delicate line you'll be using. The choice of a rod and terminal tackle will then follow naturally from your decision on which reel style to master.

In Chapter Three, on fishing reels, we'll explore the pros and cons of each basic type, and you'll learn the necessary bits of information you need to know before you buy. You'll also learn about a few elementary tests to determine a reel's quality and how to do those tests without spending all day at it.

The Reels

There are two basic types of ultralight reels: the *spinning reel* (also called a *fixed-spool* or *thread-line reel)* and the *bait-caster (overhead, casting,* or *rotating-spool reel).* On a spinning reel the line runs over a very hard roller-bearing when it's being retrieved. This bearing is the most important part of the reel; it must roll freely under pressure to avoid unnecessary line wear as the monofilament passes over it.

ABU GARCIA INC.

The Abu Garcia C4, the spinning reel I prefer for 1-kg line.

When you cast with a spinning reel, the roller-bearing is pulled aside and the line flows off the reel while the fixed spool remains stationary. The spool moves only when the bail is closed and the drag is activated by a hard pull on the line.

When a fish pulls line off a spinning reel (with the bail closed), the spool rapidly revolves. With each revolution, the line twists once. This line twist can weaken the line by up to 15 percent and increases the chance of a tangle as the torque builds on the fragile line. If you're having a bad day and allow a twisted line to slacken while you're playing a fish, the line can tangle around your rod tip. This usually means you'll lose the fish and terminal tackle; if you're having a *really* bad day, the rod tip will break too.

Line twist can be an especially grievous problem for the angler who panics and keeps reeling in while the line is running out and the bail is closed. On a reel with a 5:1 gear ratio, the bail arm rotates five times for every turn of the handle. That means more than five twists will be added to the line with every turn of the handle if the fish is running as the angler is reeling!

In everyday fishing you can relieve the twist by removing all terminal tackle and letting the line flow freely in the current or towing it for a few seconds behind the boat. But you don't have that option when you're engaged in an ongoing battle with a large fish. All you can do then is try to adapt to working with a line that behaves like a rubber-band motor on a balsa-wood airplane.

This doesn't happen with the bait-caster. Since its spool rotates whenever the line is cast or retrieved, the line never develops a tendency to twist. It can, however, run off faster than the spool rotates, resulting in the horrendous situation known as *backlash,* or a *bird's nest.* This usually occurs during casting but can happen just as easily when there's a big fish on the line if the angler has set the drag too light or accidentally touches the spool-release button.

ABU GARCIA INC.

The Abu Garcia 5500C, an excellent bait-caster for ultralight lines.

Another danger is that the line can slip between the spool and the frame of the reel and wind itself around the gear shaft. The angler usually becomes aware of this about a tenth of a second before hearing the pop of the parting line. And a further, minor difficulty with bait-casters is the level-wind feature. Although this is a great asset with heavier lines, the rubbing causes unnecessary stress to ultralight gear. The level wind is easily removed, though; and it's easy to get in the habit of moving the line manually (with the thumb or index finger) instead. In Chapter Three you'll learn about another problem with bait-casters that will probably make you choose a spinning reel for your ultralight fishing needs.

The Rods

For every reel you see in a sporting-goods store or catalog, there are probably five or six appropriate rods. Faced with so many choices, you may be tempted to just throw up your hands—pick out something that looks nifty and call it a day. But that would be a costly mistake.

For the fact is that your selection is limited to those slow-action rods with the handle length and number and style of guides that are right for you. Rod length is simply a matter of personal preference, and it matters little whether the rod is made of fiberglass, graphite, or a combination. You don't need a wilderness guide to find your way through that forest of fishing rods. Once you know how to determine your few requirements, the way will be clear.

In our tendency to glamorize fishing rods, we often lose sight of the fact that they're just sticks, used as lever arms to cushion our delicate lines from the movements of fish. The line and the reel are far more important to your success than the rod.

The Line

Which line to buy is the most important and the most difficult decision to make. Your line selection determines your gear (reel, rod, lure) selection, and your gear selection determines your boat selection.

Ultralight lines are 1 or 2 kg (by our definition), and they are all made of monofilament nylon. Be thankful there are no other materials to choose from (yet) because you'll have a hard enough time selecting a suitable monofilament strand. The variations in quality and character, owing to differences in the manufacturing process, are mind-boggling.

Monofilament fishing lines are made of nylon polymers. Cheaper lines are made of just one polymer. Single-polymer lines tend to be extreme in their characteristics; generally they're very stiff and awkward to use.

Premium lines combine desirable characteristics like limpness and abrasion resistance, but they are more expensive to produce. One way to manufacture these premium fishing lines is to blend various polymers to yield a spectrum of desirable qualities. Another technique is to layer the lines—for instance, an inner core made of one polymer that resists stretch and imparts strength, and an outer sheath made of another polymer that provides flexibility and waterproofs the inner core. More on this in Chapter Two.

These are some of the factors to be considered when you evaluate monofilament: line consistency, knot strength, tensile strength, stiffness, abrasion resistance, water absorption, fatigue rate, and elasticity. When you understand these properties, you'll know why fishing lines may have failed you in the past, and you'll be able to pick better lines in the future.

Rods, reels, lures, and boats (the "glamour items") may be the hot topics among anglers—they're showy and pretty and shiny and pricey, and they perform. But the line supports it all.

Chapter Two

The Line

WHEN CHOOSING ULTRALIGHT TACKLE, your most fundamental and consequential decision will be selecting the appropriate line. If you change lines, you may have to modify your reel spools and change rods too.

Since any rod can perform perfectly with only one strength of line, your line choice determines your rod choice. If you change lines and the new monofilament is even half a kilogram weaker, your rod will be too powerful for the new line, and fish will break off before your rod forms that neat parabolic curve you'll learn about later on.

Similarly, since the thickness of identical-strength monofilament lines can vary by as much as 30 percent, you will probably have to change the backing on all your spools if you alter the diameter of your line. In Chapter Three you'll learn that you should always fill your spool right to the lip to improve casting and reduce line twist. You can't do that unless the spool has the right amount of backing to begin with.

Starting to sound complicated? Sure it is—people spend their whole lives researching and designing fishing line. You don't need to be an expert, but you *will* need to focus on a few of the characteristics of monofilament line that are most important to the ultralight angler.

The Basics

Monofilament fishing line is made from nylon. But that doesn't tell you much at all because there are many varieties of nylon, each manufactured from different combinations of *amides*. These amides are like beads on a string. When they are joined together so they can't slide around anymore, the amides are said to be *polymerized,* and the material they create when joined together is called a *polymer.* In chemist's language, nylon is a polymer formed from amides.

There are many sorts of amides, just as there are many varieties of beads. When you string different sorts of amides together, you get different sorts of nylon. Some amides form a brittle, hard nylon, while other amides form a wonderfully pliant, soft nylon. There are so many possible combinations that chemists are still developing new varieties more than 55 years after nylon was first invented.

But the chemists don't have to make their nylons from just one sort of amide. They can mix different types of amides together before polymerizing them into a string. This is like making a necklace from two different sorts of beads. It's more difficult, but it can produce a superior result.

When chemists mix amides, they try to combine the best characteristics of the individual forms. For instance, they can combine a hard, brittle nylon with a soft, supple type and hope to end up with a fishing line that is supple but hard enough to resist abrasion.

A nylon blended from two sorts of amides is called a *copolymer;* from three sorts, a *tripolymer.* Sometimes line manufacturers combine the characteristics of different nylons by layering them instead of mixing them together. In fishing line, an inner core of a soft, supple nylon combines nicely with an outer-layer nylon that is rigid but abrasion-resistant. No matter how it's done, combining amides is very difficult and expensive since they all melt at different temperatures and have different blending characteristics. That's why you pay more for a copolymer or tripolymer line.

Manufacturers add still other materials to the amides when they make fishing line, including heat stabilizers to prevent the nylon polymer from weakening in your tackle box, antioxidants to keep the nylon from combining chemically with other materials, and ultraviolet stabilizers to keep the sun from weakening the fishing line as you use it. Some manufacturers also apply an exterior coating to the nylon to prevent water absorption, increase abrasion resistance, or make the surface smoother so it glides easily through the rod guides.

Now that you know how nylon is made, you can appreciate why

different fishing lines have different qualities. Some are stiff and some are limp. Some are elastic and some are rigid. Some are hard and some are soft. The list goes on, but you'll get the idea during the rest of this chapter. Then you'll be able to decide for yourself which fishing line is best for your purposes.

Line Consistency

When fishing line is manufactured, the molten nylon is forced through tiny holes in an extrusion machine to form filaments a millimeter in diameter. The filaments are then stretched and relaxed until the desired thickness is achieved. The process is actually quite complex, and the potential for error exists at every step.

The diameter of any given length of cheaper monofilament line can vary by as much as 30 percent. With very thin strands like 1- and 2-kg, this variation is most dramatic. An inconsistent diameter creates weak spots all along the line that will mean lost fish for the unsuspecting angler.

Consistent line strength is critical to the success of the ultralight angler, and your line is only as strong as its weakest section. For this reason alone it's best to avoid cheaper lines and concentrate on evaluating the better brands. More expensive lines have fewer and smaller weak spots; they have the greater consistency you want.

But the only way you can be sure of line quality is to buy small spools of various lines, take them home, and test them yourself. One evening spent line testing will teach you more about how monofilament behaves under stress than you'll learn in a year of fishing, and that will mean fewer lost fish and more good times.

Line Testing

To test line at home you'll need a variety of weights—from about 30 grams (about an ounce) to 500 grams (about a pound). But there's no need to go out and buy a fine set of scientific weights; just collect a small stack of old, lead fishing weights and metal scraps. Then take them over to a local shop with a digital scale. Measure each weight separately and mark the amount in *grams* on its side with an indelible marker.

Those of you in countries that have not "gone metric" will have to go through the slightly painful process of learning about grams and kilograms because that's the language of international fishing today. Here's all you need to know:

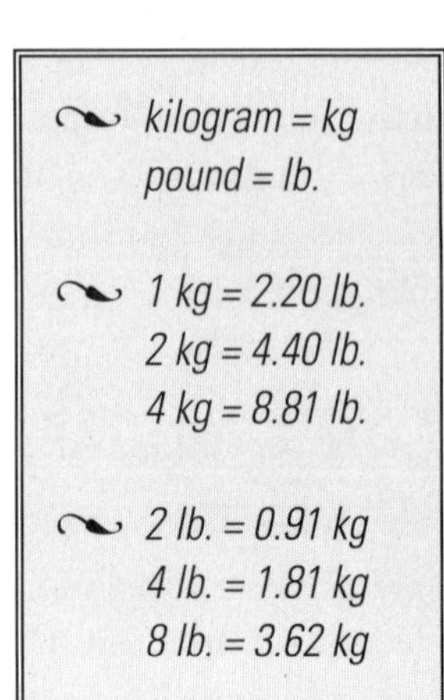
kilogram = kg
pound = lb.

1 kg = 2.20 lb.
2 kg = 4.40 lb.
4 kg = 8.81 lb.

2 lb. = 0.91 kg
4 lb. = 1.81 kg
8 lb. = 3.62 kg

With these conversion factors in mind, take your "metric" weights home and fashion two hooks out of heavy wire, or simply use two 10/0 fish hooks. To test a line, tie each end of a 6-foot (2-meter) length of monofilament to the hooks and hang it from a secure point on the ceiling. To avoid major trauma to your floor, place a small pad under the lower hook and you're ready to go.

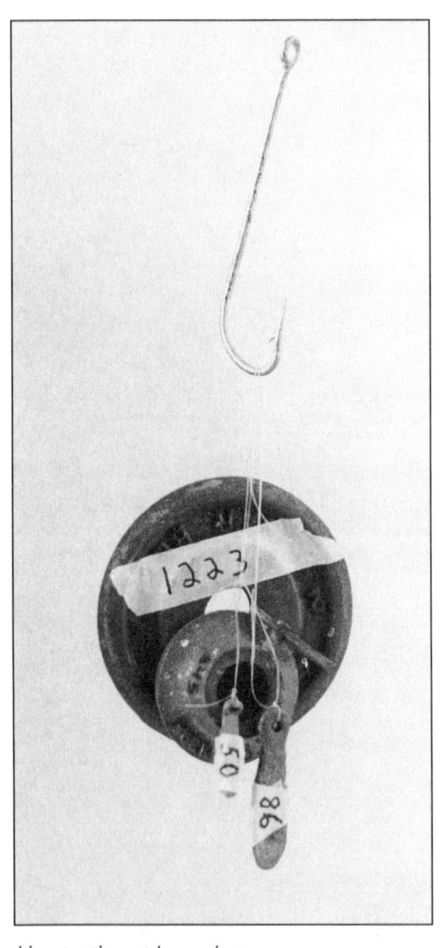

Line testing at home is as easy as hanging a few weights on a hook. Keep a pad under the weights to protect the floor.

The first step is to place a weight equal to half the line's breaking strength on the lower hook. For example, if you're testing 2-kg line, place a 1-kg weight on the hook. Then gradually and cautiously add more and more weight until the line breaks. It's very important not to add the weights abruptly since the force of a sudden impact will break the line and invalidate the test. You'll know when the line is getting close to breaking because it will start to stretch. Once that happens, be careful to add only very small weights (30 grams) each time, or you'll overshoot the line strength.

If the line breaks at or near either knot, the test will also be invalid. If you're a well-read angler, you probably expect the line to break at the knot because you "know" that any knot is weaker than the line it's tied from. Fortunately, that is not the case at all! There are several knots that will preserve full line strength if they are tied correctly. The key is to tie the knot without twisting the line or rubbing the surface coating off. Let's talk about how to do that next.

The Right Knot

When you fish ultralight, the strength of your line is the critical, controlling factor. The line is no stronger than its weakest section, and the weakest point in a quality line is *usually* the knot you tie. However, there are knots you can use that will actually be stronger than the line itself. The knot you should know is what I call the *double clinch*. I have never seen it in a book (though someone must have written about it before). I learned it from an Inuit in the Alaskan Arctic. There are some other knots that preserve line strength, but none are as easily tied as the double clinch, and none are as versatile.

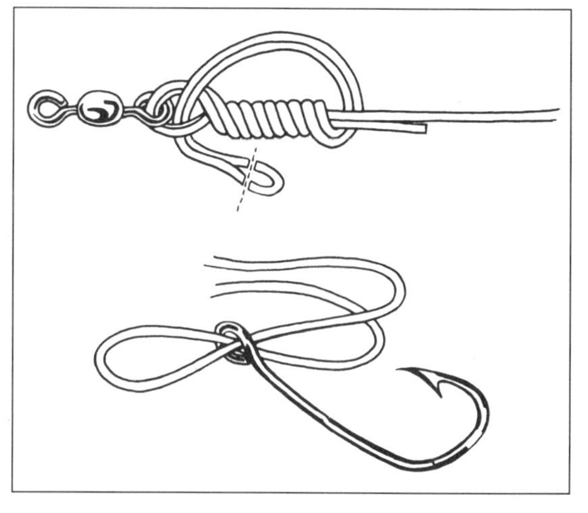

The double clinch knot is nothing more than a simple clinch tied with a doubled line.

Study the drawing of the double clinch for a minute, but read on before you rush off to tie the knot. You'll need a few details to make the knot work for you. The most important thing to remember is to double the line before you start to tie the knot, then pull the doubled end through the swivel and twist it four times. It is imperative that you wet the line with saliva before you tighten the knot; otherwise, the line will abrade itself as it's pulled tight, and that abrasion will weaken the line significantly.

Practice tying this knot over and over before you go fishing. Each time you tie the knot, examine it closely. If the line near the knot appears kinky, you know it's been abraded because you failed to lubricate it well, pulled it tight too quickly, or put too many twists in the doubled section of the line.

Test yourself by using a double clinch to tie a large hook to each end of a 6-foot (2-meter) section of 2-kg line as described under "Line Testing" above. After finishing the knots, pull steadily on the lower hook. If the

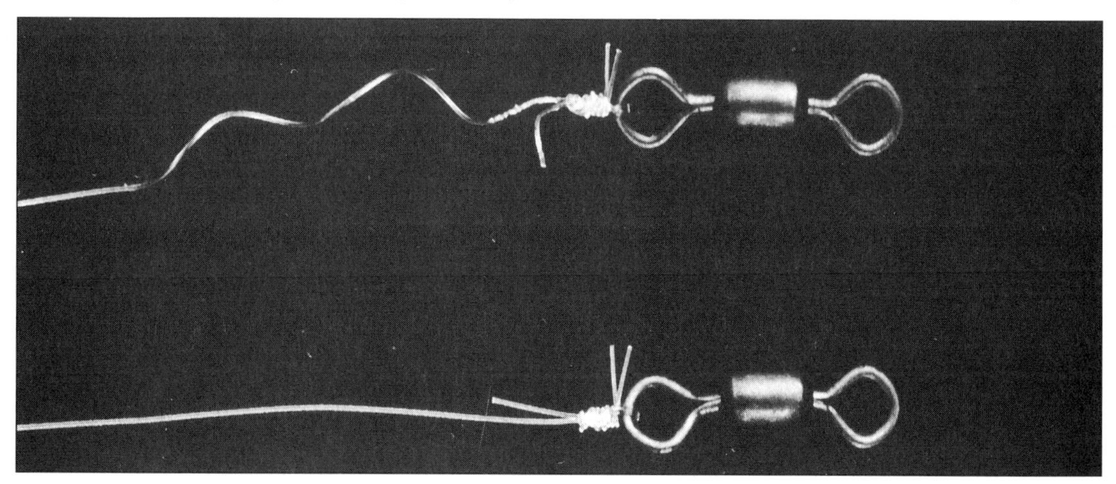

The double clinch on the bottom is correctly tied and will be stronger than the line. The example on the top was tied in a hurry. The result is a kinked and weakened line that will break easily.

line breaks within 1 inch (2 to 3 cm) of the knot or if you see the knot twist and slip, you blew it!

Go back and try it again. If the knot slipped and twisted as you pulled, you failed to tighten it adequately. If the line broke near the knot, you probably abraded it as you tightened it. When the line breaks well away from your knot most of the time and when the knot never slips, you've got it right.

The double clinch is the best knot I've found for tying ultralight lines. If there are any other knots that work as well, I doubt they would be so simple to tie. It is not important to know lots of knots to fish ultralight. The double clinch for your ultralight lines and the simple clinch for your leaders are the only two you need. If you learn to tie the double clinch so well that you can rig it in the dark, you will be far better off than if you can tie a great variety of knots with no great skill.

The best knot for your leaders is a simple clinch made with five turns of the single line. See the accompanying illustration for details. This is a common knot you can see in any fishing book, and I'm sure you already know how to use it. Nevertheless, I suggest you experiment with this knot at home so you can tie it quickly and correctly in the near dark of dawn, when you'll need it most. Since your leader material will generally be 10- to 20-kg (20- to 40-pound-test) nylon, the toughness of the leader knot usually doesn't matter because the ultralight line will be far weaker.

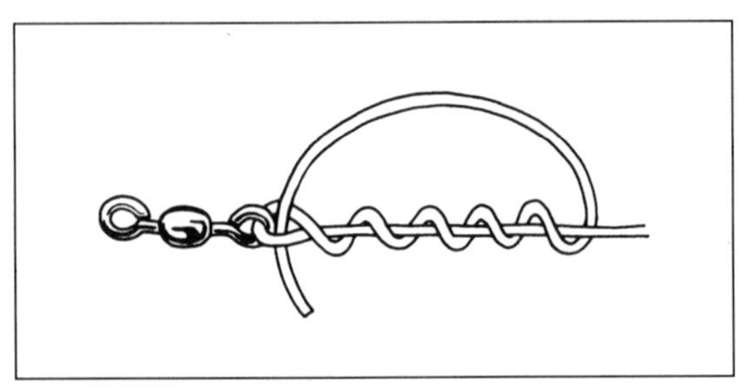

The simple clinch knot (also called the single clinch). This is the best choice for your leaders, where knot strength is not critical.

Some manufacturers claim that their lines have greater "knot strength" than other brands. This is almost always because the lines are more abrasion-resistant and/or supple. If you learn to tie the double clinch correctly, you'll find that knot strength, as a reason to buy a particular brand of line, will be irrelevant.

Tensile Strength

Another advertising claim of no significance to the ultralight angler relates to tensile strength—a measure of the line's strength for a given diameter. High-tensile-strength line is stronger than a lower-tensile-strength line of identical diameter.

This is important if you need a narrow line to cast as far as possible or want to pack as much line as you can on a reel spool. But ultralight lines are often too thin to work with comfortably, so it's actually to your advantage to use a line with a lower tensile strength. That's right, you want the opposite of what every manufacturer is trying to sell; you want a low-tensile-strength, thick line.

Stiffness

Some lines are stiffer than others; they behave almost like thin wire. This means they "set" into a fixed shape on the spool and come off in coils when you cast. It is a myth that the stiffer a line is, the more difficult it is to cast. In actual fact it's the diameter of the line, not line stiffness, that determines casting distance.

Castability is not an important factor with 1- and 2-kg lines. Casting weakens these lines by stretching and abrading them. It's best to move up to 3- or 4-kg line if you'll be casting a great deal. If you must do some casting with 1- and 2-kg line, you'll have to avoid the snap-of-the-wrist method of throwing the lure. Ultralight gear does not tolerate sudden stress. A classically powerful cast with ultralight generally leaves the lure and leader 50 yards from your boat and a broken line in your hand.

Even though stiffness has little to do with castability, you should avoid stiff lines nonetheless. They tend to lie in coils while you're fishing; and these coils soak up the movements of terminal tackle like a spring, so you remain blissfully unaware that a fish is slowly removing the bait from your hook. Limp monofilament is much more desirable. It will form a straight line between your rod tip and bait, so you can detect minute movements that could mean action is on the way.

There are two things you can do at home to reduce the line set that results from the inherent stiffness of monofilament. One is to fill your reel spools fully so the coils on the reel are as wide as possible. To do this properly, wrap the right amount of backing (garden cord makes a nice, soft

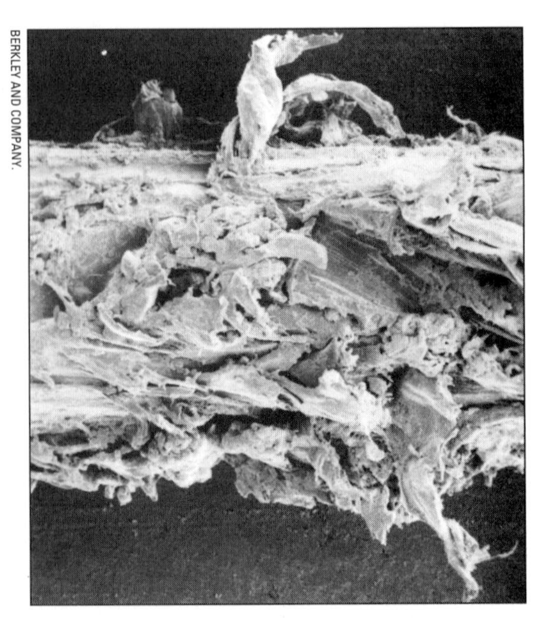

Line abrasion is not a pretty sight under a microscope.

backing) on the spool first so you don't end up with 500 yards (400 meters) of ultralight line on a single spool. The other is to select reels that have the widest possible spools to begin with. I'll go into more detail on these points in Chapter Three, on reels.

Abrasion Resistance

When you're using ultralight lines, the slightest nick while the mono is under pressure may mean the end of the fight. My wife and I frequently fish for sharks in the 45-pound (20-kg) range with 1-kg line. It takes hours to land a shark with such light tackle. During the fight we travel great distances and inevitably pick up a few strands of seaweed. If the weed remains undetected, it can wear its way through the line in minutes. Many a great fight has ended with a stream of angry curses because of the Dreaded Seaweed Factor.

The moral of the story is this: Look for lines with lots of abrasion resistance. Stiff lines offer abrasion resistance, but you now know that stiff lines are to be avoided. Some manufacturers achieve the combination of abrasion resistance and suppleness with coatings that also provide some waterproofing. These double-layered lines are more expensive, but they can have definite advantages. Another effective way to make a supple line tough is with a variety of polymers blended to form a sealed surface while retaining an inner limpness (copolymer or tripolymer lines). Either method works well.

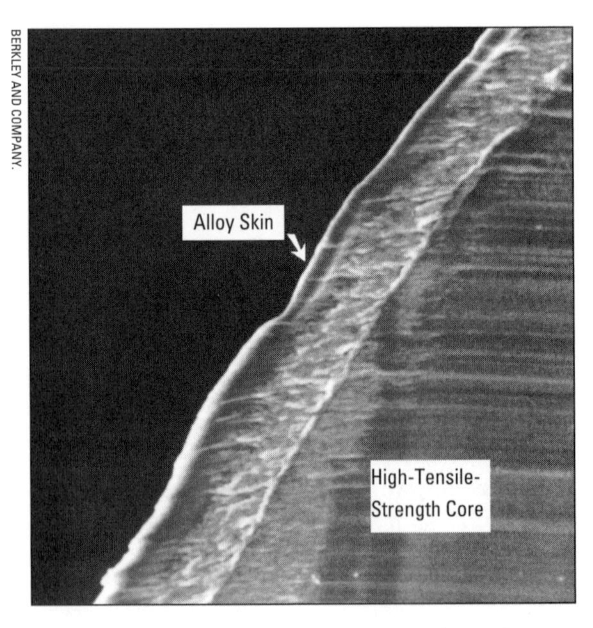

A cross section of a coated line as seen under a microscope.

It won't be long before there will be other ways to toughen the surface of a monofilament line, and I'm sure they'll be well advertised. But a manufacturer's claim of high abrasion resistance cannot always be trusted. You can test for abrasion resistance at home by putting the line under maximum stress with weights and rubbing it a bit with your fingernail. You'll be surprised to see how easily it breaks!

Water Absorption

All nylon lines absorb water. It's absorbed as a vapor at the boundary between the mono and the water, so it takes a while before the line is saturated. The more water the line absorbs, the weaker it gets. Prolonged immersion of unwaterproofed lines can cause a 10- to 20-percent reduction in strength.

Some manufacturers claim their lines have "dry to wet stability." These lines are said to absorb virtually no water and to maintain their full power when submerged. You can find out for yourself by testing the strength of a given line while it's dry, then soaking a few pieces for two hours in water and testing it again.

Since the International Game Fish Association (IGFA) uses wet lines to test strength, it is the wet strength that counts if you're pursuing world records. In the ultralight category the IGFA recognizes 1- and 2-kg line classes. In the 1-kg-line class, the lines can test up to 1 kg (1,000 grams) in wet strength and still be acceptable. That means you will be fishing with a handicap if you use a line that tests out at 2 pounds wet strength, since 2 pounds equals only 907 grams.

If you're after world records, you want to get the maximum allowable strength from your lines. So select lines with a wet strength as close as possible to the IGFA limits of 1 and 2 kg. Just be careful when analyzing a manufacturer's label. By law, a fishing line must be as strong as or stronger than the label indicates. On the other hand, if a manufacturer states that a line meets an IGFA category, the line must be weaker than the label indicates.

That's all pretty confusing, so here are some examples: Let's say a given label says "2 pound, IGFA class 1 kilogram." This means the line will test out at more than 2 pounds (907 grams) and less than 1 kg (1,000 grams). Another label might say "4 pound, IGFA class 2 kilogram." This means the line will be stronger than 1,814 grams and weaker than 2 kg (2,000 grams).

If all this is too much for you, just look for lines labeled "tournament grade" or "class" lines. They're usually guaranteed to pass the IGFA tests in their line-class category.

Some manufacturers pretest their lines for you—they test the line strength at the factory and give you an exact strength, in grams, on the label. For instance, a label might say "IGFA class 2 kg, pretest strength 1,850 grams." That means the line broke with a stress of 1,850 grams at the factory. What you don't know is how much weaker the line will get when it's wet or how many areas of the line are weaker than the sample that was tested!

So it still pays to do your own line testing at home, and it's better to do it in grams. Although manufacturers often indicate line strength in pounds, it's worthwhile to learn the metric system because the IGFA ultimately determines the strength of ultralight lines in grams.

Fatigue Rate

The more a line is used, the weaker it gets. When a fish runs, the line is dragged over the guides and through the water; it becomes worn and stretched. Such abuse can easily cut the line's strength in half, and you'll end up losing the next fish without knowing how it happened.

It's best to discard any line on which you've caught a big fish or any line you think has been damaged by repeated use. A spool should be replaced when it has 70 meters (or less) of line. Always carry two or three extra spools full of line in your tackle box. You don't want to spend your precious fishing time putting line on an empty spool.

Keep each spare spool in a small plastic bag so it doesn't get nicked by metal edges in the tackle box. Be sure to rotate your spools frequently. The longer a spool sits in a hot place (like your tackle box or car), the weaker it gets. Sustained exposure to heat or light can weaken nylon lines by up to 20 percent.

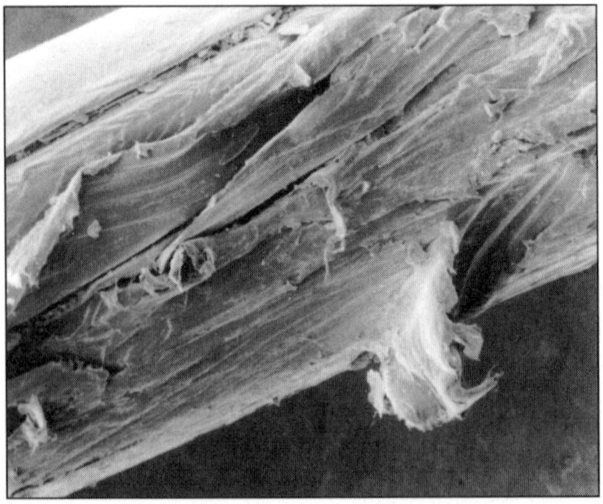

BERKLEY AND COMPANY.

A microscopic nick in ultralight monofilament can reduce line strength by 25 percent.

By now you're probably beginning to realize how fragile monofilament fishing line really is. It can be weakened by heat, light, rough surfaces, knots, and water absorption. I don't want you to become paranoid about your fishing line, but there is one other invisible way to damage it that you should know about: excessive stretching.

Elasticity

All monofilament lines stretch. The degree of expansion varies a great deal and can easily go to 30 percent if you're using cheaper, stiffer lines. Why do stiffer lines stretch more? Because the manufacturers will counteract the inherent stiffness of the polymer they're using by leaving more stretch in the line when it's being extruded and processed.

Just what does a 30-percent stretch mean to you? It means that 100 meters of line will become 130 meters under maximum stress. When your line stretches this much, there is a corresponding decline in strength that makes it difficult to set a hook since the force of the hook set is not fully transmitted down the length of the line. (For this reason it's easier to hook a fish with ultralight when there's less line in the water.)

But line stretch has its advantages too. The energy required to stretch the monofilament is dissipated as the line expands, so it doesn't break. The longer the line you have out, the greater protection you have against sudden surges by the fish. Most broken lines occur right near the boat because the mono is short and there's not enough elasticity left to cushion against those sudden shocks.

You must be careful not to allow monofilament to stretch too far. Fishing line behaves like a metal spring. Once it's stretched beyond a certain point, it will no longer rebound; instead it will become permanently weakened and deformed. The point at which the line will no longer rebound to its full strength is called the *elastic limit.*

To maintain maximum strength while fishing, try to avoid pushing the line to the point where it starts to stretch at all. Remember that line stretch is an emergency backup to be utilized when you make a mistake and need all the help you can get to land your fish. If you make a really bad move and the mono exceeds its elastic limit, you'll be left with a fishing line that's about half as strong as it was when you started—good news for the fish but not for you.

How will you know when your line is starting to stretch? First, wet-test its strength. Once you know how much weight is required to start the stretching process, tie that much weight together. Then take the rod you've selected for that line strength and run the line up the guides. Attach the selected weights to the end of the line and try to lift the weight off the ground. Study the flex of the rod at various angles and memorize the feel of the rod as you see the line stretch. (More on this in Chapter Four.)

When you're on the water and have a fish on, don't let the flex of the rod exceed what you saw at home. And, more importantly, never let the feel get heavier than it was at home. (Practice-fishing, described in Chapter Three, will help you develop these skills.) Remember, success in ultralight angling depends far more on your sense of touch than sight.

Color

This is simple. Don't buy colored lines, especially fluorescent yellow lines. Studies have shown that fish see fluorescent yellow lines without any trouble and can also distinguish colors as subtle as fluorescent purple and blue. Field studies have shown you'll get the best results with clear, clear blue, or clear green lines. Frankly, I wouldn't get bogged down in those color refinements. Just buy clear line; you can't go wrong with that.

Applications

Which line you use for any given situation is a very personal decision, but I can give you some suggestions that might make your initial attempts more fun. First of all, don't use ultralight gear in areas near reefs, large patches of weed, pilings, or marinas. It is not fun to spend your day losing fish because they've dragged your line around every obstacle in sight and broken you off. Make an exception to this rule only if you're pursuing a clean fighter—a fish that will not use structure against you. The only clean fighters I know of are bluefish (tailor), rainbow runner, skipjack (bonito), and kahawai (Australian salmon). For these fish 1- or 2-kg lines provide the most sport in any situation.

If you're after steelhead (sea-run rainbow trout) in clear water, use the lightest possible lines and terminal tackle. You'll get far more strikes with thin mono, and you'll be surprised by how quickly a powerful steelhead will succumb to 1-kg line.

Bluegills, crappies, bass, carp, and trout pursued in obstruction-free water are far more fun with 1-kg line, and you'll get more hookups too.

Large or powerful surface fighters like sailfish, bonefish, dolphin (mahi mahi, dorado), or inconnu (sheefish) are best attempted with 2-kg gear. You can go after these and similar species with 1-kg, but you must be very careful and committed to a long battle.

Tope, sand sharks, tiger sharks, nurse sharks, permit, tarpon, and other fish found on tropical sand flats are the most fun with 2-kg. The challenge on the flats is to keep your line from touching the rough bottom. If you go lighter than 2-kg line, your margin for error is far smaller; but then again, the excitement potential is greater.

Leaders

When fishing ultralight, you can expect long battles. Even fish with no visible teeth have rough lips that can easily rub through a light leader in a few minutes. On the other hand, the lighter your leader, the greater your chance of hooking fish. The best bet is to use the thinnest leader possible for any given situation. A good way to decide how strong to make the leader is to guess how long it will take to land the fish.

It usually takes 15 to 45 minutes to land a fine-toothed fighter like the kahawai or coho (silver) salmon. A leader of 10-kg monofilament is usually adequate for such a fight. Larger, more powerful, fine-toothed fish, like yellowtail and other big jacks, require 20-kg leaders to prevent line wear during the two- to four-hour battles.

What sort of monofilament should you make your leaders from? The best material will have a high tensile strength so you get the strongest mono from the thinnest line. It used to be that all high-tensile-strength lines were stiff and awkward to use, but now that problem has been solved. It shouldn't be difficult to find a high-tensile-strength line that's still reasonably limp.

Make the leader two to three times the length of the fish you plan to catch so that your ultralight line won't rub on the fish's back as it runs. But keep the leader length under 15 feet (5 meters)—the IGFA limit for ultralight fishing. In real life a leader more than 6 feet (2 meters) long is seldom needed unless you're shark fishing.

Many people advise using wire leaders for pickerel, pike, and bluefish. It's true that these fish won't gnaw through wire, but they won't often get through heavy monofilament either. Most of the time a 30-kg mono leader is all you need with 2-kg line; but if you're using 1-kg line or if you're targeting sharks, you must use wire, or you'll lose almost every fish you hook.

Fish with small, sharp teeth are deadly on monofilament line. For these species wire leaders are absolutely necessary.

Wire can be colored or black, braided or single strand, coated or plain. I don't like braided wire. I've lost too many sharks because they managed to bite through one thin strand after another until nothing was left. Coated wire doesn't do anything useful either; it just gives the sharks something to grab onto with their many rows of teeth.

The best bet is a darkened, single strand of 50-kg wire. I try to make my shark leaders about 10 feet (3 meters) long—long enough to protect my line from the shark's coarse skin and to control the shark when it gets near the boat. Leaders longer than 10 feet are difficult to manage and usually end up tangled with other gear in the bottom of the boat. A lot of people like to twist the wire repeatedly (called a *haywire twist*) when attaching it to terminal tackle. I prefer a crimp at each end and a simple fold of the wire to ensure it won't slip. The choice is yours.

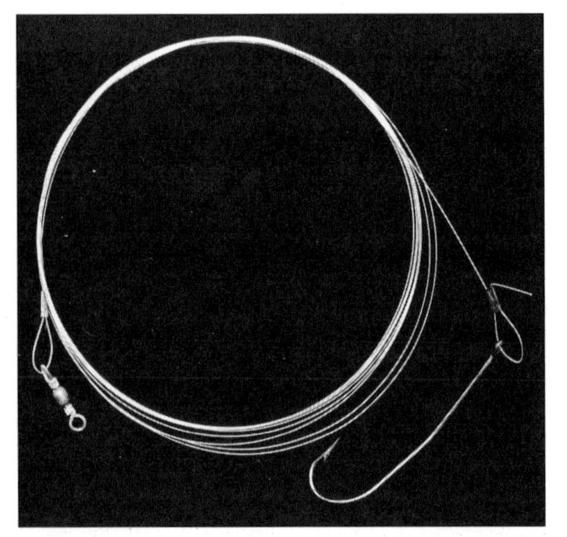

A fully prepared wire leader ready to be put into a plastic bag for storage.

No one wants to waste fishing time making leaders. So you'll need a storage system if you're going to make them in advance and still be able to get to them quickly on the water. My approach is to make 10 to 20 leaders at a time.

Monofilament leaders consist of a swivel and the line. When they're made up, I wrap them one on top of the other onto an old line spool. When I'm ready to fish, I pull one leader off the spool, attach a hook, and tie the leader to the main line. Wire leaders consist of a swivel, the wire, a small weight, and a hook. I bend the wire into 6-inch-wide (15 cm) loops, bind each loop with a single twist tie (the loops are large enough that the wire pops straight when freed), and package the leaders individually in small plastic bags to avoid tangles.

Let's move on now to the first glamour item—the fishing reel.

CHAPTER THREE

The Reel

BACK IN CHAPTER ONE we went over the basic differences between bait-casters and spinning reels. You probably remember that the biggest problem with spinning reels is the Dreaded Line Twist that develops when a big fish takes line out against the drag. Each time the spool rotates, the line twists once. That means that, for every 6 inches (15 cm) the fish runs, your line gets one twist. Of course, fish seldom run just 6 inches, so let's be realistic and say your line will twist 120 times if the fish goes on an uncontrolled 20-yard (20-meter) run. That's a lot of twists, and each one will weaken the already delicate line.

You'll also remember that bait-casters don't have any problems with line twist, so you never have to worry about your line getting weaker with every run or getting hopelessly balled up if you let it go slack. It would seem as though bait-casters are the way to fish ultralight. But things are not always as they seem.

The Bait-Caster at Sea

It was 1985, and it had been a great fishing season in New Zealand—lots of hookups, some great battles, and even a few world records. The Blue Water brought by the warm currents had made its way down from the South Pacific Islands, and with it had come hordes of gamefish looking for new sources of food. As luck would have it, the Blue Water was unusually close to shore that year, bringing big fish within reach of my dinghy and ultralight gear.

On a perfect fall morning I went out looking for trouble. The only rods in the boat were two identical 2-kg bait-casting outfits. Leaders, weights, and hooks were already rigged; and the bait box was full of live mackerel. Having nothing but ultralight gear on board, I had no choice but to use the 2-kg line, no matter how big the fish would be; by definition that meant trouble.

As the dinghy motored out of the harbor, I beheld a scene of utter carnage: for several hundred meters in every direction the air was alive with screaming birds—the otherwise quiet water was being churned up by millions of anchovies desperately seeking refuge from the marauding kahawai (Australian salmon), mackerel, yellowtail, and skipjack (bonito).

Gazing in awe at the events around me, I came to a slow realization—if there are lots of medium-size fish on the surface eating anchovies, there are probably some bigger fish down below trying to eat the medium-size fish. It was not an exceptionally brilliant insight but one worth pursuing.

I picked out an active mackerel from the livewell, attached it to the live-bait rig, and tossed it into the mayhem around the boat. The mackerel, being a reasonable fish, made right for the bottom and relative safety. Unfortunately for him, his descent did not go unnoticed, and within seconds the telltale tug of a powerful pelagic fish started to put a bend in my ultralight rod.

I couldn't have asked for better circumstances. For a mile (about 2 kilometers) in every direction the water was free of obstructions. The bottom was sand or mud, there were no other boats in sight, and the wind was negligible. It was 6 A.M., and I was already hooked up to a big fish. Everything was A-OK!

For the first hour the battle was more-or-less routine. I kept the boat within 30 yards (27 meters) of the fish with one hand as I held the rod with the other. Since the fish was staying deep, I didn't have to make any sudden maneuvers; and both my hands were usually free to take up the slack line and keep maximum pressure on the unknown pelagic below.

As circumstances began to change, I fondly remembered that first hour. The sun was rising higher, and the land was beginning to warm. As the warm air rose over the land, the cool air over the ocean rushed in to take its place, creating wind over the water. And wind is not the ultralight angler's friend.

As the wind began to rise, a chop developed on the surface. Whenever the bow of the boat rose and fell through the chop, I had to compensate with the rod and reel so the line would stay tight and the fish would sense no lessening of pressure. As the chop began to rise, the fish came up to the surface to see what was going on. My eyes lit up at that glimpse of him! He was a southern yellowtail, about 45 pounds (20 kg)—a big fish on 2-kg line but not impossible to land. If I were careful, it might mean another world record. My heart beat faster as the yellowtail started on the first of many surface runs. I did not want to lose that fish. I resolved to be super cautious, even if the fight took all morning.

The boat followed the fish as it ran, and the sea rose as we traveled. After the second hour, water started to accumulate around my feet from the spray coming in over the bow. As the chop grew, I was forced to stand so I could cover enough distance with a quick body movement to compensate for the increasing rise and fall of the bow.

By the third hour things were not going well. We had traveled about 7 miles (11 kilometers) and were now out of the bay on the open ocean. The fish was tiring, but so was I. All the water in the dinghy made for slippery conditions. And since I'd had to stand to fight the fish effectively, I took quite a few falls when unexpected wind gusts turned the bow around without warning. The falls were taking their toll; not being a limber 20-year-old, I was starting to hurt in places I didn't know I had. But the fish was still on, and my chances of landing him increased with every minute that passed—or so I thought.

Previous experience had taught me that southern yellowtail usually succumb within three hours. My hopes were high even though conditions were growing worse: I was getting tired, and everything hurt when I moved, but I was full of confidence as I felt the fish slowing down and coming ever closer to the surface. Suddenly the rod went slack. I was dumfounded! My pressure on the line hadn't increased, and the fish was moving in open water. There was no obvious reason why the line had broken so unexpectedly. I was unable to understand what had happened but decided the investigation could wait. I bottled up my disappointment, reeled in the remaining line, turned the boat around, and rode the following sea back to the harbor.

The Discovery

After a day or two nursing my wounded ego and aching body, I ventured into the garage to have a close look at the line on the reel. There were signs of wear all along the section of the line that had been subjected to repeated movement over the spool. The wear pattern was fairly evenly distributed, and the reason the fish got away was obvious.

But why had the line been worn over such a great length? Similar fights using spinning reels had produced no such wear pattern. After some testing and pondering, I realized that there was a problem of hidden line wear. Because a bait-caster has no roller-bearing for the line to run over, the full stress of a running fish is transmitted to the layers of line on the spool. And therein lies "the rub"! Every time the spool rotates while the drag is operational, the mono that's moving off the reel is biting into the layers of line below it. This causes a slow but steady erosion of line strength that becomes significant after an hour's battle with a big fish.

The following year I actually had the opportunity to determine the life of 1-kg monofilament line while using both spinning reels and bait-casters. It was a fabulous fishing season in New Zealand, and I hooked and played many potential world-record fish. Although I lost most of those possible records, I had dozens of one- to three-hour battles before I heard the heart-wrenching pop of breaking line.

The events of the season taught me an interesting fact: 1-kg line almost always wears out within an hour on the bait-caster but usually lasts up to three hours with the spinning reel *if* it is artfully handled.

To master a spinning reel you'll need to know how to use your drag, fingers, and boat to best advantage. Nevertheless, the spinning reel seems to be the ultralight angler's best choice. Here's how to make it work for you.

Using the Drag

The key to landing large fish on ultralight is to push your line to the limit but not beyond. To do this you must understand the dynamics of the line you use. How much does it stretch before it breaks? Does it stiffen up in the early-morning cold? How much abrasion will it tolerate? All these things you can learn at home by line testing and practice-fishing.

Practice-fishing will quickly teach you how to use your ultralight gear. (To do it, you find someone—a sympathetic angler or a cooperative child is good—to act as the fish, and you play your "fish" as it runs around the yard by using the rod and reel to control its movements.) We'll talk about this effective training technique later in the chapter.

By practicing at home you'll find it relatively easy to determine your line's *elastic limit*—the point at which it starts to stretch. You never want to reach that point on the water. Once the monofilament has stretched past the elastic limit, it will never regain its strength; and the fish will surely win.

Most ultralight beginners rely on the reel drag to maintain the proper tension on the line. Unfortunately reel drags, even the best, are not consistent. All reel drags require more pressure to start moving than to keep moving. The accompanying graph shows what happens when the reel drag starts to move. You can see that it requires more than 2 kg of force to start the drag moving if it is set at a 1½-kg *running drag.* This means that you will lose every fish at the hookup if your drag is set properly for the fish's first run! That could really ruin a day on the water.

The solution is simple: Adjust the drag as you fish. Set the strike drag (for setting the hook) far below the stretch point of the line. This will protect the line from breaking when the fish feels the hook and takes off on a sudden run. Then, as the fish continues its run, slowly tighten the drag until the maximum pressure is applied to the fish. Once it finishes the run, loosen the drag. With the next run tighten up again, but remember that the drag can vary: use the bend in the rod as the best indicator of excessive line stress. You also have to remember to reduce the drag when the fish is close to the boat. This is because a shorter line has little elasticity and breaks very easily.

It takes a lot more pressure to get the drag moving than it does to keep it going.

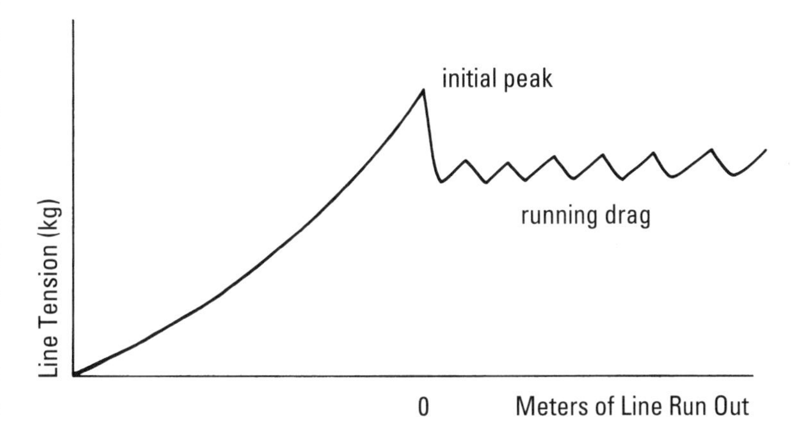

If you are going to play your fish by using the

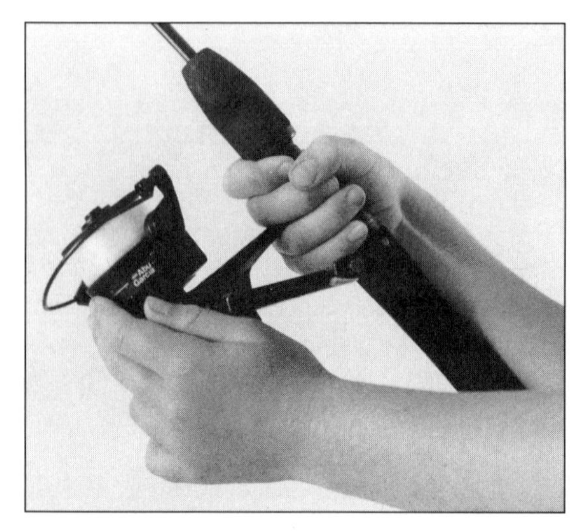

drag adjustment, it is probably best to buy a reel with a rear-mounted drag that you can get to without looking. You *can* adjust a drag mounted on the spool while there's a fish on, but it's not easy. Before reaching for a front-mounted drag, you must look down and make sure the bail and line are out of the way. A careless fingernail can easily cut through 1-kg line that's under pressure; you've got to be super careful if you try to adjust a drag mounted on the spool while you're fighting a big fish.

There is another way to slow that fish down, however; and it's a better way too.

The Hand

Living in a mechanical age, we tend to place great faith in machines. But the human hand can be much more consistent than any reel drag and much more effective in controlling a fast fish. With some practice you can learn to apply an incredibly even pressure to your line by using your fingers to regulate the rotation of the spool.

To do this, simply place your fingertips against the reel spool. To increase the drag, force your fingertips against the spool or put two fingers there instead of one. Using this method, simply set the reel at the strike drag and then use your fingers to increase the pressure during runs. With this system it becomes impossible to maintain maximum drag when reeling in (because you need both hands to hold the rod and turn the reel handle), but you don't want the maximum drag applied anyway since a sudden surge by the fish during the upward rod sweep would break the line.

Top: The human hand can produce a far smoother effect than any mechanical drag.

Bottom: Raise the rod tip and point the handle toward the deck to increase the drag when the fish runs or when you need to reel in line.

To compensate for the loss of drag as you move your fingers off the spool, all you need to do is raise the rod tip and point the handle down toward the water. A rod under full bend can increase the drag on the line markedly and give you that extra bit of fine-tuning you need.

Some ultralight salmon and steelhead anglers in North America carry this method to an extreme. They virtually disengage the drag on their bait-casters and allow the line to run through their fingers to create a drag. In order to avoid cooking their fingertips, they use a very long rod (noodle rod) and hold the rod so it forms a "C" when they want to create maximum drag. The extra-long, extra-soft, C-shaped noodle rod creates so much drag with its bend that little or no additional fingertip pressure is required.

In order to regulate the line pressure by hand, you have to be able to "read your rod": estimate line pressure by feeling and seeing the flex of the rod at any given angle. The best way to develop this skill is to practice-fish, with a friend acting as the fish, until you've acquired enough sensitivity to control the reel by touch alone.

Increasing the drag by raising the rod can be carried to an extreme when using a noodle rod. This noodle rod is being bent into a "Big C" with 1-kg line!

If your friend is an angler, attach the line to a small hand-held spring scale. That way you'll be able to follow the changes in line stress as you raise and lower the rod or apply your fingers to the reel spool. If no "volunteer fish" can be found, just tie your line to a piece of wood and reel it in over a rough grass surface to simulate the varying resistance a fish offers.

You must use the same rod and reel all the time to get good at this. Once you've mastered the technique, it will be surprisingly easy to switch from rod to rod since a good sense of tension will be imprinted in your hand, and visual feedback will no longer be necessary.

Selecting a Reel

Going to the tackle shop to buy a spinning reel can be an awesome undertaking. The variety of reels can leave an angler feeling hopelessly bewildered. Most manufacturers produce a range of reels that vary markedly in quality and features, so you cannot depend on any particular brand name to help make your choice. The best approach is to learn enough about spinning reels so that you can identify the important features, quality materials, and construction that will help you land big fish with ultralight lines.

Buy the very best reel you can afford. A high price doesn't always mean top quality, but a low price usually indicates poor workmanship or inferior materials. On ultralight spinning reels the three most important

ABU GARCIA INC.

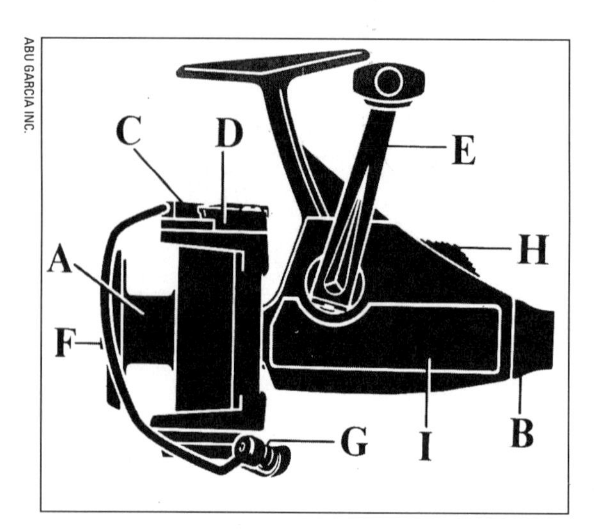

When you buy a reel, the critical parts are: (A) the spool, (B) the drag, (G) the line-roller on the bail arm. Almost as important are: (E) the handle, (H) antireverse, (I) the body.

features are the drag, the line-roller on the bail arm, and the size of the spool. After we've covered those features, I'll talk about other, less important elements of the ideal spinning reel.

The Drag

If you're a beginner you might not want to buy a spinning reel unless the drag adjustment is on the reel body (usually the rear). You'll need to continuously adjust the drag as you play the fish, and a drag adjustment on the spool can be difficult to reach without touching the line. Since the line is always under stress while a fish is on, touching it abruptly with your fingers can break it.

However, there is an advantage to having the drag on the spool: larger drag washers. When the drag is mounted inside a reel, the drag washers have to be small enough to fit inside the body. Small drag washers heat up faster, wear out earlier, and get rough with age. I know it seems hard to believe, but back in the early 1980s, when I was using one of the early-model rear-drag reels, I had to change my drag washers every week. Of course, the reel was struggling with fighting fish for at least 12 hours a week, but changing washers every seven days is not fun even if it is warranted.

Drag washers mounted within or near the spool can be much larger. This means less wear as you fight the fish, so you get a smoother, longer-lasting drag. Because the larger drag washers heat up more slowly and don't wear out nearly as quickly, you'll have fewer breakdowns while fish are on, and fewer reel overhauls at home.

With this information in mind, your first step is to decide if you want a rear-mounted drag or a front, spool-mounted drag. The next step is to make sure the drag is very smooth. The best way to test the drag is to put line on the reel and mount it on a sensitive rod. Pull the line through the guides and tie it to a fixed object. Walk backward slowly and keep your eye on the rod tip. The tip should bend abruptly as the inertia of the reel drag is overcome. (Remember that graph earlier in this chapter?) After the initial abrupt move, the rod tip should maintain an even bend as you continue to back up at a steady rate. If the rod tip quivers and jumps, the drag is too rough. It's possible to fix a rough drag, but why bother? A well-engineered reel should work right from the start.

If you don't have a rod, you can do a similar test by standing on a chair with the reel. Adjust the drag so the weight of the reel will pull the line off the spool. Then hold the line and let the reel drop slowly to the floor. If the reel falls slowly and smoothly, the drag passes the test. If the reel jerks and dances its way to the floor, put it back on the shelf. Don't forget to place a pad on the floor or have a friend catch it on the way down. You don't want to have to pay for a reel you don't want!

Fiddle with the drag adjustment and be sure there's a wide range of settings suited to the line you've chosen. If the drag goes from non-engagement to breaking your line in less than a 360-degree turn, it's not sensitive enough.

Size is only one of the factors that determine washer longevity and reliability. The substance they're made from is the other. Leather, felt, cork, and asbestos were popular in the past. But the new synthetics—Teflon, Delrin, and others—have increased the life of a drag by a factor of 10. So look for synthetic washers—they make life a lot easier.

An easy way to test the reel drag. The reel should fall to the floor smoothly and slowly. This is an old Ryobi 200—a unique reel on which, to avoid line twist, the rotor turned instead of the spool when line was running out. Unfortunately, the rotor wobbled excessively as it turned. Too bad; it was a great idea.

The Roller

The line-roller on the bail arm must rotate smoothly as line passes over it. If it does not, pressure and heat will build up at this crucial point, producing excessive line wear. The bail-roller is a critical feature of the reel, so examine it with care.

The manufacturer who has put a ball bearing or two in the roller system probably agrees that the roller is critical. That's a vote in favor of buying the reel.

To be sure the roller turns freely, run a piece of mono or a rubber band over it. You should not have to press hard to make the roller move; the motion should be steady and smooth. If it's not, put the reel back. You don't want it.

You also have to check the housing itself. Is there any free space the line can fall into? Are there any sharp edges that can nick the line? If things look good, go on to checking the spool.

The Spool

The wider your reel spool, the less difficulty you'll have with line set and line twist; but if you choose a spool that's too large, the reel will feel exceedingly awkward on the rod. For 2-kg lines an ideal compromise is a diameter of about 2¼ inches (57 mm) at the lower lip of the spool. For 1-kg line, 2 inches (50 mm) is about right. The line capacity of the spool is not important because you'll never use much more than about 100 yards (90 meters) of line at a time anyway. I know that seems unbelievable, but you'll see why when we review how to fight big fish.

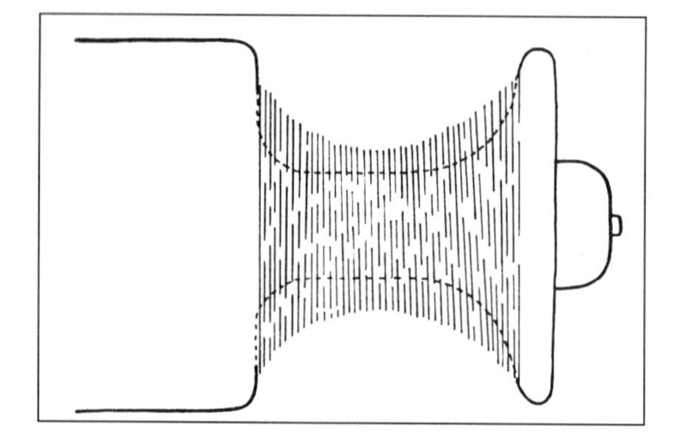

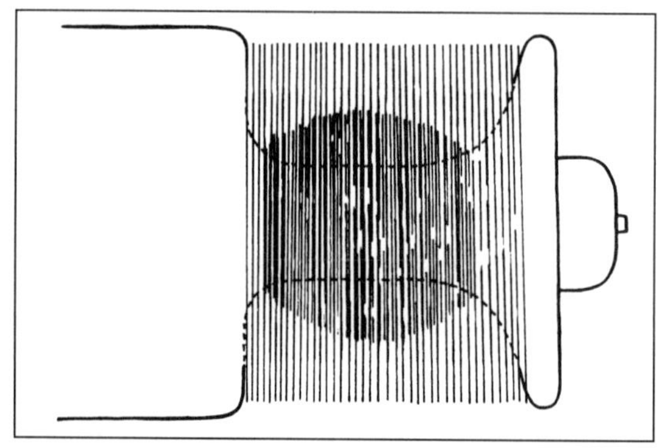

Top: A cross section of the spool from a medium-size spinning reel after it's been loaded with ultralight line but no backing. Note the bulge of line on the edges.

Bottom: A properly loaded spool from a medium-size spinning reel shown in cross section. Note how the backing is bunched in the middle so the spool will take ultralight line evenly.

Avoid all the cute little spinning reels that crowd the market and look so nice on 5-foot (1.5-meter) ultralight rods. They are made for appearances only and will cause you nothing but trouble unless you only fish for brook trout or crappies.

A problem with using 2¼-inch (57-mm) spools for ultralight lines is the "bunching" effect when the spools are filled—excess line at both lips of the spool and too little line in the middle. It happens because manufacturers generally design such spool sizes for 4- to 8-kg lines, and the undulations of the spool while you're reeling in don't quite synchronize with the thinner diameters of 1- and 2-kg lines.

To get around this problem, arrange cotton garden-cord backing so that it bulges slightly in the middle of the spool. Cover the cotton cord with tape, or wind a few layers of 4-kg line over it to smooth out the highly irregular surface. Since you'll be putting only about 100 yards (90 meters) of line on a spool, the backing will take up most of the spool's capacity. It takes a while to get the backing distributed just right, but once it's on you can leave it for many, many line changes.

Maybe, one day, some manufacturer will design a perfect reel for ultralight lines. Such a reel will not be pretty, though; and, unfortunately, good looks still sell more reels than good design.

Other Features

Although they're not as critical as the drag, line-roller, and spool, certain other features are worth considering. If you fish in salt water, you want to be sure the reel is corrosion-proof. Materials that stand up to salt water include graphite, bronze, anodized aluminum, and stainless steel. I don't like to clean my reels meticulously after a day on the water, and I bet you won't want to either. So save yourself a hassle and buy a reel made with the right materials.

Choose a high gear ratio: 5:1 is about right. This will enable you to retrieve line quickly when the fish comes toward you or when you close too quickly while following with a boat. Since power is not an issue with ultralight, there's no need to consider lower-gear-ratio options. Some reels come with dual gear ratios—a single lever switches from a 5:1 ratio to 3:1. The design is fascinating; but you don't need the power of a 3:1 ratio, and extra complexity always means less reliability.

Look for a reel that has a silent antireverse. The constant clatter of an antireverse ratchet can shatter the peaceful calm of an otherwise lovely morning on the water.

Mount the reel on an appropriate rod and get a feel for how it sits. Use the reel handle and make sure it fits your hand comfortably. If things go well on the water, your hand will be spending lots of time on that handle, so make sure it feels good. If you're left-handed, make sure the reel is designed for the left hand or has an optional right-side handle position.

Some reels are made with a bail that closes only when you wind the handle. This makes it difficult when you want to close the bail manually while the line is slack. Slack line has a greater chance of being caught under the spool or around the bail hinges. So look for a reel with a bail that can be closed manually as well as automatically.

While you're fooling with the reel, turn the handle rapidly and then let it go. The bail should spin around freely without wobbling. A few ball bearings at the rotor and a counterbalancing rotor weight help the reel stay smooth. Look for these features.

Try to avoid buying reels with lots of gadgets. Line holders on the skirts of your spools will catch and nick your line while it's loose, so avoid them or cover them with tape. Some spinning reels have a switch that disengages the drag so the fish can run freely with the bail closed. This is unnecessary since you'll be bait-fishing with the bail open. And, of course, each revolution of the reel spool with the bail closed means another twist in the line.

Another attention-getter is the one-handed bail-trip device. This might be useful if you cast lures all day long, but ultralight anglers don't do that. The triggers that trip the bail are likely to become clogged with salt and grit, and they get in your way while you're fighting big fish. Stay away from them.

Also avoid closed-face spinning reels. The face stresses the line, the internal bail nicks it, and you can never tell how much line is left on the spool. Closed-face reels are not for ultralight lines.

Spare Parts

You can expect a top-quality fishing reel to last for many years. If you use one reel all the time, it becomes so comfortable that it seems to be part of you. This is a great asset on the water; it can mean the difference between success and failure when you're fighting a powerful fish.

I've had several reels for more than 10 years now. They are used a lot, and they take a hell of a beating on the water. They were top-quality products when I bought them, and they're still working well. I get attached to my equipment and don't like to retire gear just because new models are available. It's nice to own a reel long enough to know it won't let you down when that special fish comes along.

When you keep a spinning reel for years, you will invariably require spare parts for it. To be sure those parts will be available, I'd suggest buying from a firm that has been in business for a while. It's a shame to have to retire a good reel because there's no way to get parts to repair it.

As insurance buy 5 to 10 sets of drag washers, one or two extra bail-rollers, several bail and ratchet springs, and two or three extra spools when you buy a new spinning reel. When you go on prolonged fishing trips, take a few tools and the parts with you. It could save your holiday.

Bait-Casters

There are several good reasons to buy a bait-caster for ultralight fishing. Perhaps your arm and hand feel much more comfortable with a reel above the rod. Maybe you won't be casting much or don't anticipate any battles lasting longer than an hour. Certainly a bait-caster is a reasonable choice if you will be fishing with 4-kg line in situations with lots of structure or if you'll be trolling a lure.

Much of the information about choosing a spinning reel applies to bait-casters as well. For instance, a uniform drag motion is as critical on a bait-casting reel as it is on a spinning reel. Test it in just the same way. Because of their construction, bait-casters generally have larger drag washers than rear-drag spinning reels. This means they last longer and usually perform better over prolonged periods.

Other factors are important for bait-casters specifically, such as the tolerance between the spool and the reel body. If there is a large gap, your line will slip behind the spool and all will be lost. If you buy a reel with too large a gap, you can reduce it by building up the edge of the spool with several coats of epoxy or other similar material. If the reel you pick has a level wind, you might want to remove it. Level winds can cause a great deal of line wear. Check out the reel before you buy it. You might be able to keep the level wind on if the line passes cleanly through it and if the areas of it that contact the line are hardened and smooth so they will not erode the line.

You'll need to buy spare drag washers, ratchet springs, and spools just as you would for a spinning reel. Though the washers last longer on a bait-caster, they will fail eventually. When buying a bait-caster, you need to be especially careful to avoid choosing one because it looks good. Some of the new reels are so pretty and full of buttons they'd probably be a greater success displayed in the living-room cabinet than on the water.

Having selected a reel, you can go and pick out a rod.

CHAPTER FOUR

The Rod

ONCE YOU DECIDE TO START FISHING ultralight, you will find unlimited opportunity to spend lots of money on new fishing tackle. Unfortunately, decent ultralight gear really is expensive, so it's important to choose carefully. As with most things, choosing carefully means buying top quality. To catch fish consistently with 1- and 2-kg lines, your equipment must work perfectly. That will mean buying the best you can possibly afford since the gear will be used to capacity (and beyond) once you become experienced. As an introduction to this chapter, I'd like to tell you a story about how not to buy your fishing rods.

A Cautionary Tale

Back in 1982 I was preparing to travel to the Brooks Range in northern Alaska. My plan was to walk in the mountains for 10 days and then float down the Kobuk River toward the Bering Sea. It would be a fantasy realized; and, for that, I'd need a new fishing rod. To be suitable for long-distance hiking, it would have to break down into four to six pieces, or it would have to be one of those horrible telescoping rods.

Even in those days I was wary of telescoping rods. They tended to jam open at the most inappropriate times and always seemed to flatten out where the segments joined. So I set out in search of a multipiece, sturdy little pack rod, light enough to cast small spinners for grayling but stout enough to handle a fair-size salmon on 2-kg line. The tackle shops were full of pack rods, and a dozen had already passed my eye when I saw the little beauty I wanted.

It was love at first sight; the rod was made of hollow fiberglass (no graphite in those days), and it was light as a feather. The pieces fit together well, and it was a lovely tan color with white wraps. It felt good as I wagged it in my hand and, best of all, it was remarkably cheap. The little rod and its case would cost me only $18—what a find! I dashed home to assemble the pieces and practice fishing on the lawn.

A month later, on the waters of the Kobuk River, the rod seemed to have proved its worth. Numerous grayling and arctic char had fallen victim to its action, and soon we'd be reaching the deeper downstream waters where the salmon were in better condition for a battle on ultralight tackle.

One cold, fall morning I was casting a spinner into the broad reaches of the Kobuk when a powerful fish struck the lure and took off downstream. The shores of the river were sandy and clear, so it was easy to follow the fish as it ran. After an hour the fish started to weaken; I figured another half hour's hard work would bring him to shore. As the fish came closer, the bend in the little rod became greater and greater.

Toward the end of the battle I was on a small ledge and could see clearly into the deep water just below. The fish was a salmon, and it was a real beauty too. I was feeling quite proud of myself, when a "shot" rang out in the cold Alaskan air. Looking up with alarm I saw no one, but I did notice that the fishing rod was feeling very light in my hands.

I gazed back down upon a strange sight: the entire shaft of the rod seemed to be sliding down the line, ever so slowly, toward the blackness of the swirling waters below. Soon the lovely white wraps had sunk, one by one, and I was left with only the rod handle and reel. The line was still intact, and the salmon was swimming with the shaft of the rod bouncing up and down like a pogo stick on top of his nose.

As if in slow motion, the salmon came closer to shore, the angle of the line changed a bit, and then I heard a little pop as the mono parted and the fish disappeared into the depths with my lure, line, and rod. About this time I realized that the "gun shot" I'd heard was the crack of the rod shaft!

An hour later I was still on the ledge dragging the bottom with a weight and treble hook in a futile attempt to recover the lost shaft. With a final barrage of feeble curses, I gave up and sat down on the rock to contemplate my loss.

I made several resolutions during those moments on the rock:

1. I will not buy pretty little fishing rods any more.
2. I will not look for bargains when buying tackle.
3. I will test my rods before going on the water.

BERKLEY AND COMPANY.

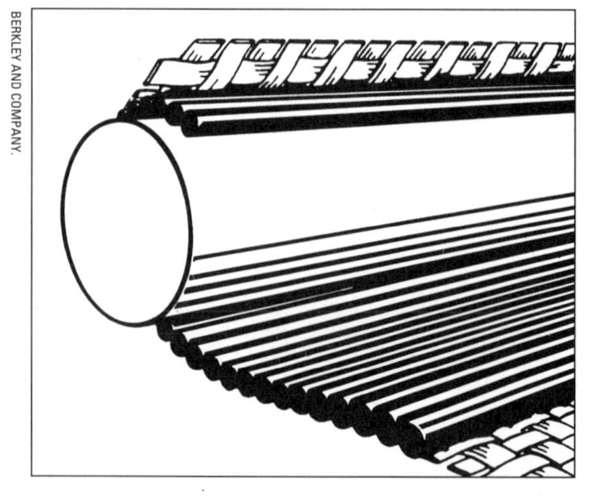

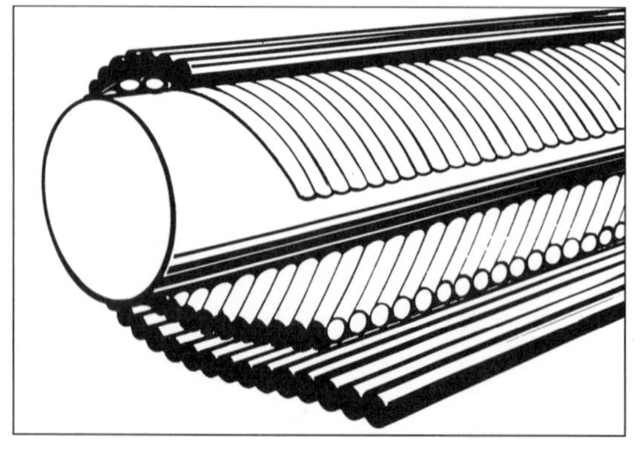

Two of the many possible ways to combine fabrics in a fishing rod.

Fast or Slow?

Fishing rods are made out of cloth. The fibers in the cloth are usually some combination of graphite (called *carbon fiber* outside the United States), glass, boron, or Kevlar. The fibers of the cloth are impregnated in one of a variety of resins to help maintain their alignment during the manufacturing process. Graphite and glass are by far the most commonly used materials in making cloth for fishing rods.

Graphite is a mixture of carbon and other elements that are heated to very high temperatures and then extruded through small holes to form incredibly strong fibers. Although graphite is occasionally used in a "pure" form, it is usually woven together with glass into a fabric that makes a very tough cloth.

Fiberglass is a woven fabric made of glass fibers that are thin enough to be supple and soft. Each of the many varieties of fiberglass available has its own characteristic suppleness and strength. "S-Glass" is one of the well-known varieties most suitable for fishing rods.

The fibers that run along the length of the cloth have to be very strong since they will usually run the length of the rod. These fibers are made of some combination of graphite, glass, boron, and/or Kevlar. Glass fibers are usually used across the width of the fabric. These glass fibers are far less numerous than the fibers that will run the length of the fabric, so the rod will be able to bend freely.

There is an infinite number of fabrics available to rod manufacturers. The quality of the fabric can vary in many ways. The individual fibers can be thick or thin. They can be woven together very closely (high modulus) to produce a relatively stiff action or left far apart (low modulus) for a softer effect. The fibers can be of just one substance or any combination of materials. The list of possibilities goes on, but the bottom line is that making a fishing rod involves making a lot of choices, each of which influences the characteristics of the rod you buy.

After deciding which fabric to use, the manufacturer determines which resin to impregnate the cloth with. The resin helps to hold the cloth together and maintain its shape when it is finally molded into a fishing rod. Once the fabric is impregnated with resin, it has to be cut into the right pattern before it is wrapped around the *mandrel.* This pattern is called a *flag.*

(A) This combination of flag and mandrel will produce a fast-action rod. (B) This combination will produce a slow-action rod suitable for ultralight fishing.

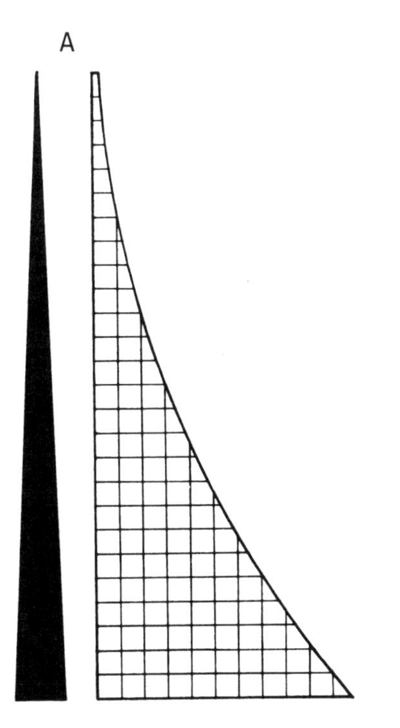

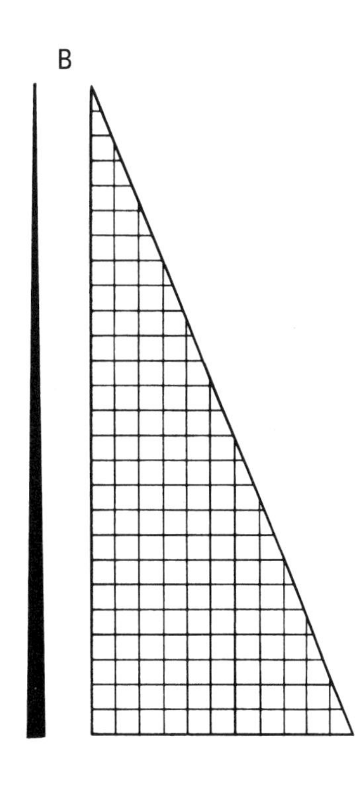

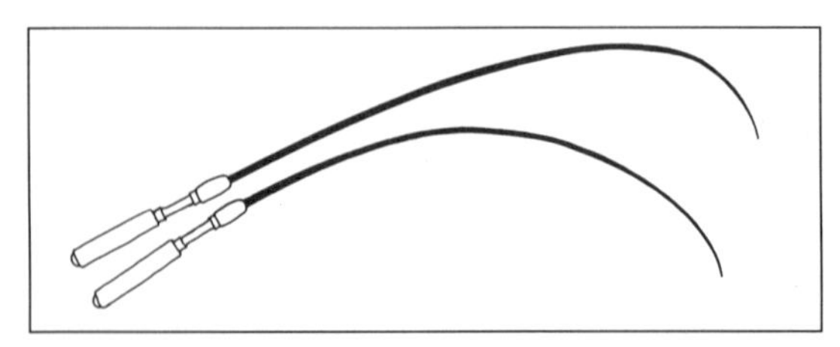

The upper rod has a fast action: it bends more at the tip than at the butt. The lower rod has a slow action: it bends evenly from tip to butt.

As you can see from the illustration on page 37, the shape of the flag will influence where the rod is strong and where it is weak. If the flag has a fast taper, then the rod will bend more at the tip than along the shaft. A rod like this is said to have a *fast action* because it will bounce back quickly after being bent. If the flag tapers slowly along its length, then the rod will bend evenly right to the handle. Such a rod has a *slow action;* it recovers slowly after being put under load. A slow-action rod is what you will be looking for when you go shopping.

The power of a fishing rod is determined by the width of the flag and the diameter of the mandrel. The wider the flag, the more often it is wrapped around the mandrel. More wraps mean more power. Ultralight rods don't need to be very powerful, so the flags are relatively narrow and the mandrels, thin.

Once the flag is cut, it is wrapped around the mandrel and coated with cellulose film. The mandrel is then baked, and the excess resin runs off during baking. When the mandrel is removed from the oven, the cellulose wrap is cut off. The raw rod then has to be cleaned or sanded down to even off the ridges formed by the joins between the edges of the flag. Once the rod is smooth, the ends need to be trimmed. If too much of the tip is cut away, the rod will become too stiff for ultralight. If too much of the butt is removed, the rod will become so slow it will lack the power to support even 1-kg line.

At the tackle shop you'll want to look for a slow-action rod. A rod that bends right down to the handle will act like a buffer between your line and the fish. Should the fish move off suddenly, the full length of the rod will absorb the force of the run, so you'll have a chance to react before the line breaks. But a big fish on a fast-action rod can easily break the line because only the tip of the rod will bend when suddenly stressed, and the line might part before you can react. *Do not buy a fast-action rod!* Ultralight anglers need the cushion that only a slow-action rod can provide.

The Line and the Rod

Now it's time to go off to your favorite sporting-goods store and buy that first ultralight fishing rod. The strength of the line you intend to use is the prime consideration. Since 2-kg line is meant to be twice the strength of 1-kg, you'd expect that a rod designed for 2-kg line would be twice as powerful as a rod designed for 1-kg.

There's no way a rod can be suitable for both line strengths. A rod that has just the right suppleness for 2-kg line would be hopelessly stiff for 1-kg. Yet, when you go to the tackle shop, you'll see rod after rod with a manufacturer's recommendation on it saying something like "1–4 pound," "1–6 pound," or even "2–8 pound." When you see this sort of label on a rod, just remember that the company that makes those rods wants to sell as many as they can. To do that, they make the rods appear to be very versatile.

Your goal, however, is to buy just the right rod for *one* line strength. You'll have to be skeptical about the manufacturers' recommendations and make your own decisions. Since 1-kg line is for hard-core ultralight addicts, I'd suggest you begin with 2-kg and work your way down.

Buying the Rod

When you go into a store to pick out a rod, bring your reel and some 2-kg line. After mounting the reel on the rod, run the line up through the guides and tie it to a suitable weight or fixed object on the floor. Jam the butt of the rod into your belly and hold it at a 45-degree angle to the floor. Tighten up on the line until it begins to stretch. With the rod butt at 45 degrees to the floor, and the line just starting to stretch, the rod tip should be almost vertical and pointing down toward the place where the line is tied. It's best if the stress is distributed throughout the rod so a smooth curve is formed from handle to tip. A rod that forms a smooth, parabolic curve under load has the slow action you're looking for.

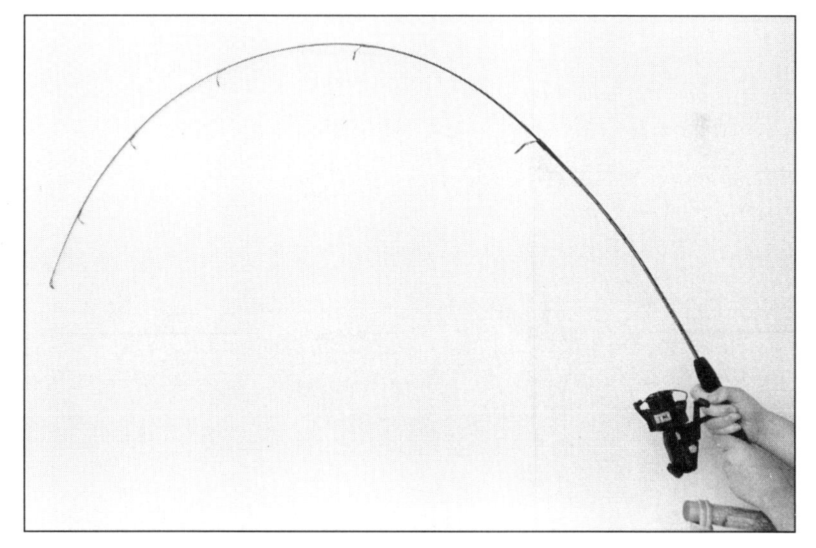

This is what an ultralight rod should look like under full load when you're testing it at the store. Shown here is my preferred 1-kg rod, a Berkley Bionix X-20.

If the rod is too flexible, it will assume that same degree of bend *before* the line begins to stretch. This means that you won't have enough strength in the rod to use the line to maximum advantage while you're fishing. If the rod is too stiff, the parabolic curve you're looking for will not be formed until after the line starts to stretch. On the water such a rod will not bend enough to soften the stresses of the fight, and the line may break before you have a chance to accommodate any unexpected runs.

By testing rods this way, you'll be sure to end up with one that's truly suitable for a single strength of line, and that's the most you can hope for. The rod will be compatible with the line, and you'll be able to use the rod's flex as a reliable sign of line stress. Once you become experienced you will depend on this flex to determine how hard to push the fish.

The Guides and the Bend

For a rod to form a smooth, parabolic curve under stress, it needs guides that don't flatten out its slow action. If the feet on the guides are too long or too firm, their rigidity will create a flat spot in the curve of the rod. This produces uneven stress on the rod and line, which leads to line wear and lost fish. Single-foot guides are the most desirable since they interfere the least with the rod's action.

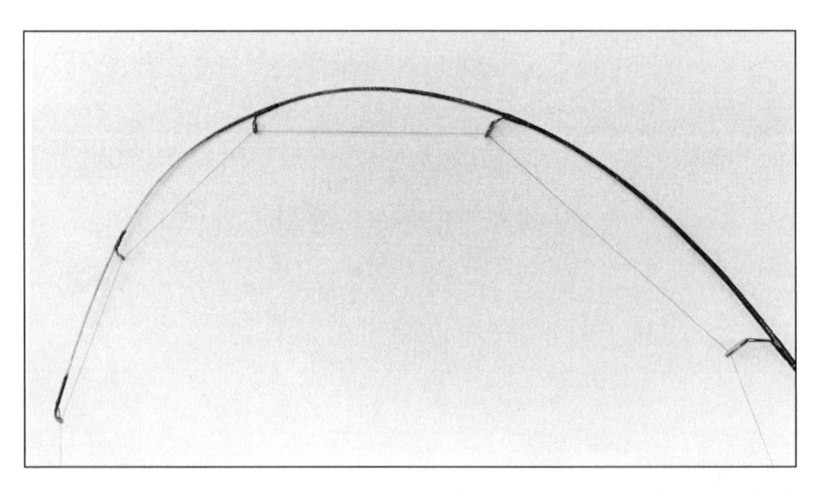

The guides on this rod are too widely spaced. The line wears more quickly when there aren't enough guides to support it.

The rod you're going to buy also has to have the right number of guides. It is cheaper for a manufacturer to place fewer guides on a rod, and the poorer rods are made just that way. On an ultralight stick in the 5- to 6-foot (170-cm) size range, you'd expect to find at least five guides and probably six. The guides should be closer together toward the tip where the maximum bend is. To check that the guides are correctly positioned, just look at the line while you're testing the rod. When the rod is under stress the line should flow evenly from guide to guide. If it forms a sudden angle at any one guide you know the rod was poorly designed.

I've lost so many fish with worn metal guides that I don't trust them and will never use them again. Do not buy a rod with metal guides. They wear out, rust, and crack with astounding frequency. Once when I was fighting (and losing) sharks with 1-kg line, tiny grooves appeared in my metal guides after only 2 hours of continuous use. (When I discovered the reason for the lost fish, I was angry but relieved that the fault lay with the guides and not with me.) The next week I stripped the rod and put on all new aluminum oxide guides. The rod is still in use today, and the replacement guides are as smooth as ever.

To cope with the amazing abrasiveness of monofilament nylon, the guides need to be made of a ceramic material like aluminum oxide or silicon carbide. These materials are smooth yet hard enough to resist the wear and tear that monofilament can produce. Smooth guides also reduce line wear during long battles with hard-fighting fish. You can make it even easier on your line by lubricating the guides regularly. To do this, simply dip the rod into the water to wet the guides while you're fighting a fish. By keeping the guides moist, you can reduce resistance to line flow to a point where line wear from the guides becomes negligible, even after a two- to three-hour battle.

Length

The length of your rod is a matter of personal preference. A pole less than 6 feet (2 meters) is easier to use in a small boat than a longer one. A "noodle rod" can be up to 12 feet (4 meters) long. The advantage of a noodle rod is that it distributes the line stress over so many guides that there are no abrupt angles in the line. The noodle rod's length and excessive flex also cushion the line against sudden runs by the fish. It is awkward, though, and less responsive than a shorter rod.

I use a noodle rod if I'm fishing from shore for big or powerful fish like steelhead, salmon, or kahawai (Australian salmon). For boat fishing I use much shorter sticks; 5½ feet (1.7 meters) seems to be my favorite length when there's a boat to help me fight and follow the fish.

A lot of ultralight rods are also made ultrashort. These short rods look quite nice in the store, but they're a problem on the water. A rod less than 5 feet (150 cm) provides very little length to cushion your line; you end up with far more break-offs than you otherwise would. Avoid them unless you'll be fishing for brook trout on small mountain streams or panfish in farm ponds.

Handles

Fighting a big fish for several hours is somewhat easier with a long handle (18 inches or 45 cm) on the rod because you can wedge the handle under your forearm or into your body. But it also makes the rod heavier and less precise. I'd suggest a long handle or an extension if your wrists tire easily or if you expect to have fish on the line for hours at a time.

Make sure the handle is made of a firm material like cork or EVA foam so that your hand doesn't sink into it while you're holding on for dear life. It should conform to your fingers comfortably as you grip it tightly. With luck, you'll be holding onto it a lot, so make sure it's a good fit.

Another design element that aids sensitivity is a rod blank that runs completely through the handle. These rods are a little more expensive, but having the blank literally in your hands enables you to pick up a lot of signals that would otherwise have been absorbed by your tackle.

Pistol-grip handles are great if you're bait-casting with lures all day, but they're awful if you're fighting a fish for several hours. Stick to the longer, smoother, conventional designs.

Materials

The last factor to consider is the composition of the blank. Varieties of fiberglass, graphite, and composites of fiberglass and graphite are your main choices. I don't think it matters much what the rod is made of if its flex under stress feels and looks appropriate when your reel is mounted on the handle.

Don't bother to stand in the store and wave the rod around to get a feel for it. Fiberglass and composites are heavier than 100-percent graphite and seem to flex more freely as you swing them around because their greater tip weight has more momentum. What counts is how the rod performs with the line running through it and the shaft under stress. Waving it around the store is fun, but it will tell you next to nothing.

Another issue is "toughness." Don't be impressed by exaggerated claims for toughness. Most modern, quality rods are more than adequate for the ultralight angler. Toughness is usually irrelevant while you're fishing. But if you regularly step on your fishing rods, crush them in car doors, or let the kids take them down to the local wharf, a tough rod with a solid tip might be a good investment.

Putting It All Together

When you use the same rod and reel over and over again, they become an extension of your body. At that point your chances of doing well on the water rise dramatically. The magic moments of fishing—the ones that you'll remember for the rest of your life—can happen only when you are at one with the fish, and you won't be if you're fumbling with a new reel and an unfamiliar rod.

To make those magic moments happen, you need top-quality equipment and the spare parts to keep it going for many years. Once you've picked out your line, reel, and rod and given them a few test runs, it's time to put together your long-term outfit. This is the outfit you'll fish with for years, so it's worth investing some time and money in its selection.

My suggestion is that you buy three identical fishing reels and three or four spools to go with each reel. A reel that performs well with 2-kg line will be okay with 1-kg line too. (Remember that reels and rods differ in that respect.) The only difference will be in the amount of backing you put on the spools. Divide your spools into three lots. Dedicate four spools to 1-kg line, four spools to 2-kg line, and the rest to 4- or even 6-kg line for those days when you find yourself fishing around weed or reef.

With three reels you can have two on the water with you every day; if one dies, you always have the other. Though one reel will be mounted on a 1-kg rod and the other on a 2-kg rod, it takes only a few seconds to switch reels and pop on another spool. The third reel sits at home as a back-up. After every five or six trips, rotate the reels so they take turns sitting in storage.

A 1-kg rod is good for only 1-kg line, and a 2-kg rod is good for only 2-kg line. (A final reminder: rods and reels differ in that respect.) If you find a 1-kg rod you really like, buy two of them. Ditto for your 2-kg rod. Then, if a guide breaks, you have a substitute rod while the other's being fixed. Buying a 4-kg rod is a good idea too if you have the money; it will be most useful when you have to fish around structure.

Now that you've got your outfit put together, the next step is to decide which hooks to use; and, believe me, there are lots of options.

CHAPTER FIVE

The Hook

MOST OF US BUY FISH HOOKS based on the size of the fish we hope to catch, following the old rule that large hooks are for large fish and small hooks are for small fish. And this is certainly understandable—not many of us are knowledgeable enough to select just the right hook from the overwhelming variety of styles available in any large tackle store. But the old rule is usually misleading, so you'll need to know a little more in order to select the correct hook for ultralight fishing.

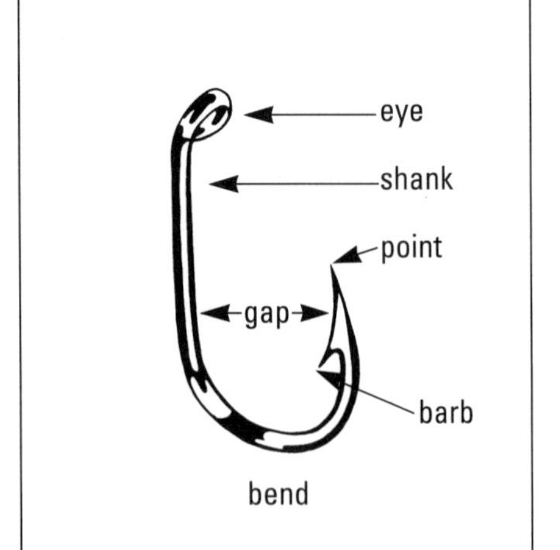

The humble fish hook has many parts, and each part has many design variations.

The Factors in Hook Selection

If large hooks are not necessarily for large fish, how do you decide which hook to use? There are a lot of factors involved, especially if you'll be fishing ultralight. Let's go over them one at a time.

The Fish's Jaws

The amount of force required to set a hook varies with the species of the fish and where in its mouth you try to hook it. You can see this for yourself by experimenting with a fish that's freshly caught and dispatched. You'll find it takes about 5 pounds of force to set a 2/0 hook into the upper or lower jaw of an average fish and about ½ pound to set it into the side of the mouth. A fish with tough jaws—like a snapper, muskellunge, shark, or tarpon—will require more force to set a hook than a more delicate species like a bonito, weakfish, or trevally.

Hook Size

You can decrease the force required to set a hook by reducing the size of the hook. Sit down at the kitchen table with a hard apple and compare the force necessary to sink the barb of a 10/0 hook into the apple with the force required to set the barb of a 2/0 hook of similar pattern. You'll be surprised by the difference.

You can appreciate an even bigger difference if you remove the barb from the 2/0 hook. To remove a barb, simply take a pair of pliers and squeeze the barb toward the bend of the hook. If it doesn't break off it will end up lying flat and out of the way. You'll see that barbless hooks are far easier to sink in than barbed hooks, regardless of size.

There's a much better chance of setting a small hook than a large one, and an even better chance of setting a barbless hook. The next time you get into a big enough school of fish (mackerel, bluefish, kahawai, perch, or crappie would be good species) you can prove this to yourself by comparing the results you get using different-size hooks, both barbed and barbless. You will unquestionably find that you hook more fish with small, barbless hooks. If you allow no slack to develop in the line, you'll also land

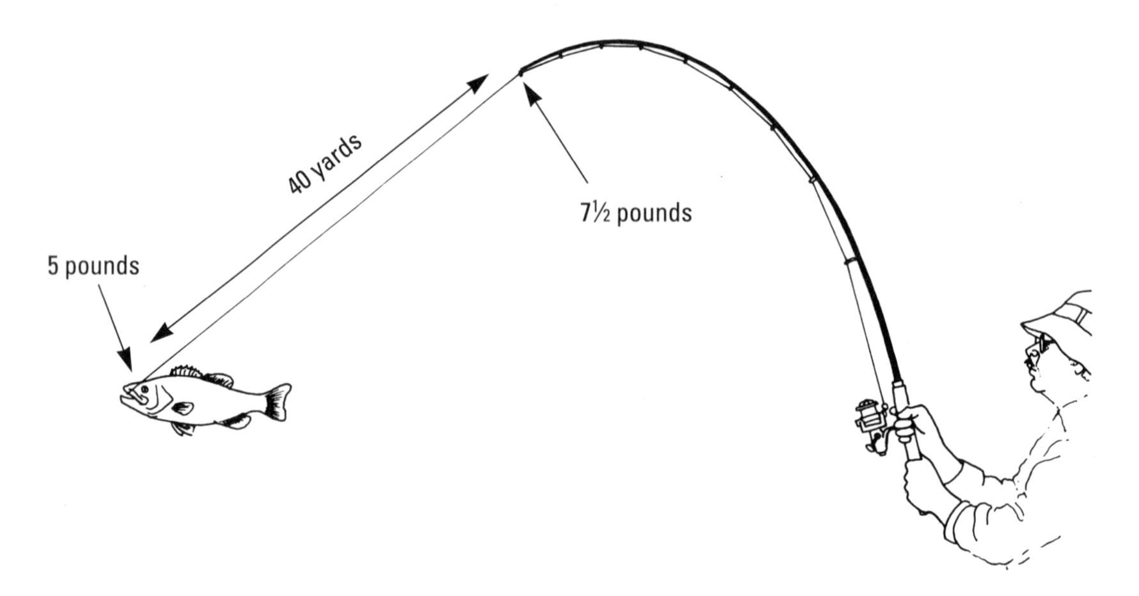

When you set the hook, some of the force of the strike is absorbed by the stretch of the monofilament line.

just about as many fish with barbless hooks as with barbed hooks. It's also a lot safer and easier to remove a barbless than a barbed hook from the mouth of a struggling fish.

The Line

After you've seen just how much force you need to set a hook, common sense will tell you that it's just not possible to set a big hook with a 1- or 2-kg line. It can be just as impossible to set a hook with 4- or 6-kg lines! This is because the amount of force you can apply to the hook decreases as line length increases. Since wet monofilament nylon has built-in stretch (up to 30 percent), it absorbs the force you put into the strike. For instance, a 7½-pound force applied to 4-kg line will provide only 5 pounds of hook-setting pressure at the end of 40 yards (36 meters) of wet line. If you try to increase the hook-setting pressure by pulling harder on the line, you'll just snap it at the rod tip and lose the fish and the terminal tackle.

To get around the problem of line stretch, use the smallest possible barbless hooks. The other approach is to use hooks that set themselves. You'll learn more about these unique hooks under "A Bent Hook" later in this chapter.

The Point

There's nothing you can do about line stretch or fish anatomy, so the only way to increase your success is to improve the hooks you use. A sharp hook makes a great deal of difference. You can reduce the force required to set a hook by 50 percent just by sharpening it properly.

There are several approaches to hook sharpening. Some people advocate a triangular or diamond-shape point. A few insist a short barb is all-important; they suggest cutting the points off all store-bought hooks and resharpening them so the barb length is decreased by 40 percent or so. Although these strategies might be effective for heavier lines, they won't do for ultralight.

A diamond or triangular point has a cutting edge that will invariably enlarge the hole created by the point, thereby loosening the hook. After the first 30 or 40 minutes of a good battle, the hook will simply fall out if the line slackens or the fish jumps. A better point style for ultralight is the needle point, which has no cutting edges but is smooth all around.

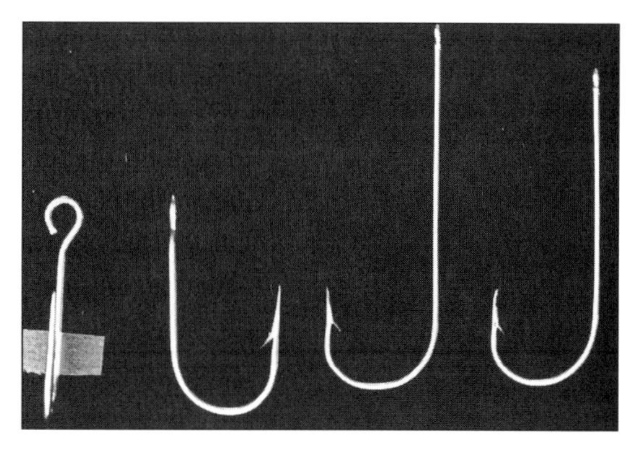

The open-eye, Salmon-style hook on the left has a much longer barb than the Aberdeens on the right.

A hook with a short barb can be driven in faster but may require more force than an ultralight line can muster. A hook with a long tapered barb (or no barb at all), sharpened to a needle point, without cutting edges, is the ideal hook for ultralight.

The Fish's Size

You don't need a big hook to catch a big fish unless you like to pull hard. Since you can't pull hard with 1- or 2-kg line, there's usually no need to use a big hook.

Hooks will just straighten out if the force applied by the angler exceeds the strength of the hook's bend. Even hooks as small as a 1/0 wire Aberdeen will land a 10- to 20-kg gamefish with ultralight lines because the lines are just too weak to allow the angler to accidentally straighten the hook.

The Bait

For the ultralight angler bait size is the most influential factor in hook selection. For species that require live bait or species like sharks that require a large slab of dead bait, you must use a large hook. For live bait the solution is to use wire Aberdeen hooks with the barbs left on. (More about

The size of the hook has to match the size of the bait.

that in the next section.) And there's just no way to put a fist-size hunk of bonito bait onto a 1/0 hook; for this situation a specially shaped 9/0 hook is required. I'll tell you all about those hooks too in "A Bent Hook."

Wire Hooks

The Aberdeen wire hook is designed for live bait like crickets and 2-inch (4- to 6-cm) minnows and is seldom used to catch larger fish. It is frequently used for freshwater fishing in America and Europe, where people use small live bait to catch small gamefish like pike, pickerel, crappie, and bass.

The Aberdeen features a long shank, wide gap, and curved-in or straight point. The eye can be straight or turned down. The bend is not kirbed. The hook is made of round wire and comes in two varieties: light and extra-light. If you compare an Aberdeen to another hook style of similar gap, the most striking difference is the light wire construction.

Aberdeens are actually supposed to bend if you pull on them too hard, which makes it possible to straighten the hook and retrieve your line if it gets hung up on a snag. Such snags are common in the freshwater environment where pickerel, crappie, and bass live. The fine wire design also makes it possible to rig small live bait without killing it.

The fine wire has yet another advantage: it's easy to sink the hook into the gamefish. With large-diameter or forged hooks, you need a strong line just to force the hook in. But Aberdeens can be set with just a twist of the wrist, and this makes them ideal for live-baiting with ultralight lines.

Aberdeens come in sizes from #10s to 5/0s. I've found sizes 2/0 to 5/0 to be the most suitable for 3- to 6-inch (8- to 15-cm) live bait. A 4/0 Aberdeen will not straighten with lines as strong as 4 kg; yet it's thin enough not to injure live bait as small as 4 inches (10 cm) in length. When live-baiting in fresh water with shiners, chubs, or other small bait, use a 2/0 Aberdeen to avoid major trauma.

There are two basic ways to hook small live bait. If the fish is capable of withstanding some injury—like a mackerel, killifish, or herring—you can hook it just in front of the dorsal fin. Although this is the most popular technique, it is fraught with difficulty. The most common problem, of course, is ending up with dead bait. This usually happens because

Two effective ways to hook live bait. Mouth-hooked bait will live longer and be more active than back-hooked bait.

the hook is set too far under the skin or because the hook shaft rotates and the point gets buried in the bait's side. Hooks with turned-in points are especially likely to bury themselves. (There will be more on this in Chapter Seven.) As you can imagine, buried points don't snag many fish. Also, you'll have used a large-size hook (4/0 or bigger) to secure a medium size bait by the back, and that will make it harder to sink the barb when a gamefish does strike.

A better way to hook delicate live bait—like mullet, menhaden, pilchard, or English mackerel—is to mouth-hook it. This has two advantages: the fish can swim more freely, so it isn't dragged downstream in the tidal flow; and the bait is not injured by the hook. The main disadvantage is that the hook can fall out if it isn't placed properly. (This is why you need to keep the barbs on hooks used for live-baiting.)

Accurate hook placement is critical in mouth-hooking. If you put the hook into the thin membrane around the jaw, it will quickly erode a hole so large that the hook will fall out when the line slackens. If the hook is placed too far back, it gets into important places like the brain; and that does not lengthen your bait's life span. The trick is to place the hook just behind the thin membrane around the upper jaw and right in the midline. If you do that, your bait will survive for hours, and there will be no need to change it every 20 minutes.

Aberdeen hooks are made in the United States by Wright and McGill under the Eagle Claw brand and by Mustad in Norway.

The Eagle Claw variety comes in two styles, "F" and "EL." The "EL" stands for extra-light, and these hooks are probably too thin for lines over 2 kg. They have a curved-in point and come in three finishes: bronzed, gold, or blued.

The Mustad hook comes with straight or curved-in point and with a straight or turned-down eye. It has a bronzed, gold, or blued finish. My choice for mouth-hooking delicate live bait would be a 2/0 Aberdeen with a curved-in point, bronzed or blued finish, and straight eye. For back-hooking larger live bait, a 4/0 or 5/0 Aberdeen with a straight point would be a better option.

A Bent Hook

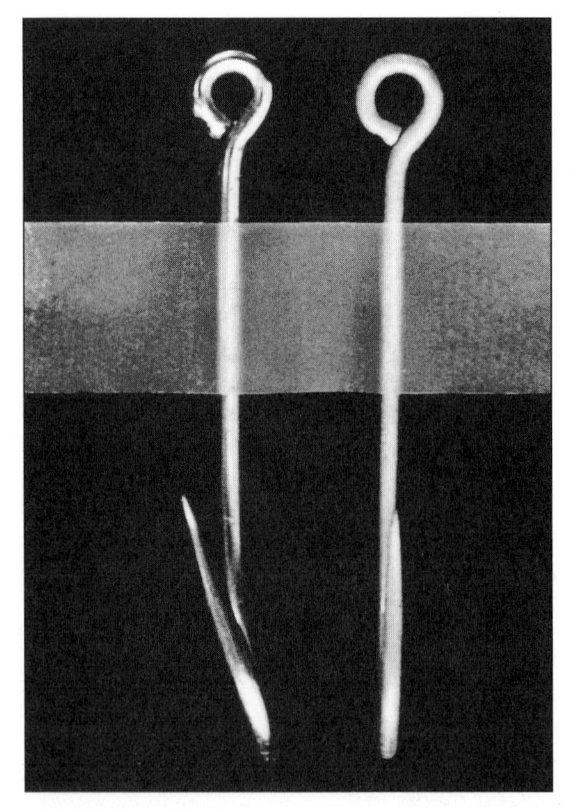

When the spear of a hook is bent away from the shaft, it is called "reversed" or "kirbed," depending on the direction of the bend.

One of the biggest problems for the ultralight angler is setting the hook. When using thin lines it's difficult, and sometimes impossible, to drive a large hook into the armored mouth of a predatory fish. For this reason hook selection is *numero uno* when it comes to choosing terminal tackle.

Back in 1986 I knew all the basics of hook selection, but it didn't seem to matter. We were after sharks, and we seemed to be spending most of our time losing them. We could spend hours looking for a school and then, with hundreds of sharks around us, proceed to lose one after the other. There were lots of things that went wrong, but most of the time the hook would simply fall out in the first 10 minutes of the fight.

The situation was driving us nuts. We experimented with different bait presentations; but no matter how the bait was mounted, most of the hooks fell out. We tried hooks as small as 4/0 but they ended up buried in the big bait. Experiments with point-curved-in tuna hooks were a dismal failure. We even tried fishing shallower water to reduce the inherent stretch of the nylon, but that didn't help either.

It seemed to be a hopeless predicament, and for that summer we had no choice but to accept our losses. A solution unfolded during the following winter in, of all places, New York City. I was looking through a hook catalog and noticed a little item designed to be a cod hook. It had a most unusual shape.

Cod live deep down on the floor of the Atlantic, and it's difficult to hook them because the stretch inherent in the long length of fishing line absorbs all the energy of the strike. To overcome this problem, the designers of the cod hook intended it to be self-setting. The hook had a curious bend in the shank that paralleled the kirbed point. When the fish clamped its jaws around the bait, the curved shank acted like a camshaft and forced the barb into the fish's mouth.

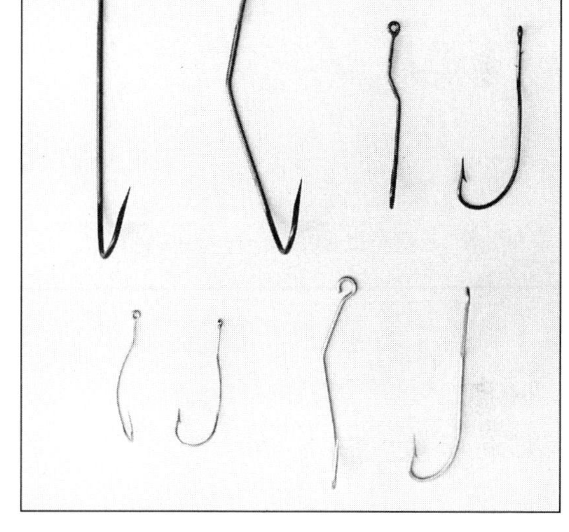

An unmodified 9/0 Carlisle hook is shown at the top left. The shaft on the Carlisle next to it has been bent to produce a cam action to help sink in the point. The hooks on the top right are 4/0 Tru-Turns; on the bottom left are two views of the Eagle Claw 1/0 Aberdeen Auto; and on the bottom right are two views of a 4/0 Shank Bent Aside Superior Mustad Limerick.

Unfortunately the hooks in the catalog were made of heavy-gauge stainless steel—not at all suitable for ultralight fishing. So I ordered 200 9/0, thin-gauge, kirbed, bronzed Carlisle hooks and bent them myself.

Experts will tell you that bending hooks weakens them, so that they tend to self-destruct under stress. But I figured that ultralight line was not going to stress a 9/0 hook under any circumstance, and indeed that proved to be the case. After experimenting with a variety of bends I came up with the design shown in the accompanying photo. The following summer the hooks proved to be a tremendous success. Our hook drop-out rate was less than 10 percent, and we got to spend more time fighting sharks than cursing our gear.

You can make these hooks yourself, or you can order them. There are three styles available that I know of:

- Mustad makes a Shank Bent Aside Superior Limerick hook, which is tinned and kirbed, in sizes 1/0 to 12/0.
- Eagle Claw makes a Messler hook, which is bronzed and kirbed, in sizes 2 to 4/0. It features a compound curve in the shank to produce the cam action. Eagle Claw also makes an automatic rotating Aberdeen in sizes 8 to 3/0.
- Tru-Turn specializes in the bent-hook style and makes a worm hook of similar design. It features a double bend in the shaft, no kirb, and bait holders on the shank. I use numbers 3/0 to 5/0; other sizes are available as well. They also make a cam-action

Aberdeen hook in sizes 8 to 2/0, which combines the virtues of a bent-hook and wire construction.

If you fish with ultralight in deep water or have lots of trouble with your hooks falling out of the mouths of your intended victims, try these hook styles. They may reduce your "anguish rate" next season.

The Long Barb and Other Hints

Of the thousands of other hooks available, I'd like to mention just three more styles that might interest you.

- The Mustad 95141 Hollow Point Salmon hook is a handy item. This hook has a very long barb that easily takes a needle point. It also has an open ring instead of a closed eye. This makes it very handy for attaching to lures in place of cumbersome trebles. The wide gap and long barb of the hook also make it useful for fishing with medium-size soft bait that might otherwise cover the point. The hook comes in a variety of sizes, but the most useful are the 1 and 1/0.

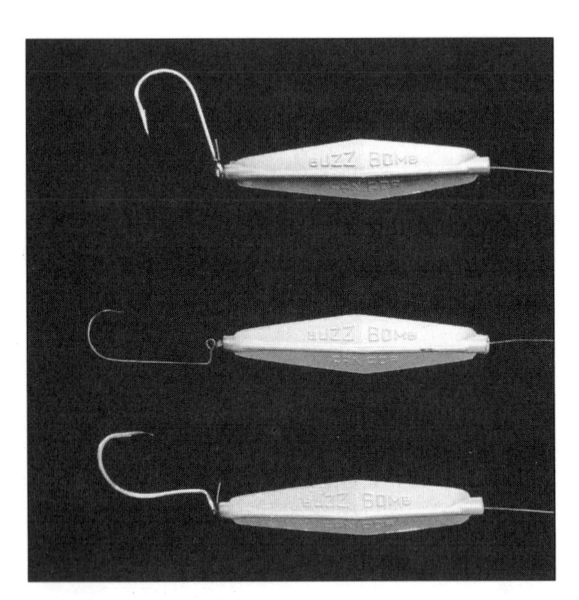

One problem with sliding jigs like these Buzz-Bombs is that the hook can swing away as shown at the top. The cure is to use a jig hook with a bent shaft (middle) or a hook with a turned-up eye (bottom).

- When you place an ordinary hook under a sliding jig, the hook will often ride up toward the side of the lure (see the photo). The net effect of this little trick is no hookups because the hook is tilted away when the fish strikes. You can solve this problem in two ways: with a jig hook or a hook with a turned-up eye (see the photo). The jig hook has a 60- to 90-degree bend in the shank, just a bit below the eye. The bend in the shank is designed for making lead-head jigs, but it also helps keep the hook from riding to the side.

  There are many sorts of jig hooks. My favorites, Extra Short Shank Aberdeens, are made by Mustad. They have a 90-degree bend and are available in bronzed, gold, and tinned finishes. For a turned-up eye, try the #92550 Mustad beak hook; it works well too.
- The suicide or circle hook is relatively unknown in North America but very popular in the Far East. It is often used for tuna fishing;

but, for bottom species like snapper and trevally, it's the most suitable hook for the ultralight angler. It's called a suicide hook because the fish commits suicide when it takes the bait.

A variety of hooks that are suitable for tough-jawed fish like snapper. From top to bottom: a 4/0 Tru-Turn, 1/0 Eagle Claw Aberdeen Auto, Eagle Claw 4/0 Aberdeen EL, #16 HP Tainawa (suicide), Black Magic 4/0 KL (circle), and 6/0 Mustad Wide Gap.

The curve of the hook forms an almost complete circle. Every angler's initial impression is that there's no way any fish could get hooked on one of these; but after you think about it a while, it's easy to see what happens when the fish bites. As the fish's jaws put pressure on the hook, it rolls in the fish's lips, and the rounded point nicks the corner of the mouth. As soon as the fish begins to pull away, the rounded point responds by circling around, driving the barb all the way in. Like the bent hook, the suicide hook requires only that the angler keep a tight line. If you try to set the hook, you'll just pull it away from the fish, denying him the opportunity to commit suicide.

Chapter Six

Lures

Lures are great fun to use and even more fun to buy. They're lovely to look at—they gleam in the sun and look terrific in a tackle box. And, of course, there is a bit of cult status attached to using lures. In general, however, properly presented bait—even cut bait—will catch more fish and cost a lot less money.

Lures are often difficult to use with ultralight. Repeated casting is tough on 1- and 2-kg lines. Twenty or 30 casts of a heavy lure, followed by rapid retrieves, can reduce line strength by 10 percent or more. Many lures also cause line twist because of their movement in the water. One- and 2-kg lines are so supple that they have virtually no resistance to this twisting process. There's no way to prevent it either; even the most expensive, ball-bearing–based swivels are not sensitive enough to prevent twisting with ultralight lines.

Despite all these negatives, lures are sometimes indispensable—like when you run out of bait. And because lures are selective (each one selects for a certain type of fish), you can avoid hooking up with "undesirables." There are also those days when there are so many fish around that you can't help but hook up on the first cast—get out those lures and enjoy yourself! There's no doubt that fishing with lures, especially surface types, is more fun than handling smelly bait.

There are so many lures on the market that no one person could fish with all of them. The variations in design, color, and action are fascinating but also a source of endless confusion for the angler who just wants a few artificials for the tackle box. Fortunately, there are some principles of lure fishing that will help you make your way through the morass of possible choices. They are presented below in order of importance.

Having Faith

The most important aspect of fishing with artificials is an emotional one. It's imperative that you "believe in" the lures you use. If you have faith in a lure, you will use it often. The more you use a lure, the more proficient you become in varying its actions to suit any given situation.

I have an infatuation with a lure called the Buzz-Bomb (see the illustration on page 62). Buzz-Bombs are a dense, jigging-type lure made in British Columbia, Canada, for salmon fishing. (For more information on these lures contact Buzz-Bomb Lure Corp., 2498 Cousins Avenue, Courtenay, B.C., Canada, V9N 7T5.)

During my first trip to British Columbia, I watched with wonder as my local mentor caught salmon after salmon while very skillfully jigging his Buzz-Bomb. I was impressed, and the first glimmer of faith entered my mind. In the years since then, my proficiency with these lures has grown, and therefore my faith in them has deepened. I've taken Buzz-Bombs all over the world and fished them in every sort of situation; they always seem to work. But they work because I'm used to them—I've learned through hard experience how to vary the pattern and speed of the retrieve to suit any fish, anywhere. I'll tell you more about these lures later in this chapter.

I know, in my heart of hearts, that there's nothing special about the Buzz-Bomb. Many other lures are as good, possibly better. Skilled anglers who use other lures with equal effectiveness will tell you the same thing. Pick a few lures, use them a lot, and you too will have faith.

Form

You will usually catch more fish with artificials if you match them to the situation. Try to identify what the fish are eating, and then dupli-

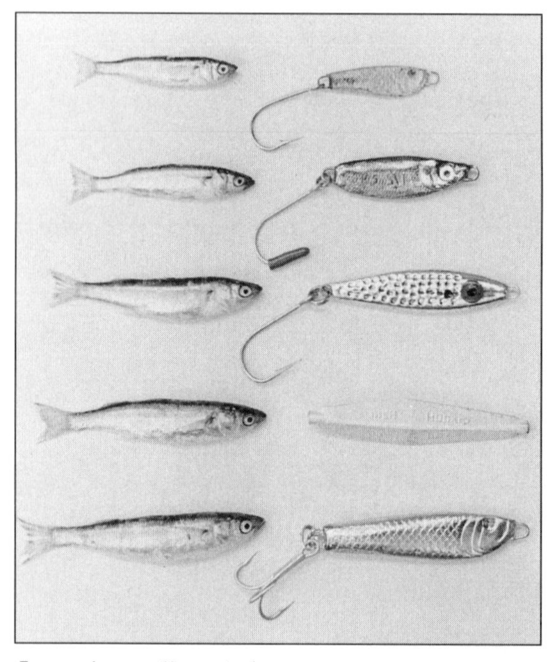

For maximum effect a lure needs to match the size and shape of a fish's natural prey.

cate with your lures the form, size, location, motion, and color of the fish's prey. Like us, fish are creatures of habit. If they are actively feeding on one species of prey, they will tend to concentrate on that one species to the exclusion of all others.

I have drifted past large schools of feeding kahawai as they were tearing through masses of silver-colored anchovies. The action was spectacular, but there was no way those kahawai would take anything other than a lure resembling those anchovies. Despite my repeated efforts, the kahawai would not respond to a larger live bait, halfbeaks, or anything else they would normally gorge on. Similar experiences with bluefish, yellowtail, trevally, and walleye have convinced me that the rule is close to universal. As the fly-fishermen say, "Match the hatch!"

An Example

If you encounter a school of pelagics plowing through a mass of baitfish, use a lure that looks like the species of baitfish they're eating. Since fish respond primarily to the lure's silhouette in the water, your first job is to match the size and shape of the artificial to the form of the prey. To do this you'll have to analyze how the gamefish approaches its prey. If the fish attacks from below, then match the shape seen from underneath the prey. If the fish attacks from the side, then match the shape seen from the side.

Once you've determined the right shape for the lure, the next challenge is to imitate the motion of the prey. Does the intended victim skip across the surface? Does it flee in a jerking motion with rapid turns? Does it dive or jump out of the water? If you imitate the prey's shape and movement pattern, it's hard to go wrong.

Another Example

If you come across a school of mackerel, jacks, or trevally feeding on crustaceans near the surface, use a soft-plastic lure, wet fly, or crappie jig that resembles the feathery form of the crustacean from behind—where the fish will be. What the lure looks like from the side or the top doesn't matter. It's the fish's perspective that counts, not the fisherman's.

Location

You have to get your lure to the area and depth of the natural food supply. If you can see that the baitfish are near the surface, use a lure that will stay on top. If the baitfish are fast-moving, you'll need a dense minnow imitation that's heavy enough to stay under the water despite a fast retrieve.

If a large school of baitfish shows up in midwater, you'll have to drop down a metal jig, lead-head bucktail, or similar minnow imitation to try to attract the gamefish around or under the school. Since you cannot imitate fleeing baitfish in 30 feet (9 meters) of water with ultralight, you have to do the next best thing and imitate injured bait. Injured baitfish follow a jerking motion through the water as they try to move, so that's what you have to do. Just remember that an injured fish 4 inches (10 cm) long does not make 8-foot leaps through the water. Move your jig as the injured bait would move, a foot or two at a time. Another way to deal with such a situation is to slowly troll a diving lure or dense spoon around the school of baitfish.

Keep in mind that gamefish wait underneath and downstream from areas where large schools congregate, so concentrate your activities there. Predators are put off by a lure that comes toward them; their victims are supposed to run away from death, not toward it. The solution is to guess where the fish might be and make your lure behave as though it's trying to get away from that area.

If you're fishing for species that wait in ambush—like pike, pickerel, bass, and trout—then get upwind and cast a lightweight minnow imitation or spinner, and retrieve it slowly enough to resemble a casually swimming baitfish. By speeding up the movements of the lure intermittently, you can imitate the sudden panic of a frightened fish that has just detected approaching doom. The sudden acceleration is often the key factor in producing a hookup, and that brings us to the subject of a lure's action.

Action

As a gamefish evaluates the form of a potential prey, he also examines its pattern of movement. The basic rule of retrieve is to make the lure travel fast enough that the fish can't get a good look at it, but slow enough that he can catch it. Situations that illustrate the rule are a quickly retrieved silver spoon simulating a healthy, fast-moving herring; an erratically jigged, silver-colored plastic worm simulating an injured halfbeak; or a soft-plastic lure—retrieved with the sudden, erratic motions characteristic of crustaceans—to entice bottom feeders. A bizarre application of the rule is keeping a hair bug motionless to seduce the clever carp that's feeding on dead, floating insects.

If your first idea on the correct motion of a lure is unproductive, try other patterns of movement. Anglers succeed by being flexible: if something doesn't work, try another approach. There's no way to know exactly what's happening under the water, so you just have to keep guessing. In moments of desperation remember that sometimes the most "inappropriate" actions catch the most fish. I can remember times when we've caught one smallmouth bass after another by jigging a gold spinner up and down. Totally inappropriate, but it worked.

No matter what retrieve pattern you're using, remember to continue it right up to the shore or side of the boat and then move the lure in a figure-eight pattern before pulling it out of the water. Some gamefish are especially notorious for following the lure right to the angler. Pike and pickerel typify this behavior pattern. Their life habit is to wait in ambush and then dash out to grab their prey. Once they've launched themselves, they don't give up easily and tend to follow the lure to the end of its path. When the lure demonstrates some enticing new motion, they finally strike. That last figure-eight movement can be the delectable new effect that you need. It can make the difference between lots of exciting action and an empty hook.

Color

Most gamefish have some sort of color vision, and they use it to help identify their prey. For this reason it is of some importance to match the color of your lure to the bait it imitates. Again we come to the issue of the fish's approach. If the gamefish attacks from below, it is the color of the bottom of the lure that counts. For example, if you're using a popper to imitate the panicked flight of halfbeaks, make sure it's silver on the bottom side. The upper half might as well be pink polka dots because the fish will never see it.

Sometimes color is of critical importance. If you're in an unfamiliar area, find out what lure color the locals prefer. It may be important. I learned this lesson the hard way fishing for inconnu in northern Alaska in the early '80s. These giant whitefish grow to 40 to 60 pounds (20 to 30 kg). I tried all sorts of spinners, spoons, and jigs but caught only salmon, grayling, and an occasional small inconnu. I didn't understand what I was doing wrong until an Inuit fisherman suggested I try an orange spoon. That was it! After tying on an orange lure (it didn't much matter what sort) I couldn't keep the inconnu off my line. To this day I have no idea what those fish saw in the color orange.

On this particular fall day, these inconnu would take any orange lure, but no other color would do. These fish were all sun-dried for winter food.

But the significance of color is sometimes obvious. While fishing the high mountain lakes of the Wind River Range in Wyoming, I found that the larger cutthroat trout would take a lure with a red stripe before they'd attack anything else. Since these larger trout often ate their smaller relations, I figured the red stripe must represent the red streak below the cutthroat's neck. With that insight I touched up a few lures so the front end had a red stripe. The results were impressive indeed. We ate well that trip.

Good Vibrations

Fish don't have the world's greatest night vision, yet they can hunt on the darkest nights. They also seem to be able to find food in waters clouded by silt and churned up by the wind. How do they do it? Probably by detecting low-frequency vibrations. The pressure waves produced by low-frequency vibrations are so long that the vibrations are not heard but felt.

Gamefish have a lateral line along their flanks, made up of dozens of tiny holes containing sensitive nerve endings that respond to the minute changes in water pressure caused by low-frequency vibrations. Because the lateral line is an elongated organ, the fish can use it as a direction finder. If the vibrations are stronger to the right, the fish knows its prey lies to the right. If the vibrations are evenly detected by both flanks, the prey is straight ahead.

Stealth

Water is a wonderful conductor of sound. The noise of pounding on the floor of a boat will travel at thousands of miles an hour through the water and will be heard by fish miles away.

Some fish are frightened by alien noises. Others, like sharks and yellowtail, are often attracted by low-frequency sound. The South Pacific peoples used to beat rocks on the bottom of their wooden canoes to attract certain species. But unless you know which sounds attract the fish you're after, try to be as quiet as possible. Suspicious sounds and doubtful lures make a poor combination.

All fish are sensitive

If you want to catch fish in a stream, stay low and stay quiet.

Any creature moving through the water generates these low-frequency vibrations and long pressure waves. An injured fish moving erratically will produce a different sensation in the gamefish than a healthy bait moving smoothly. Each species of fish makes its own particular sound pattern, and even from a great distance a gamefish can determine the species and the motion pattern of a prospective meal by the feel of its vibrations. With the information provided by its lateral lines, the feeding fish can close in on its intended victim without visual contact. Of course, the baitfish can also detect the bigger fish closing in. When that happens, the bait usually panics and generates even more pressure waves, which tell the gamefish that it's on the right path.

Lures moving through the water produce pressure waves too. Since each species of fish is attracted by particular patterns of waves, the trick is to, again, "match the hatch" by using a lure that generates the waves the gamefish is looking for. A good example of this is the wildly successful plastic worm.

Any idiot can figure out that plastic worms don't resemble anything a bass would eat naturally. How many 6-inch (15-cm) chartreuse worms have you seen bouncing along the bottom 20 feet from shore? It's not what the plastic worm *looks like* that makes it so effective; it's what the worm *feels like* to the bass as it moves through the water. A properly retrieved plastic worm creates long pressure waves that the bass feels and finds irresistible. That's the key to the worm's success.

This phenomenon also explains why some anglers do better than others in identical situations. Have you ever had this contest with a friend:

both of you fish from the same location, have identical rods and reels, and use the same lure; yet your friend outfishes you 10:1? How can this be? Your friend has learned the secret of retrieving that lure as effectively as possible, of producing just the right pattern of movement to create the vibrations that drive the target fish crazy with desire. That particular pattern of movement may not work for all species of gamefish, but it works for the one you're trying to catch under those specific conditions.

This level of skill comes only with experience. It takes a long time to learn the subtle movements that bring life to a lure and make it irresistible to feeding fish. Give yourself time to gain the experience to make lures work—don't try to master too many lure types. Pick a few, use them often, and know them well.

Although a skilled angler can vary a lure's vibratory pattern by varying the retrieve, each lure has its own intrinsic identity; and that's difficult to alter. Some lures are just not attractive to some fish in some situations. For instance, the Panther Martin is an extraordinary spinner. It produces vibrations that pickerel, pike, and trout cannot resist, and will catch fish when other spinners won't. Yet I've never been able to catch a saltwater fish with a Panther Martin; saltwater fish are just not interested in what that lure has to offer.

There is one lure that produces a vibratory pattern attractive to a wide variety of species in both fresh and salt water, and that's the Buzz-Bomb (the lure I mentioned earlier). I warn you that I am highly biased toward the Buzz-Bomb, and you should take that into consideration as you read the next section.

Jigging and the Buzz-Bomb

Buzz-Bombs don't shine or look pretty, but they are, without doubt, one of the world's most versatile and effective lures. I'd like to tell you how I fell in love with this particular lure; perhaps a similar romance will come your way.

While fishing in the crystal-clear waters along the coast of Glacier Bay in Alaska, I had a chance to observe the Buzz-Bomb in action. I was on a high wharf and could watch the lure's movements as I jigged it in the waters below. When I pulled upward, the lure would rise smartly; but when the tension came off the line, the lure would fall through the water with a turning motion, generating vibrations as it fluttered down.

to the sound of someone stomping along a riverbank or through the water; they know it means danger. If you must move along water that holds fish, move in an upstream direction so the sounds won't be conducted as well. If you're in a boat and approaching a big school of surface feeders, swing the boat upwind or uptide of the school; then drift into it with the engine off and everyone sitting low in the boat. Don't start the engine again until you've drifted right through the school and out the other side. If you're quiet enough, you may get a second or third drift and a lot more action.

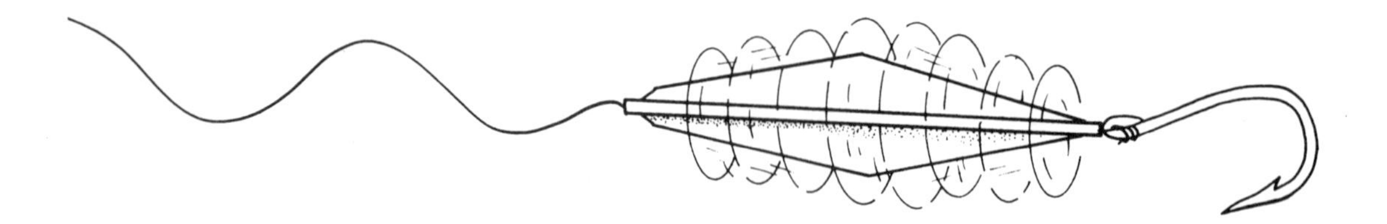

Because the fishing line runs through the middle of the Buzz-Bomb, the lure will spin and vibrate as it falls through the water.

On the other side of the channel, a school of salmon was actively feeding. It wasn't hard to tell—the water was disturbed, and there were birds hanging around, looking for an easy meal. As I stood there, mindlessly jigging away, I was astonished to see several silver salmon swim toward my lure from across the channel. They'd deserted their productive feeding ground to find the source of the vibrations they were picking up. One of those salmon, a lovely 10-pounder (4.5 kg), took the lure and ended his days nailed to a cedar slab next to the evening campfire.

Buzz-Bombs were designed by Rex Field in British Columbia, Canada, more than 30 years ago. They are strangely shaped lead jigs that you attach to the line by running the monofilament through the center of the lure, which causes the Bomb to rotate around the line as it falls through the water.

The Buzz-Bomb's eccentric, rotary motion produces underwater vibrations that attract gamefish, and it's the rotation that sets this lure apart from others. If you don't have a lot of experience with the Buzz-Bomb, you've got to follow the instructions to make it work properly. If you do study the instruction sheet that comes with the Buzz-Bomb, you'll be glad you bought the lure; otherwise, you might as well have spent the money on beer and peanuts.

If you're the sort of person who hates using instruction sheets when there are better things to do, hold off on the beer and peanuts while I tell you how to use this lure. First of all, the Bomb is not for every occasion. It does not troll any better than other, cheaper lead jigs, and it's also nothing special for a fast retrieve on the surface. The time to use the Buzz-Bomb is when you can take advantage of the vibrations produced by its rotating motion as it free-falls through the water.

If you're fishing from shore, the Bomb is especially useful when you're near a steep drop-off so that you can cast the lure, retrieve it a bit, let it free-fall for a while, and then retrieve it again. Since you're trying to imitate the activities of an injured baitfish, don't retrieve the lure too quickly and don't let it fall for too long.

An injured baitfish usually flutters in the water for a bit and then, when it senses an attacking gamefish, tries desperately to swim away. That's what you're trying to duplicate. A 4-second fall followed by a 4- to 6-second retrieve is usually about right. If that doesn't work, vary your technique until you hit on a combination that catches fish. Even small changes in your timing can dramatically alter your results.

The Buzz-Bomb really comes into its own when you're fishing from a boat. There are two basic ways to use the lure: one is to free-drift over any potential fishing area and jig as you move; the other is to find a school of fish by using a sounder or observing birds, and then go to work. Let's go over each method in some detail since these techniques apply with other jigs as well.

Free-Drifting the Bottom

The right water depth for successful jigging with ultralight is 15 to 30 feet (5 to 9 meters). The fish scare too easily if the water is shallower, and in deeper water it's hard to use a jig without causing excessive line stretch and loss of control when you hook up.

Pick out your prospective fishing area and then pass over it at low speed while surveying the depth with a sounder. Get an idea of how the contours vary so you won't end up leaving all your lures on the bottom. Then move your boat upwind of the area so you can drift over it slowly. You can't free-drift if the wind is blowing hard unless you use a sea anchor to slow you down. A fast drift will force your jig off the bottom and out of the productive bottom zone as you move.

To start your drift, cast the lure in the direction you're going; it will strike bottom about the time you pass directly over it. When it strikes bottom, reel in a bit to avoid being snagged, then start to jig. Don't try to jerk the lure 10 feet off the bottom with each upswing of the rod. Remember that you're imitating a small injured fish, and injured fish don't go streaking off into the void.

Another thing to keep in mind is that you're targeting bottom fish. Bottom dwellers are usually flat-bodied fish, highly maneuverable but relatively slow. They can follow the Buzz-Bomb for short distances, but they cannot chase it at light speed. After you pull the jig 3 feet (a meter) or less off the bottom, let it drift down. But don't let a belly of loose line form as

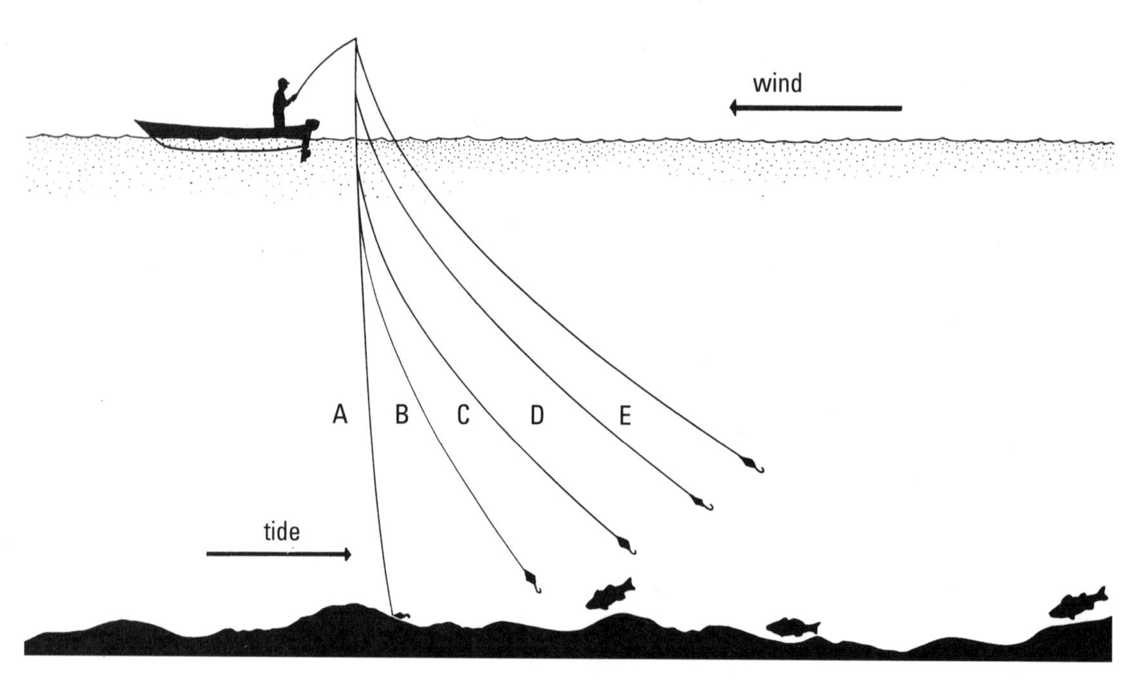

If there's a wind, your lure will gradually shift position from A to E as you drift.

you drop the rod; make it a controlled fall. Most fish strike on the downstroke, and you'll miss the bite if the line is loose and you can't set the hook.

Unless you're drifting quite slowly, the lure will gradually ride up as the force of the water flow lifts it off the bottom. As that occurs, you'll need to let out a little more line to keep the lure near the bottom. When the lure is finally riding behind the boat at a 45-degree angle, retrieve it and start again. For reasons I don't understand, jigs work best at an angle between 45 and 90 degrees. At any rate, if the angle becomes more than 45 degrees you'll have too much line out to fish effectively, so the lure will have to be brought in.

The same technique will work in midwater. Just remember that midwater species are usually fast-moving pelagics and can catch a speeding lure. The price these fish pay for speed, however, is reduced maneuverability. So, in midwater, make your rod sweeps longer and faster. The erratic movements that work so well on the bottom will not work with many midwater species.

If this advice fails you, remember that flexibility is usually the key to success. Try varying your technique before you scramble around changing lures. For instance, a straight, fast retrieve, with no downstroke at all, will sometimes succeed with bluefish, amberjack, and yellowtail when nothing else will.

Jigging the Schools

When you spot a school of baitfish on the sounder or see a flock of feeding birds, it's time to slow down and take advantage of the situation. If the fish are on the surface, do not try to approach the school directly; nothing will make gamefish sound faster than a screaming outboard and a wake that looks like a tidal wave. Bring the boat around the school and stop the engine well upwind of the activity. Once the boat's positioned, drop your jig as you drift into the feeding fish.

Gamefish generally patrol the perimeter of a cluster of baitfish. Over time, sick or weak baitfish tend to be forced to the edge of the school, where they are easy prey for the pelagics waiting for dinner. Your job is to work the lure where the pelagics are holding around the school. Since a school of baitfish has three dimensions, the gamefish could be above, below, or around it. But the biggest pelagics will be downstream from the school, where there is the greatest chance a free meal will come drifting toward them. That's where you want to concentrate your activities.

Again, try to vary your techniques until you hit on the right combination of depth, drift speed, and jigging motion. The best place to start is at a depth about halfway down the school, using rod sweeps about 3 to 4 feet (about a meter) long. If that doesn't work, try altering the depth or reducing the length of the upstroke as you drift past the school. If all else fails, let the jig drop to the bottom and then start a rapid, smooth, vertical retrieve right to the surface.

Other Jigs

Jigs are probably the world's oldest fishing lures. In antiquity they were made of carved bone or hardwood and weighted with rocks. Ancient Native Americans used jigs to catch fish through holes in the ice. With the development of metals, the jig became far less cumbersome; the tin squid dates from that era,

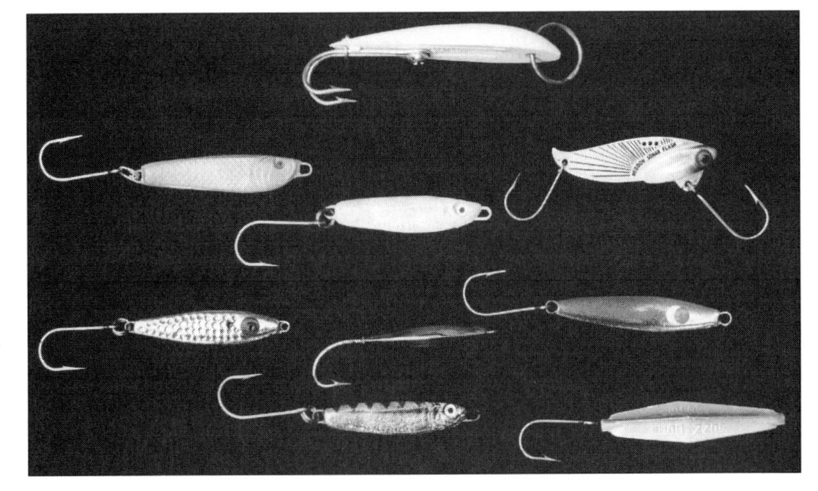

All these metal jigs have evolved from the modern version of a bone jig shown at the top.

and we would all recognize it even today. It was usually made of some combination of lead for weight and tin for glitter.

Not a whole lot has changed in the past thousand years. There are a lot more varieties of metal jigs, but they are all pretty much the same. The results obtained depend primarily on the skill of the angler, not any inherent action of the lure. Appearance doesn't seem to be too important either—painted eyes, patterned surface scales, and fancy paint jobs just don't seem to matter. What does matter is that the lure is reasonably bright. I keep a can of chrome and a can of white spray paint in the garage, and every few weeks I touch up the jigs that have become discolored and chewed up (making no effort to paint on eyes or scales or to use contrasting colors). The best weight for ultralight jigs is about ½ ounce (15 grams). Heavier lures produce too much bend in the rod and too much stretch in the line; lighter lures tend to drift upward with even the mildest currents.

Plastics

The Plastic Age gave us another sort of jig, modeled on the worm lures used so successfully for bass fishing in the United States. Today there are so many varieties of plastic squids, fish, frogs, tubes, and worms available that it's a nightmare trying to make a choice. But they're also so cheap that it doesn't much matter if you make a mistake. I've settled on squids between 2 and 3 inches (5 to 8 cm) long and plastic fish about the same size. Although there are lead-head hooks available for these lures, those hooks are usually too thick for ultralight lines. I prefer to use a 4/0 Mustad Aberdeen (#37353) or an Eagle Claw 5/0 Aberdeen (#202).

Soft-plastic lures come in a mind-boggling variety of shapes, sizes, and colors.

All you need to do to rig the lure is to force the hook, eye first, through the plastic. For trolling, run the hook right through the center to reduce line twist. For bottom-jigging, it's best to place the hook at an angle and upside down so the hook point rides up, away from the snags on the bottom.

You can rig a sliding weight on the leader ahead of the lure or clamp a couple of large split-shots just above, or on, the hook. If you're going to be bottom-bouncing with the plastic lure, it's best to fix the weight on the hook, just under the eye. This will also help reduce snags.

The soft-plastic fish at the bottom can be rigged in the three ways shown above. Maximum action is created with the sliding sinker mounted on the leader ahead of the lure, but this rig also has the greatest chance of snagging on the bottom.

The best way to fish with these lures is on a free drift or downstream from a school of feeding pelagics. If you're free-drifting, try to let the lure hit bottom every time. This will kick up some mud and create vibrations that will attract bottom feeders to the area. Remember that most bottom feeders are slow swimmers but highly maneuverable, so jerk and twist your plastic lure all you can, but not too quickly.

If you run into a school of feeding pelagics but you want a white-fleshed fish for dinner, try moving downstream from the school and jigging your plastic lure. Bottom feeders often take up positions underneath and downstream from feeding pelagics so they can eat the dead and dying baitfish that drift down. If you're there with a plastic minnow, it's relatively easy to pick up a tasty meal. Just remember to imitate an injured baitfish, and the lure will do the rest.

Always keep a tight line when using plastic lures; otherwise, you might miss a soft pickup. When a fish does grab the lure, don't strike—you might pull the lure right out of its mouth. Wait a few seconds. When the bottom feeder has a good grip on the bait, set the hook. Plastic lures feel natural, so it's unlikely they'll be spit out right away. You can increase your chances of success by soaking the lure in a little tuna oil before you use it; then the fish will never let go.

Making Noise

Remember the lateral line? That's the organ the fish feels vibrations with. But many fish can also hear, just as we do. Because sounds have a

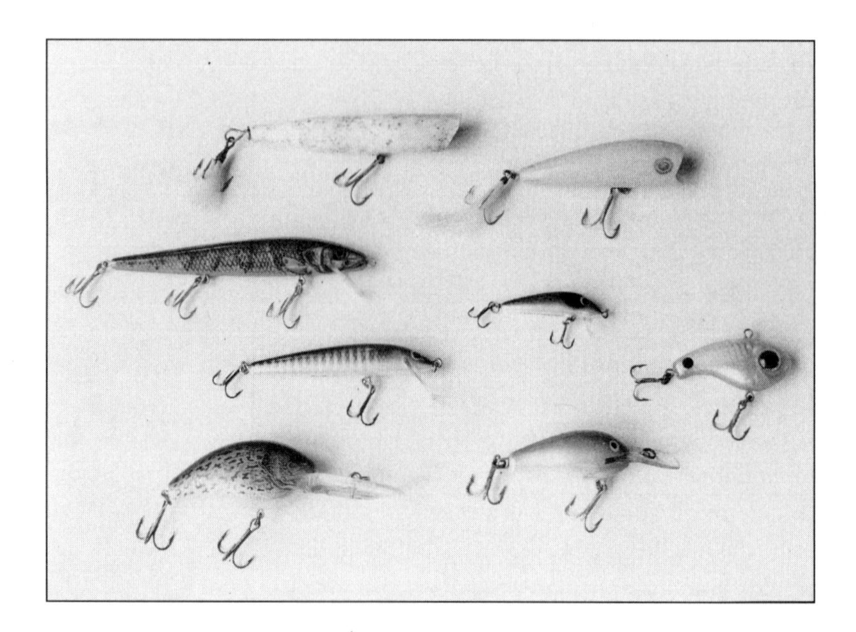

Hard-plastic lures need to be small and lightweight to work with ultralight tackle.

higher frequency than vibrations, another sort of organ is required to detect them—the inner ear.

The latest rage in lure production is noisy lures—lures that make a racket both the fish and the angler can hear. Among them are the spinnerbaits so popular for bass fishing, hollow plastic lures with metal balls inside, and poppers. Most of these lures are too heavy for ultralight or create too much resistance to be useful with soft-action rods. But some of the smaller poppers (⅛ and ¼ ounce) can be used with ultralight, and they are great fun to fish with.

Poppers are surface lures that make a lot of noise and splash as they're jerked through the water. Various retrieves are worth trying, but a rapid, irregular rate is usually best. Sometimes stopping the lure dead in the water after a fast retrieve is particularly attractive. These lures are easiest to cast with the wind at your back.

Poppers are most suitable when you find yourself in the middle of a surface-feeding school of pelagics. In this situation the rapid, continuous retrieve works best. The fast motion imitates the movements of a frightened baitfish as it skips across the surface of the water.

Of all the fishing techniques, skipping poppers is the most fun. It's exciting to watch the fish come after and take the lure, often right at the side of the boat. Remember to remove all the treble hooks and attach just one single hook to the rear of the lure for the most enjoyable time.

Saltwater Flies

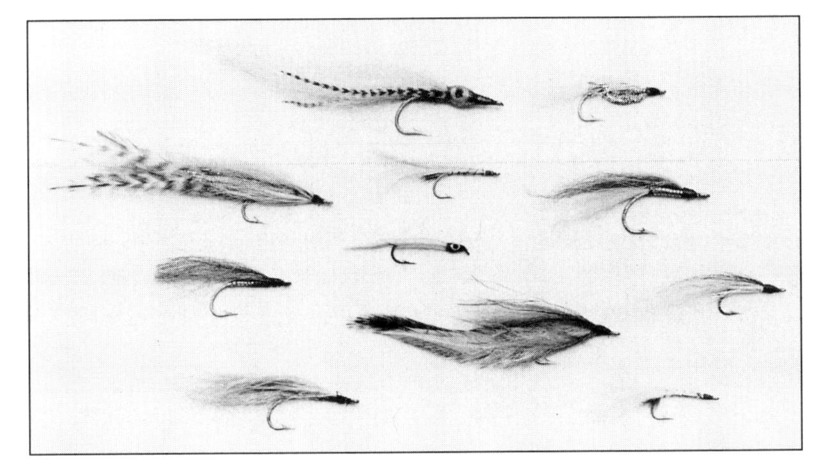

The ultralight angler usually uses metal and plastic lures to imitate fast-moving or injured baitfish, but in certain situations there's a better way to imitate minnows. If you're trolling for surface-feeding pelagics—like rainbow runner, dorado, kahawai, cobia, or bonito—with 1- or 2-kg line, the best lure is a saltwater fly.

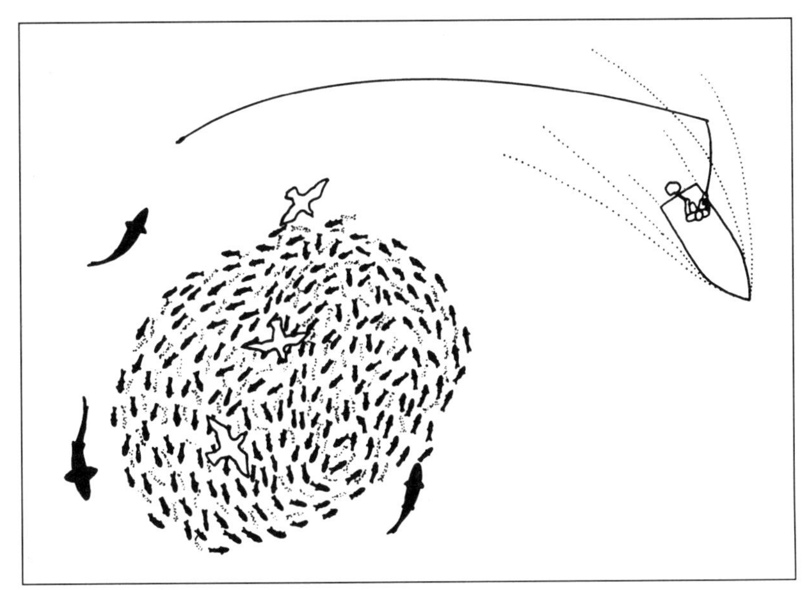

The saltwater fly has almost no water resistance, so it can be trolled at speeds high enough to attract these powerful, fast-moving fish. By adding a split-shot sinker to the leader in front of the fly, you will be able to cast it and add action to the fly when it's jigged through the water. Just remember to pick a fly tied onto a thin wire hook that can be set with light line. Many of today's saltwater flies are tied on quite large, thick, stainless steel hooks, so you may have to look around a bit to find what you want.

Top: Saltwater flies are the best lures to use for trolling with ultralight line.

Bottom: Stealth is critical if you want to catch fish. If you see a school of fish on the surface, troll your fly around the outside, not through the middle.

Basics

Most of the lures we've reviewed will not cause excessive twisting, and none will cause excessive line stress because they're all relatively lightweight. There are many other possibilities I've experimented with over the years and many more that I haven't. I'm sure you can come up with other options not mentioned here that may be even better than anything I've discovered. Just remember the basic principles of enjoying ultralight lure fishing: avoid line twist, and pick lures with minimum drag.

Before we finish up, I'd like to point out that treble hooks are usually more trouble than they're worth. Although there's a chance that they produce more hookups, they often become entangled in the line during casting or jigging, and they are exceedingly difficult to remove from a fish's mouth. Replacing trebles with single, sharp, unkirbed hooks is well worth the effort. As mentioned in Chapter Five, the Mustad Salmon hook with an open eye is an excellent choice for this purpose. If you're planning to release your catch, remove the barbs so the fish have a chance to fight another day.

A Last Note

It was the mid-1960s, and we were teenage boys on our first international fishing trip. Excitement was at fever pitch as we took off in our old Chevy for the wilds of Canada. On top of the car was a decrepit, flat-bottomed, 12-foot jonboat. To go with it we had a 30-year-old, 5-horsepower outboard and an outrigger made of wood and plastic foam to stabilize the boat against the raucous movements of three young men. Our mothers had packed a 24-hour, in-car food supply in addition to the two-week food reserve in the trunk. Being young and carefree, we didn't have much of a plan. The basic idea was to drive north until we ran out of enthusiasm and then look for a place to fish.

The energy of youth carried us for a thousand miles—through New Jersey and New York, past Montreal and its World Fair, and on toward the Northwest—until we were deep in the heart of La Verendrye Reserve in Quebec. In those days there were few controls in the Reserve, and we were free to go anywhere and fish any lake or river we fancied. As luck would have it, we came upon a road-building crew preparing to head into the bush for a week's work. They told us they'd just built a road past a lake that, they were quite sure, hadn't ever been fished. Not only did they guide us in to the site, but they took a few minutes to bulldoze out a roadside camping area for us. Then they were gone, and we were just three boys alone in the Canadian bush.

Fear and excitement kept fatigue at bay as we prepared the campsite, set up trip wires to alert us to the nocturnal visits of bears, and assembled our fishing gear. By evening, darkness and exhaustion had overcome us, and we agreed to begin fishing at dawn.

True to our word, we were up and moving about at first light. We were oblivious to the cold as we launched our ramshackle craft and began to explore the lake. Though we were young, we had a lot of fishing experience among us. Over the years our pocket money had gone to expand our collection of fishing tackle, and we knew how to use every lure we had to good effect. Our confidence was high as we ventured for the first time into the "virgin waters" of the Far North. But luck was not with us—though we must have tried 30 different locations and dozens of lures, the following four hours of nonstop fishing yielded a grand total of three northern pike. That was all we caught.

Disgruntled and hungry, we returned to camp for food and rest. Over a splendid breakfast of bony old pike, we discussed our situation. It was clear that the road crew had been right: there were no signs of human habitation on the lake; there was no human litter on the shoreline; and wildlife—moose, bear, and deer—was ubiquitous. So what was the problem? Where were the fish? More specifically, where were the good-tasting, hard-fighting walleye that populated all these northern lakes?

For the next two days we cast spoons, jigs, spinners, and poppers from shore at all hours of the day and some hours of the night. We trolled lures from our boat, journeyed to far-off corners of the lake to fish the shallows and ledges, and even tried midday jigging in deep waters. We caught a few miserable pike each day, but there was no sign of those delicious walleye we hungered for.

In desperation we held another summit conference. Here we were, in the wilderness, fishing where no one had fished before, and we could catch next to nothing! We were virtually overcome by depression in the face of our incompetence. Without a sufficient supply of fish, we would run out of food in five days and would be forced back to civilization in disgrace.

It became obvious that these walleye would not eat metal, plastic, feather, or deer-hair lures, no matter how well they were disguised. So we decided it was time to abandon our artificial standards and try bait. Simultaneously, and with great excitement (realizing we were on the right track), we exclaimed, "Now what do these fish really eat?"

Worms and insects were out. Lake-dwelling walleye probably didn't survive on such foods; and it was early fall, already too cold to find those delectables anyway. Though we hadn't seen any big schools of minnows along the shoreline, they clearly had to be the major food source for the walleye. So we set off in the boat for one of the rivers that drained into the lake. There, in the shallows of the river, were hundreds of shiners (small minnows) swimming in a gala procession. They were just waiting for us, our size-18 hooks, and our rotten pike meat for bait. The skills acquired in our years of fishing the streams at home proved invaluable as we quickly filled a pail with dozens of the little shiners. We took off for camp with our treasure and waited for evening.

As the day began to cool, we set out to try our new bait. Within minutes we were all catching the prized walleye. No matter where we went or how careless we were with our tackle, if we used shiners, we caught walleye. Any attempt to use any lure, even in the face of an apparent feeding frenzy, met with failure. We were amazed but delighted that we had, at last, found the secret. Within days we mastered the art of getting the walleye to leap out of the water alongside the boat in their attempts to get at the shiners. Once or twice we even got them to leap *into* the boat! But at no time, no matter what the lure, could we capture a walleye on an artificial.

This discovery enabled three teenage boys to return home immersed in self-conferred glory. The lesson also saved us from empty creels on many future fishing trips. From then on, when faced with fishing failure, we would look at each other, wink, smile, and say, "Now what do these fish really eat?"

CHAPTER SEVEN

Bait—Finding and Using It

IF YOU WANT TO CATCH POWERFUL, pelagic fish on ultralight, the most reliable way to do it is with live bait. A living organism lures big fish by creating attractive vibrations and odors as it struggles to get free. And since you don't have to cast or jig, there is minimal stress on your light line but maximum fish-attracting potential. Using live bait, however, is a big hassle. The aggravation begins when you go out to catch it and continues right through the havoc live bait causes on the end of your hook. Let's review these problems one at a time, and I'll suggest some ways to overcome live-bait phobia.

In Pursuit of Saltwater Live Bait

Getting bait is problem number one. Worldwide, the most common baitfish are mullets, anchovies, herrings, halfbeaks, and mackerels. Their common names are quite confusing since there's considerable overlap in usage. For instance, the term "sprat" is used in the South Pacific to identify a small mullet, but in European waters "sprat" refers to a herring. Other terms used for herrings of various forms are sardines, pilchards, menhaden, and bunker. Halfbeaks, found worldwide, are also called piper, ballyhoo, and garfish. These unique baitfish are the subject of a special section later in this chapter.

Virtually every harbor and bay throughout the world shelters some species of usable live bait. Probably the very best way to find out which live bait is available in any one area is to go to the local wharf and see what the kids are catching on a Saturday morning. Watch their techniques carefully because what is described here as an effective method for catching mullet, halfbeaks, pilchards, and mackerel may not always apply to other species. Remember that children are quite inventive and, inevitably, can come up with a lesson or two for us old folks. If nothing instructive is happening around the wharves, inquire at the local fish shop or tackle store.

Sometimes baitfish are not concentrated near the local wharf. Then there's no choice but to gather bait from a boat. Once on a boat you're dependent on local knowledge, using a sounder, or searching out feeding birds to find the bait you need. If things don't go well, you can spend the whole morning looking for the bait you needed at 6 A.M.!

Mullet, halfbeaks, and herring are not as active as mackerel, but they're just as attractive to gamefish if they're properly cared for. The quickest way to get these fish is to buy them at a seaside tackle shop or marina. The next quickest way is to net them. That means, of course, that you must have the net and accessories and you must be situated on a suitable overlook or shallow arm of a harbor to get at these baitfish. You also have to be very careful not to crush them in your net (the goal is to have living bait). In short, I don't recommend netting. It's not the most pleasant activity at 5 A.M.; and, at that hour, it's likely you'll end up entangled in the net, very wet and cold.

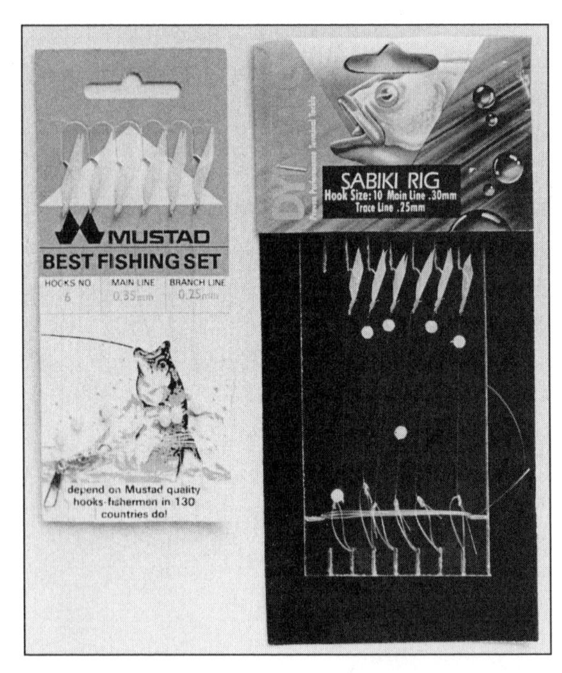

Bait flies like these are ideal for catching live baitfish. Be sure to use only three flies at a time to avoid monster tangles.

A more pleasant way to get the few mullet or halfbeaks needed for a day's fishing is to bring your boat just upcurrent from them and begin to chum (also called *ground bait, berley,* and *rubby dubby*) with very fine fish bits or oatmeal soaked in fish oil. The baitfish will be right on the surface and all around the boat within minutes. They will become quite excited, and then you'll be able to catch them on one of those Japanese or Korean fly sets (see photo) available at many sporting-goods stores.

For mullets I'd recommend using a Japanese #6 or Korean #12 set. These hooks are tiny enough to be effective on the small-mouthed fish. For halfbeaks you can use a slightly larger fly. You don't need to cast the flies or even jig them. Just leave them passively in the chum trail, and you'll get all the bait you need within minutes. If you can see the fish but they won't take the flies, try putting a tiny piece of bait on each one. That usually does the trick.

These Japanese and Korean sets come in a little package containing six or seven gaily colored flies on one line that's very easily tangled. If you put the whole string of flies on at one time, you'll invariably end up with a bird's nest that will boggle your mind and leave you cursing in the light of dawn. A better idea is to cut the string of flies in half and use only three at a time. You'll still hook nearly as many baitfish, and you'll spend a lot less time cursing. Another hint about that early morning light: don't try to put these flies on in the boat; do it the night before, when you're relatively alert and conscious. Just be careful when handling the fishing rod after that—the flies are very sharp and love to hook wool sweaters, hats, and human skin.

The tiny hooks on the flies bend easily, so carry needlenose pliers or surgical forceps to restore their curve when necessary. Use the flies until they begin to lose their luster; after that it's best to throw them out and put on a new string. You'll find this to be a rare problem, though; you probably won't have your fly set long enough for it to dull because it will usually be lost to a gamefish that comes along and eats your live bait before you get it in the boat.

These fly sets work even better on mackerel than mullet. For catching small mackerel the best choice is Korean sizes 6 to 8. The Japanese equivalent is about size 10. The smaller sizes will hook more bait, but the larger ones have stouter hooks and lines, so you'll lose fewer. My preference is for a smaller size and a light touch to compensate for the weak hooks and lines.

Look for small mackerel around reefs, wharves, and pilings, especially where there are night lights. If you catch your bait before dawn, use little or no weight on the flies since the mackerel stay right up on top, usually clustered around the lights found at most wharves. Once the sun rises, the mackerel dive down, so you'll need to put on enough weight at the end of the fly string to hold the bottom against the tide. Cast the flies upcurrent, wait for them to strike bottom, and then retrieve with a slow, jerking motion. Once you feel a mackerel on, pull it in slowly and steadily. The hooks tear out easily, especially when you lift the fish into the boat, so do this with care. A net can be helpful, but the exposed flies tend to get tangled in the mesh, and they take forever to sort out. At low tide the mackerel cluster in the deeper areas near the wharves. You'll probably need a sounder or lots of luck to locate the school if you're forced to search the channels.

Finding Freshwater Live Bait

Most popular freshwater fishing areas have tackle shops that sell live bait; but when you buy live baitfish in an unfamiliar area, be careful what you call them. The names of freshwater baitfish are just as confusing as those of saltwater baitfish. There are literally hundreds of species of true minnows throughout the world. They are known as shiners, dace, fatheads, carp, chubs, and a dozen other names I can't recall. Other popular freshwater baitfish are small suckers, alewives (another herring), and smelts. If you don't have local knowledge, just ask the proprietor what sort of live bait he or she stocks.

It's usually far easier to buy baitfish than catch them unless you know an area well. When you buy your bait, you'll need an insulated bucket and aerator so the fish will survive until you get to your boat or shoreline fishing hole. But if you know the area, it's easier to catch your bait near where you'll be fishing. Plastic or metal minnow traps are quite effective in small streams. For larger streams, seining is a better system. For gathering bait in shallow areas of lakes and ponds, cast nets are most effective.

Some freshwater baitfish (especially smelts) are large enough to take the flies we just talked about. If you can catch your bait with flies, do it; you'll have lots of fun, and you're guaranteed to avoid the damaged fish that netting often produces.

Keeping It Alive

It's very important to take care of the live bait once you have it. A live bait in a coma from too little oxygen is virtually useless. Mullet will tolerate lower oxygen levels than mackerel or halfbeaks, but they still require water changes. Since a 15-quart (15-liter) pail will hold only two to three mackerel for an extended period, you would need three or four pails for a day's fishing. Unless you want to mess with aerators, a much better idea is to build a wooden live-bait well (described in Chapter Ten) and bolt it onto the back of your boat. With a livewell, the natural tidal flow and boat motion will provide a continuous water change. A 20-quart (20-liter) live-bait tank will keep 15 to 20 mackerels lively and useful all day with absolutely no attention at all.

Do keep any live bait that doesn't survive. It can be very useful as dead bait (whole or strip) later in the day.

Using Live Bait

Understanding why live bait is so effective is the secret to using it successfully. Gamefish find their food by three main mechanisms. The obvious one is vision, but that doesn't come into the picture until the prey is just a few feet away. The other two mechanisms involve scent and vibration. Frightened or injured fish give off various scents, including the smell of blood from the wounds where they have been hooked. Even uninjured live baitfish release an odor into the water that gamefish can sense. These odors are easily detected by the sensitive olfactory apparatus of predators (the shark is legendary for its keen nose). By following the odor trail, fish are able to find prey they cannot see.

The stern of my boat has a livewell (see photos in Chapter Ten) with several holes drilled in it to allow oxygenated water to flow freely into the tank from the surrounding sea. Water escaping from the livewell travels downstream from the boat like a chum line (berley trail). Even when none of the bait in the well is bleeding or injured in any significant way, mako sharks or yellowtail come up to the boat and attempt to attack the livewell. Since their approach is silent until they smash into the stern, the makos generate considerable excitement in the well—and in the boat—when they demonstrate their olfactory skills.

The sense of smell is useful, but a far more rapid method of prey detection is to follow vibrations. Low-frequency vibrations produced by struggling baitfish travel through the water at about 5,000 feet per second. To take advantage of these clues, virtually all pelagic fish possess a lateral line (see Chapter Six)—the sensory organ that runs the length of both sides of a fish's body. The lateral line specializes in detection of low-frequency vibrations, while the fish's inner ears specialize in the higher-frequency signals that we commonly consider sounds.

A speeding pelagic fish can use its lateral line to follow the trail of "noise" from a frightened baitfish as it flails about trying to escape the hook. For this reason a healthy, lively bait is of paramount importance. If a baitfish is nearly dead from lack of oxygen and blood loss, it won't create

Top: The hook on the right has been placed so the point faces backward. This is a major error! When the bait is taken, the point will be buried, as shown on the left.

Bottom: This live bait has been correctly prepared with a reversed hook. When it is taken headfirst by a predator, the point of the hook will face up and back and will not become buried in the bait.

enough vibration to draw the gamefish toward your line. In that case you'd be much better off with a smelly strip bait.

With the onboard, live-bait tank, keeping the bait lively is no problem. The next step is to ensure that you don't unduly damage it when you prepare it for fishing. Whether you're going to hook the live bait through the upper lip or the back, the trick is to hook it as superficially as possible. The more tissue you destroy with the hook, the less time the bait will stay active. It's hard to move about with a spear in your back!

If you're back-hooking, use the smallest hook you can and put it through the muscle and skin just ahead of the dorsal fin. If you must use a kirbed hook, make sure it's aligned so the barb is pointing up when the eye of the hook is pulled toward the tail of the bait. When gamefish take your bait, they will almost always swallow it headfirst, forcing the eye and shaft of the hook toward the tail of the bait. If the kirb of the hook directs the barb downward, it will become buried in the bait's side. Then, when you set the hook, you produce a surprised gamefish and regurgitated bait, not an exciting fight. The accompanying photos illustrate, first, the effect of an incorrectly placed kirbed hook and, second, correct placement of a kirbed hook.

Do not squeeze the fish when you place it on the hook, and don't cast it out so it smashes against the water's surface. Small fish are not designed to withstand crushing injury. Such trauma plays havoc with their internal organs and causes massive bleeding. You want a healthy, active bait, not a candidate for the local trauma center.

The ideal approach to fishing with live bait is to use no weight at all. This does two things: it spares your ultralight line the stress of additional drag, and it allows the bait maximum movement. By simply placing your bait in the water, allowing it to swim freely, and drifting with the tide, you often get the best results.

Unfortunately, this technique doesn't always work. If you have to anchor the boat, the tide will pull on the line and tend to lift the bait toward the surface. Small bait cannot resist this, so you might need a ½- to 1-ounce sliding sinker. Sometimes the bait simply will not dive. That's okay if you're fishing for surface-running pelagics; but if you're after midwater or bottom-dwelling species, you'll need a weight to get the bait down where the gamefish are. Some people hook the bait just forward of the anal fin to encourage it to dive deep. I don't generally do this since the aesthetics of having a hook shoved through one's bottom makes me squirm.

Be sure to check the live bait frequently while you're fishing—it has a nasty habit of getting off the hook, resting under the hull, or swimming into some weed while you're having a beer with your mates. Fishing with live bait is an active sport that requires constant attention. If you're not hooking up at one location or depth, then try some variations. If you're not attracting gamefish, you have nothing to lose by changing your technique. You'd be surprised at the results you get by letting your bait sink down an extra 3 yards (3 meters) or moving it closer to the edge of a channel. When you're reeling in live bait, do so very slowly. Baitfish tend to struggle more when they're being reeled in, and that can attract a gamefish at the most unexpected moment.

With ultralight lines you have to use leaders, and the leaders have to be heavy enough to withstand the abrasion they incur during the fight. As you recall from Chapter Two, toothless pelagics over 10 pounds (4.5 kg) require a 20-kg leader since a thinner line will wear through in the hour or two it might take to land the fish. A 10-kg leader is usually adequate for smaller fish. You'll need wire for sharks, barracuda, and other toothy beasts. The IGFA allows you a 15-foot (4.5-meter)

leader of any strength for ultralight saltwater fishing. You'll find, however, that a 6-foot (2-meter) leader will work just fine.

Longer leaders just lead to masses of tangled line on deck. You haven't lived until you've spent 10 to 20 minutes unraveling a leader from the outboard you tried to start while the live bait was swimming gaily in circles around the prop.

So You Don't Like Live Bait?

Live bait is difficult to obtain, troublesome to keep alive, tedious to hook up, and a hassle to fish with; but it also catches more fish than anything else. If you can't tolerate the problems associated with live-baiting, if "livies" are unobtainable, or if you find the whole exercise morally offensive, there are other options that are nearly as effective and much easier to use.

I've arbitrarily divided the other choices of bait into two sections: halfbeaks and cut bait. Let's start with the halfbeak, the most effective bait I know of.

Halfbeaks

Depending on where you live in the world, halfbeaks are also called piper, balao, garfish, or ballyhoo. These slender, silvery little devils are amazingly attractive to kahawai, snapper, barracuda, yellowtail, dolphin (dorado), sailfish, large mackerel, amberjack, trevally, albacore, kawakawa, sharks, and probably every other fish in the sea. They are the most versatile bait I know of. Although live bait probably yields more hookups, halfbeaks are almost as effective and a lot easier to use.

Halfbeaks can easily be gathered with a dragnet along appropriate beaches and harbor shores where they school heavily at night. They are also easily caught with flies or small hooks with bits of bait. Personally I find it much easier to buy them frozen at the local tackle shop, or fresh at a fish shop. If properly cared for, these baitfish will last for months in the freezer and provide bait for many fishing trips.

It's best to buy halfbeaks in bulk the day they are delivered to the fish shop. Ask the shop assistant to save a bag of small halfbeaks in the back refrigerator for you and to call as soon as they arrive. If you wait until they've been hanging around the shop for two or three days, their soft flesh will have started to decay. The gamefish don't seem to mind the flavor of fetid piper at all, but the flesh is so soft that it falls apart the first time a fish strikes. In ultralight fishing a little more staying power is required for consistent success.

After bringing your bag of piper home, you need to break off all the beaks. (They get in the way when you put the fish on your hook.) Then lay the fish side by side on a metal tray. To maintain maximum firmness, freeze them as quickly as possible (uncovered, in the coldest part of the freezer). Once they're frozen solid, place them into small plastic bags in groups of 5 to 10. On fishing day, pull a bag or two out of the freezer as you head out the door. Defrost the piper by throwing them into a pail of water when you need them. A rapid defrost is best because the flesh stays firmer than if you thaw it slowly.

To rig a fresh halfbeak, put one unkirbed 1/0 Salmon hook through the eye sockets as shown in the photo. Aberdeen-style wire hooks are a poor choice for piper because the point is short and tends to get lost in the bait. Salmon hooks feature a much longer point and a long barb as well. To increase their effectiveness, pinch the barb down or break it off.

The ganged hooks placed between the piper are far more difficult to use and no more effective than the double-hook rig above them. The single-hook rig below the gangs is almost as good and can be put together instantly. All the hooks shown are 1/0 Salmon.

After hooking the halfbeak, place a ¼- to 1-ounce sliding sinker on the leader. This will pull the piper down against the current and provide lots of action (and vibration) as you slowly jig it or simply let it undulate in a brisk tidal flow.

In the underwater world, a wounded fish will struggle to escape an attacking predator as it closes in. But a wounded baitfish can swim only a short distance. To imitate the bait's futile attempt to escape, try jigging the piper. The trick is to pull the piper upward through the water with a single, short upsweep of the rod tip. Then allow the bait to sink down slowly as the rod tip drops so that there's constant tension on the line. The upward sweep of your rod while you're jigging provides the motion that makes the piper look as though it's making a futile attempt to flee.

An educated fish may avoid your bait if it fails to see the halfbeak struggle to get away as it approaches. Unfortunately, rapid jigging puts lots of stress on the bait and the ultralight line, so you should avoid using the technique unless you're sure a gamefish is close by.

Many people feel that piper should be gang-hooked to ensure maximum success. Making the gangs is a time-consuming chore, however, and it creates a bloody mess out of the bait. Since gamefish often take their prey headfirst, a single hook in the right place usually does the job. That is, it usually does the job if you remember to leave the reel bail open and let the fish run with the bait for five seconds or so before you set the hook. A spastic lunge at the first sign of a pickup will usually cost you both the piper and the fish. The best way to ensure a solid hookup is to let the fish take the bait for a few seconds or until it stops to swallow the meal. At that point, close the bail and wait until the line tightens up again. Then set the hook; success is guaranteed!

If you're bottom- or drift-fishing and confronted by a plague of tail-biting bottom fish, you can rig the piper with two hooks. To double-hook, tie an extra hook about 6 inches (15 cm) up from the end of the leader. Both hooks can be tied to the leader with separate, simple clinch knots. Put the upper hook through the eye sockets and the lower one through the tail area, as shown in the photo on page 81. Before you drop the piper into the water, check that the points of both hooks are well clear of the bait. Be sure that there's no stress on the tail hook (the leader should be limp between the two hooks), as it will pull out easily. This is a sure cure for the tail-biting woes and the only effective way to utilize overly ripe, mushy piper.

Cut Bait

Sometimes there are so many fish around that you don't need to lure them from far away. In these situations there's no need for the vibrations of frightened live bait or the sight and smell of an undulating piper; a small piece of something desirable will do the job just as well. This is when cut bait is the ideal choice for the ultralight angler. Cut bait is cheap and convenient. Unfortunately, it is really effective only when large numbers of fish are around. But this is a common occurrence in channels or gullies where the fish gather at low tide. The use of chum can produce the same effect, as can the judicious observation of sea birds, leading you to schools of surface-feeding pelagics (and the bottom fish that always lurk underneath).

By "cut bait" I mean any sort of fish or shellfish that can be cut up to fit on a hook properly. "Properly" means that the bait is arranged so it is all gathered around the hook, and the barb of the hook is completely exposed. Since bait comes in different sizes, you'll need a variety of hooks to suit your needs. Again, Aberdeen hooks, with their long shanks and wide gaps, are excellent for cut bait.

Strip bait presents an exception to the general rule of keeping your bait clustered on the hook shank. Strip bait attracts fish by its scent and movement in the water (as it's jigged, drifted or left to undulate in the tide). It is made by cutting a fresh fillet, up to about 8 inches (20 cm) long, from a small mackerel, herring, mullet, or other oily fish. If you scale the fish before filleting it, the scales won't get stuck on the point of the hook. Preparing the fillet just before you use it will preserve as much of its body oil as possible, making your offering highly attractive to the fish. Although freshly caught fish are best for this, bait frozen in good shape does nearly as well.

After you fillet the strip bait, make sure the hook comes up through the meat then *through the skin so the barb is completely exposed.*

Be sure to put the hook through the tail of the fillet, where the skin is toughest. This will produce maximum motion and staying power. To keep the tough skin just below the point by the barb of the hook, push the point of the hook first through the meat of the fillet and *then* through the skin. As with whole piper, give the fish time to take the bait, or you'll end up with no fish and an empty hook as well.

Squid tentacles are another very effective strip bait. Use three to four at a time and watch out. It's such a seductive bait that you'll often get a "follower" fish trying to wrest it from the mouth of the fish you've already hooked. This can be a disaster on ultralight since the follower fish

To improve the effectiveness of small dead bait, use a syringe to inject fish oil and then make small cuts in the side of the bait so the oil will ooze out and create an odor trail.

can easily cut the line if he touches it.

Similar in effect to strip bait are small, whole, dead fish like mullet, herring, or mackerel up to about 6 inches (15 cm) long. The best way to hook this bait is through the eyes or both lips with a 2/0 to 4/0 Aberdeen hook or a 1/0 Salmon hook. If you put shallow cuts in the flesh of the dead fish, more oils will ooze into the water to attract gamefish. Using a syringe to inject tuna oil into the bait will also help. Unless your quarry is right on the surface, use a ¼- to 1-ounce sliding sinker on the leader to provide the maximum motion while jigging, drifting, or anchoring in the tidal flow.

Cube baits—solid chunks of larger mullet, bonito, or other oily fish—are another valuable tool. Bonito is by far the most effective because it's so oily, but it's also the softest and easiest to lose. If you leave a section of skin on the cube bait and put the shaft of the hook through the meat first and then the skin, your offering won't be lost as often.

Circle-style hooks are the most effective hooks for cube baits, but they make a mess of the bait if you try to insert them point first. The way to rig them is to use a needle and thread to draw the hook shaft up into the cube. Only the eye of the hook is left exposed (just above the skin). This is the only exception I know of to the basic rule that you always leave the point of the hook exposed. Although they might not look it, these hooks are ideal with untended lines or for still-baiting. Because the bait is very soft, the fish literally hook themselves if you keep a tight line and *don't* strike.

For trevally, snapper, flounder, permit, bonefish, and other bottom feeders, shellfish is one of the most useful baits. However, they are very soft and easily pulled off the hook during casting; their use demands a light touch and a sharp hook.

Don't bother trying to toughen shellfish by cooking them. Overboiled shellfish probably tastes worse to fish than it does to people. A better way to make shellfish more stable on the hook is to salt them. I gather several quarts (liters) of shellfish at a time and coax my wife into helping me open them and remove the meat. Then I spread out the meat and salt it heavily. After the fluid has been drawn off by the salt, I add more salt, bottle up the meat, and store it in the refrigerator until I need it. Whenever I go fishing, a bottle of the "goo" always goes with me. It's a versatile bait, and it lasts for months. If it's not taken by a fish within 10 minutes, just put it back in the bottle to reinforce its captivating aroma. After the day's fishing, seal the bottle well and wash off the outside. Without these precautions you may well find your bait ejected from the refrigerator by an irate family.

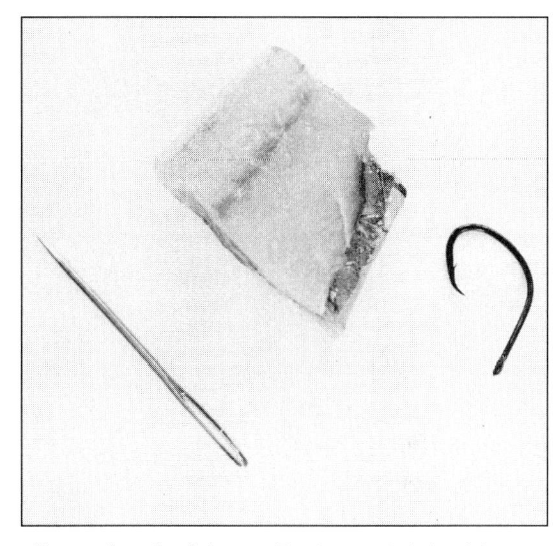

To place a circle hook into cube bait, use a large sewing needle to draw the eye of the hook through the bait.

You'll recall that cut bait is effective because it smells good to the fish. To preserve that odor, you must change it every 15 minutes or so. Use the old bait for chum, and you'll be wasting nothing. If you have a limited supply of cut bait, you can reinforce the odor by soaking it in tuna oil. Or, better yet, you can put some tuna oil in a 10-cc syringe and inject it into the bait just before you use it. That way the bait creates its own chum line as it drifts in the current.

CHAPTER EIGHT

The Boat

TO CATCH BIG FISH ON ULTRALIGHT you must choose the fishing site very carefully. Areas with reefs, pilings, weeds, or irregular, rocky bottoms are certain death to light lines. That leaves you with two alternatives: casting from the shoreline or using a boat. If you fish from shore with ultralight, the river bottom must be smooth—sand or mud. And the shoreline must be clear so you can move freely along the water's edge as the fish runs. Otherwise the fish might easily pull too much line from the spool; if that happens and the fish turns suddenly into the current flow, the water pressure against the line will break the mono while you stand there helplessly. For that reason the site can't be too wide either. Since fishing areas that meet all these requirements are quite rare, most people choose the second alternative—a boat.

A large, elegant cruiser will defeat your purpose. The basic principle of ultralight is that the angler must outmaneuver the fish in order to land it. To be aware of the fish's every move, you must be close to the water. To respond to his every move, you must be able to act quickly and gracefully. The more fishing line you have out, the less sensitive you are to the fish's movements and the less chance you have to compensate for changes of direction and sudden runs. To maintain direct contact with the fish—to stay close and move quickly—you'll need a small boat. But what sort of small boat?

The loneliness of the ultralight angler is a fact of life. No sensible person wants to hang around for three or four hours while someone else does gymnastics chasing a fish around the ocean. Unless you have a friend who shares the bizarre desire to land big fish with ultralight line, you'll often find yourself launching your boat alone.

That's no fun if you have to cope with a large, heavy craft. Even a tilt-boom trailer and a power winch don't make it an easy job for one person. And you don't want to be out at 5:00 A.M. pushing and pulling and grunting and groaning just to get your boat in the water.

For successful ultralight angling, you need a boat that will keep you close to the water; and for a hernia-free launch, you need one light enough for one person to handle. What are the other characteristics you'll be looking for?

Shallow Draft

Fish don't usually run in just one direction. When they feel the hook they can go anywhere, anytime, and you have to be able to follow. A shallow-draft craft can follow a fish onto the flats in just a few feet of water, and it can turn on a dime when the fish changes direction. But there's another significant advantage to a shallow draft that becomes critical when the fish is close to the boat.

Imagine yourself with a 70-pound (30-kg) shark on the end of a 2-kg line. You're on the flats in 12 feet (4 meters) of water, and the fight's been going on for a couple of hours. The shark is tired but it's also angry. It decides to charge the boat. You're not in any danger; the shark will realize the boat is dead and assume it's just a piece of flotsam.

As the shark passes under the boat, your fishing line will follow. That leaves you on one side of the boat with the shark on the other and your line under the hull. As the shark keeps running, the angle of the line changes; the line begins to creep up, closer and closer to the hull. If you had a boat with a keel that was well underwater, the line would then stretch across the keel. You would know exactly when that happened—when you felt the pop as the line parted and the shark swam off into the sunset. The moral of the story: you need a boat with a shallow draft.

Cabins

Having a cabin on a boat is a great luxury. It gives you a place to escape the rain and the sun, a place to have a nap or a meal. But it also makes it impossible to move around the perimeter of the boat without scrambling over all sorts of obstructions.

Remember that shark I just told you about, the one that's just gone under the boat? Let's say you were on the starboard side near the stern and the shark took off toward the bow on the port side. If there were a cabin dividing the boat, you couldn't possibly make the switch from starboard to port to follow the fish. You'd have no choice but to push your fishing rod into the water to keep it from touching the keel and, at the same time, try to get to the engine to maneuver the boat into a turn so you could again be facing your quarry. In the meantime you would lose lots of line, maybe enough for the water pressure alone to break the mono.

If there were no cabin, it would be a simple matter of pushing your fishing rod into the water and walking the rod around the bow until you were once again facing the shark. Cabins are deadly to ultralight lines. So are high windshields, running lights on poles, rod holders above the level of the gunwales, Bimini tops, and elevated handrails. Anything that sits above the level of the gunwales is a threat to your line, with one exception: a foredeck.

The Foredeck

A small foredeck with a cleat in the bow is the only item that should be at gunwale level. Life in a small boat can be unpleasant enough without a pool of water around your feet on a cold morning. So it's nice to have a foredeck to help shed water while you're moving. A foredeck less than a yard (meter) long will give you some protection, support a couple of cleats and an anchor warp, and still not get in the way of your fishing. Of course, the foredeck won't help much if the boat has inadequate freeboard or a blunt bow. This brings us to the issue of design. What sort of shape will be best for you?

The Options

The choice of a boat depends on your circumstances. If you'll be fishing in sheltered waters that are always calm, a 12-foot (3.6-meter) jonboat will be quite adequate. Jonboats have lots of room inside and a flat bottom that provides stability when you move around. They're inexpensive and can ride on top of the car. But when the wind comes up, it's a nightmare—rocking and pounding in the chop and shipping water over the flat bow. Unless you fish only on ponds, peaceful rivers, and protected lakes, the jonboat is not for you.

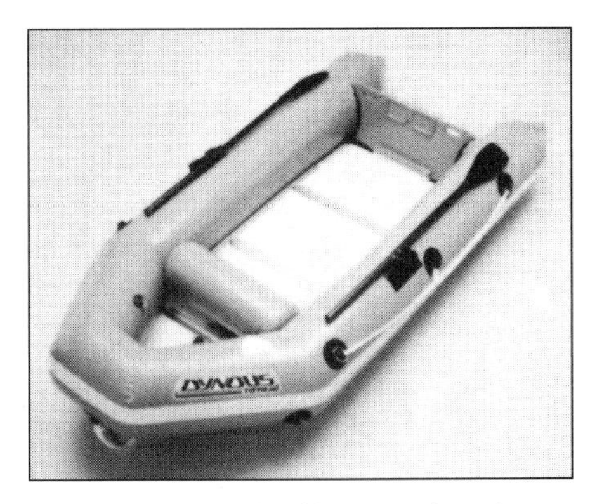

Inflatables are safe and maneuverable but wet and relatively cramped.

The same goes for canoes, with or without flat transoms. And canoes have an additional drawback: you're too close to the water to use the rod effectively if you have a big fish on the line. Kayaks suffer from the same problem.

What about inflatables? A lot of good things can be said about these boats. They are very safe, bouncing off rocks that would splinter wood, dent aluminum, and crack fiberglass. They are highly resistant to puncture; and even if one tube loses its air, the others will keep you afloat. They are easily portable. Inflatables are lighter than most other boats and can be deflated and broken down for storage and travel. They are also unbelievably maneuverable and wonderfully safe in bad weather.

Sounds ideal doesn't it? Well, not quite. Yes, it is nice to be able to deflate and store a boat; but it's not nice to have to inflate and assemble it, especially at 5 A.M. Inflatables ride very low in the water and do a poor job of deflecting water. Guaranteed: you will get very wet in rough weather.

The other big disadvantage is the soft floor. In an ordinary inflatable the floor is just another balloon, and it's not easy to stand on while you're fighting a big fish. Manufacturers of inflatables have found a solution to this problem. They now make roll-out or fold-out wooden and aluminum floors to provide firm footing. They also make hybrids, with inflatable sides and rigid, fiberglass hulls. But incorporating these features increases the weight and bulk of the inflatable. A top-quality 12-foot (3.6-meter) inflatable with a solid floor actually weighs more than a comparable aluminum boat but provides less usable interior space. It also costs a lot more.

That leaves wood, plastic, fiberglass, and aluminum boats. Wonderful boats can be made of wood. Wood is quiet, stable, and strong. But it's also heavy, and it requires a lot of maintenance. If you love working on boats, wood can be a good choice. I hate working and I don't even like boats, so that rules out wood for me.

Plastic boats are a relatively new innovation. With new molding techniques one piece of polyethylene can be formed into a double-hulled craft with a layer of air sandwiched between the layers of plastic, producing a boat that's about as light as aluminum but more flexible under load for a smoother, quieter ride. The plastic itself is lighter than water, so even if water completely filled the air space in the hull, the boat would still float.

Although a polyethylene boat is amazingly strong, it does have its liabilities. For one thing, if that air space did fill with water (and it could easily happen without your realizing it if there's an undetected hole in the outer hull), your day would be sunk even though your boat would float. And the transoms on these boats are not as supportive as on aluminum or fiberglass boats, so lighter-weight engines are required. The plastic, although UV-treated, has the potential to become brittle with age. Moreover, plastic is harder to modify and repair at home than aluminum or fiberglass. Nevertheless, these boats are inexpensive and a viable alternative for the ultralight angler.

This leaves us with two final options: fiberglass and aluminum. Fiberglass boats have a lot going for them. They're almost as quiet as wood, and the fiberglass can be formed into an infinite variety of styles. The 16- to 18-foot American bassboats, the 18-foot open skiffs used for bonefishing on the flats, the 18-foot center-console models, the unbelievably stable 15-foot Boston Whalers, and the plain old 14- to 16-foot runabouts are all good choices for the ultralight angler. A fiberglass boat has only one disadvantage: its weight. Because it's heavier than an aluminum boat, it is harder to launch and retrieve, needs a larger engine, is a little less maneuverable, and requires a little more water to float.

The Zipper. A good example of a fiberglass runabout, it provides easy access to all sides of the hull, and it's light enough (275 pounds) to launch without help.

These may not be drawbacks for you. Maybe you always fish with a friend, or maybe you always launch from a good ramp and the weight doesn't matter so much. If you don't mind a little more expense and complexity, an electric starter for your motor can compensate for the fact that the larger engines are harder to hand-start when you're coping with a fish on its first run.

If you often fish alone or venture into shallow waters or launch from beaches or estuaries, if you dislike equipment maintenance but like a boat that can take abuse, or if you have limited funds, then aluminum is the way to go.

Aluminum

I've found that a small, lightweight aluminum boat with a relatively low-horsepower engine is the most versatile option for the ultralight angler. A 12- to 14-foot (3.6- to 4.3-meter) aluminum dinghy with a 10- to 20-hp engine is about the best choice. Engine size is critical because while one hand is busy with that fish you've been looking for, the other must be able to start the engine all by itself, on the first try. With a small engine, that's easy.

A 12-foot (3.6-meter) aluminum dinghy is inexpensive to operate and can be towed behind any car.

A 12-foot (3.6-meter) dinghy will still be small enough that you don't have to move at all should the fish dash from stern to bow while close to the boat. You simply rotate with the fish as it moves—a graceful pirouette instead of a hasty scramble. If you move up to a 14-foot (4.3-meter) hull, you'll have to scramble around a bit, so make sure all your fishing gear is well stored and the floor is clear of obstructions.

A lightweight boat will turn easily and accelerate rapidly enough to catch most fish. A 12-foot (3.6-meter) aluminum dinghy with a 15-hp engine will do about 30 knots on a calm day. In rough waters you won't be going anywhere (except home) anyway since it's not possible to follow fish effectively in windy conditions.

Aluminum dinghies come in dozens of designs. The standard design features a deep "V" in the bow that cuts through the chop and provides stability when the boat is struck from the side by oncoming water. The standard hull flattens out toward the stern and has only a 7-degree deadrise (see the drawing on page 92) at the transom. The nearly flat stern increases stability

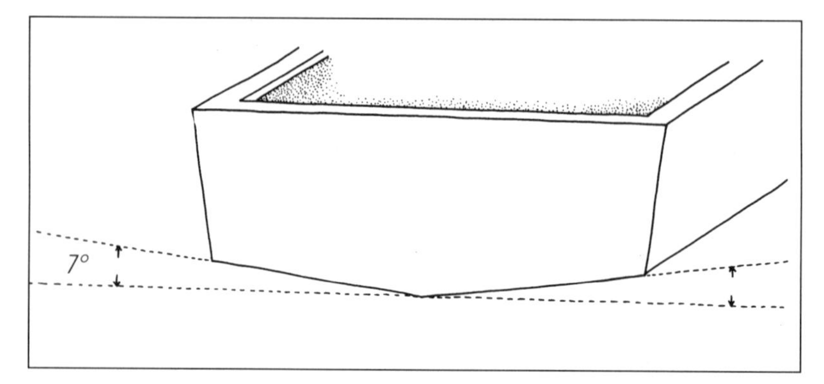

A common compromise between stability and drag is a deep "V" shape in the bow and a 7-degree deadrise in the stern.

when the angler gets up and moves around the boat, and it provides the platform necessary for the boat to plane on the surface of the sea.

There is one design that I feel is better than the conventional version. This features the same deep "V" at the bow but a transom that looks like a gull wing. This gull-wing, or cathedral, design provides improved stability when there's movement in the boat, increases the hull's ability to cut through chop, deflects spray from the stern, and offers more resistance to lateral motion when the boat is caught in heavy seas. The negatives are that a gull-wing transom necessitates a little more water to float the boat and a long-shaft engine to compensate for its own height in the middle. Despite these minor drawbacks, the gull-wing seems to be the best bet.

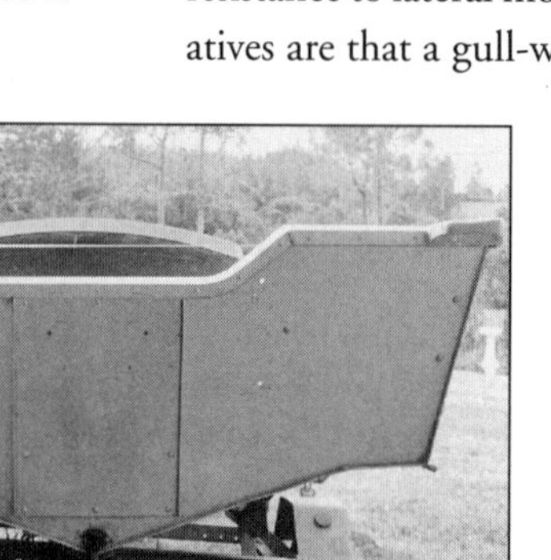

The stern of a 14-foot aluminum boat with a deep "V" in the bow and a gull-wing shape in the transom. The center height of the transom is 19 inches (480 mm), so a long-shaft engine is required.

The other advantage to aluminum is that it can be worked with. You can drill it, weld it, and bolt things to it with impunity. So you can attach all sorts of gadgets to the hull—gadgets that make ultralight fishing a lot more fun. We'll learn more about those little extras in the next couple of chapters, but first a little bit about engines.

Engines

For an aluminum dinghy that weighs in at under 150 pounds (70 kg) a 15-hp engine is just about right. There are many brands on the market, and they all have their pros and cons. The features you want are quiet running, minimal vibration, and light weight. The four-stroke engines made by Honda and Yamaha are certainly the quietest and most economical engines around, but they're initially expensive and very heavy (95 pounds/43 kg). At this writing the 2-stroke outboards made by Force are the lightest at 64 pounds (29 kg). The Mariner/Mercury engines are 7 pounds heavier at 71 pounds (32 kg). The Johnson/Evinrude models weigh in at 74 pounds (34 kg). The 2-stroke Yamaha, Suzuki, and Tohatsu all weigh around 81 pounds (37 kg).

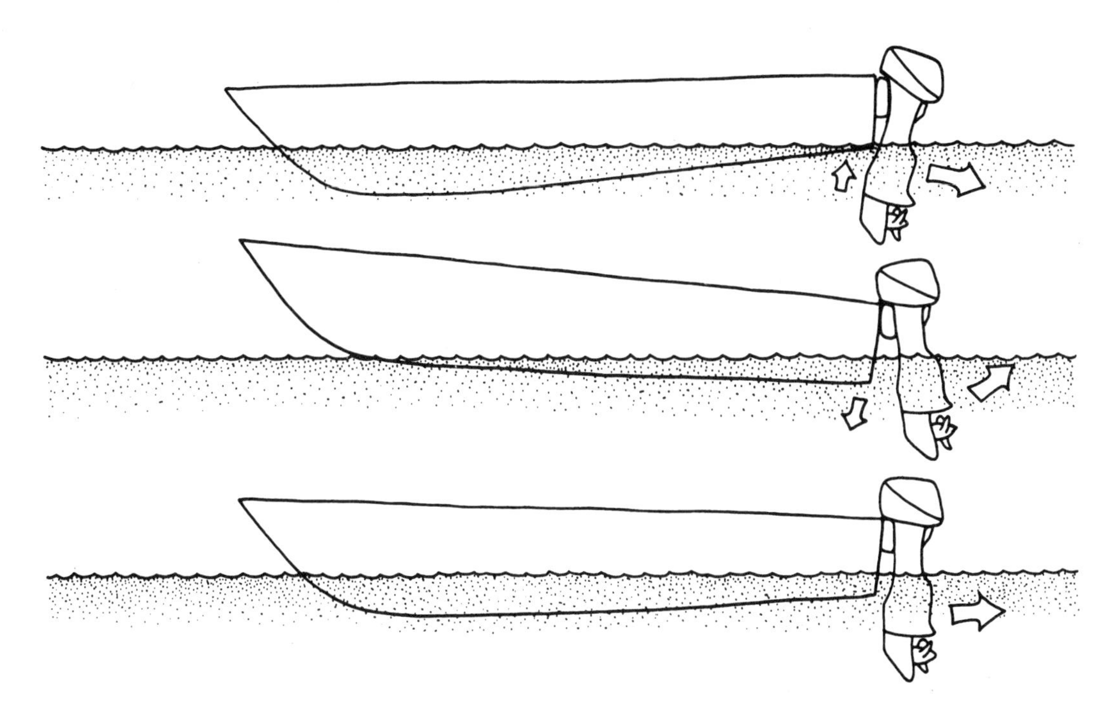

The top drawing shows what happens when an engine is trimmed in too far, forcing the bow down. In the middle the engine is trimmed out too far, forcing the bow up. At the bottom it's just right, and the boat is in trim at last!

Engine weight is important because the engine sits in the stern and throws the boat out of trim. The situation is aggravated when you wind up the motor—the force of the engine pushes the bow right up out of the water when you're trying to get started after a fish.

You can cope with this in several ways: You can reduce the weight in the stern by buying a light engine or by moving the fuel tank toward the bow; or you can use the trim adjustment on the engine to alter the angle of the engine against the boat. This is called "trimming in"; the technique uses the engine to elevate the stern (see the drawing). This works well when there's a heavy load in the stern, but it can force the bow down into the water when you're at speed. Another method to trim the boat is to use ballast (like a fat relative) in the bow.

But the easiest way to trim a dinghy is to attach a hydrofoil to the engine. This is a small wing that's placed on the cavitation plate of your engine. As you rev the engine, the wing lifts the stern and prevents the bow from riding up. It's also claimed to increase fuel economy. The two models I know of are made by Doel-fin and Permatrim. I can verify that these gadgets work very well; I've been very happy with mine. Because the hydrofoil lifts the stern, you're more apt to oversteer, so be careful when you first use it. It takes a few hours on the water to adjust to the effect.

DOEL-FIN.

A hydrofoil attached to the engine can provide enough lift to the stern to bring a boat into trim during acceleration.

There's nothing more boring then taking care of an engine, but maintenance is the key to good performance. Follow or exceed the manufacturer's recommendations. Make your own fuel-oil mixture; that way you know it's right. It also pays to clean those spark plugs frequently and keep the engine body well lubricated and free-moving.

Following fish involves lots of low-speed running that can foul plugs quickly. When you sit down to clean those plugs, just remember how much you want the motor to start on the first pull when there's a big fish taking out your line at light speed.

The Trailer

Cartop carriers are great—if you're built like Hercules. A small, two-wheeled trailer is far more practical for your aluminum boat. It's a lot easier to launch a boat from a trailer than it is to lift it off the top of a car. Of course, no boat will launch easily if the trailer is not kept in perfect shape. Well-lubricated, clean rollers on a trailer make life much more pleasant in the wee hours of the morning.

Launching is much easier when the trailer tires are well into the water, so it's best to use aluminum wheels. Unfortunately, when you put hot wheels into cold salt water, a vacuum forms within the wheel core and salt water can be sucked into the bearings. To prevent this, keep your hubcaps filled with grease so the grease, rather than the salt water, gets sucked into the bearings. You'll need to regrease those bearings frequently, and you can easily fill the hubcaps at the same time. I know it sounds like a lot of work, but nothing's worse than having to abort a trip because your bearings give out at 6:00 A.M. on Sunday morning, 20 miles from home.

If maintenance is not your forte, consider buying a set of bearing protectors. They can be filled with grease and attached to the bearing housing. When your hot wheels hit cold water, the grease reserve in the bearing protector ensures that no salt will get into the wheel's interior. Most bearing protectors come equipped with a grease nipple so they can easily be refilled.

Discovering a hole in your boat after you've launched it is also guaranteed to ruin your day. Fractures in aluminum hulls most often occur when the rollers on the trailer do not make firm contact with the boat. Bouncing along rough roads smashes the hull repeatedly against the rollers that *do* contact the body, causing metal stress and fractures.

To avoid this gloomy prospect, make sure each trailer roller sits firmly under the boat. In areas that suffer the most stress, add more or bigger rollers to distribute the weight. On most boats the transom takes the greatest weight because the engine is mounted there. So remove your engine before road trips, or be sure there is adequate support directly beneath the transom. To prevent the boat from bouncing around, secure it firmly to the trailer with rope or nylon straps that won't slip.

A Simple Safety Kit

Onboard my aluminum dinghy I carry a complete tool kit wrapped in plastic, an engine manual, spare spark plugs, a spare bung, extra split pins, extra engine starter rope, a lighter, a waterproof flashlight, a set of oars, a gallon of fresh water, a signal flag, a cell phone, and a complete flare kit. A good flare kit contains meteor or parachute flares with a launcher and hand-held smoke signals too. I know this list seems long, but most of this safety gear is stored in one waterproof, plastic box; and it could easily save your day, or your life.

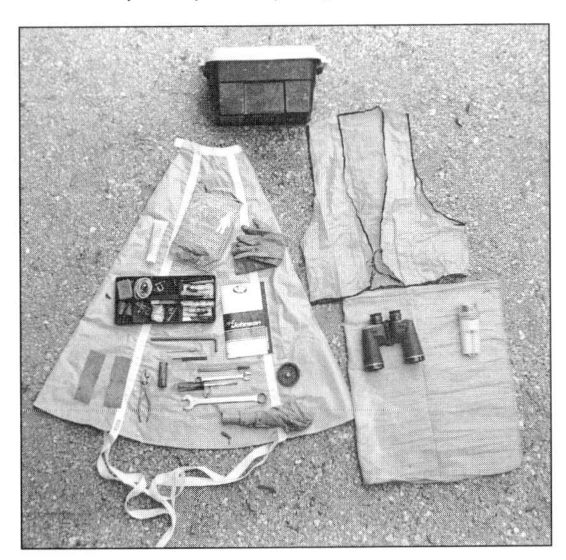

Left: The plastic box at the top contains a tool kit and a selection of safety equipment. It holds everything but the binoculars, sea anchor, and umbrella, yet it fits easily under the foredeck of a small boat.

Right: A hard-working fishing boat with all its gadgets in place. More on these items in the next couple of chapters.

When traveling to remote areas, I put an auxiliary 2-hp engine in the bow for insurance (and ballast). If my main engine suffers an untimely death, the 2-hp outboard will at least get the boat to shore. (I hate to row, but there's also a set of oars tied to the transom.) A long anchor line is also one of the most important safety devices I know of. Far better to anchor where your engine dies than to drift aimlessly and never be found. For warmth I carry an emergency aluminum cold-weather suit (very compact) and a complete PVC storm suit.

There are lots of other gadgets that can make an ultralight angler's life safer and easier. In the next two chapters I'd like to suggest a few. We'll start with sounders, the most useful of all electronic accessories.

CHAPTER NINE

Sounder Mania

IF YOU READ FISHING PUBLICATIONS, you've probably noticed the blitzkrieg of ads for sounders (also known as depthfinders, echo sounders, sonar, and fish finders). Technically, sonar is designed to detect objects in the water and sounders to define bottom configurations, but the ads for these complex new machines blur all this. You've probably also noticed how expensive they are and how confusing the advertising can be if you're not an electronics whiz.

What I'd like to do is explain in simple terms how sounders work, and then tell you what they can and cannot do for you—and there's a lot that sounders can't do. Once you can sort out fact from fiction, you'll find it a lot easier to decide which unit to buy.

Sounders Deciphered

Imagine that you're a dolphin. You've been cruising the open ocean for days, and now you're heading into a harbor to feast on the young mackerel gathered along the edges of a reef. But recent rains have so muddied the water that you won't be able to see these small fish. You must locate them another way.

As you enter the harbor you begin to emit high-pitched squeals sending sound waves through the ocean at 5,000 feet every second. Whenever the sound waves strike an object ahead, they bounce off it and come right back. When you hear the echo, you know there's something up ahead blocking your path. If the object is large, echoes will come from many points; if it's small, echoes will come from only one direction. If the object is soft, like mud, the echoes will be weaker than if the object is hard, like a coral reef. If the object is nearby, the echoes return sooner and are louder than if the object is far away.

As you swim along, you pick up a number of faint, distant echoes—"Sounds like a school of tasty mackerel." Right next to that you hear a louder, stronger echo—"Sounds like the coral reef where the fish are hiding." As you close in, the echoes become louder and you can begin to guess the size of the fish. Closer still, you know how many mackerel there are and how they're grouped. Now you begin to focus your squeals in their direction. This magnifies the echoes and gives you an even better picture of what's ahead. Finally, at the last second, you are close enough to see the fish you've journeyed so far to find. And, before the mackerel know you're there, you've had your meal.

A sounder works just like the dolphin. The sounder consists of two parts: the transducer and the recorder. The transducer is the dolphin's squeal and ears; the recorder is the dolphin's brain. The transducer sends sound waves down into the water under the boat; when the sound waves bounce off an object, the transducer hears them and sends a message to the recorder. The transducer's message tells the recorder two things: how loud the echo is and how far it has traveled (how long it took to return). The recorder then sends that message to a screen that paints a picture of the scene for the angler.

Do You Need a Sounder?

If you fish in the same general area all the time and have lots of local knowledge, you're probably better off keeping your money in the bank.

Sounders are most helpful to anglers who travel to new grounds. With a sounder you can track the bottom contours and use that knowledge to find the fish you're after. Sounders will even show a mobile school of fish in midwater whose presence could not have been predicted from either the bottom configuration or surface activity. Unfortunately, that's just about all these machines can do. They usually won't help you "see" anything besides bottom contours and midwater schools of fish.

Fish on or near the surface can be spotted by watching for birds or a stippled appearance of the water surface (called worried water). Obviously you don't need an expensive machine to help find something you can see with your own eyes.

Many companies' ads claim their sounders can pick out bottom-dwelling fish and highlight them for you. In my experience this claim is sel-

Sounders tell only part of the story. The sound waves bouncing back from bottom fish are camouflaged by other sound waves bouncing back from the sea floor. Fish in midwater without air bladders (like sharks) are also invisible because the sound waves have nothing to bounce off of.

dom accurate. I've sat in my boat over hundreds of tope (school sharks) and hordes of bottom-feeding snapper and seen nothing at all on either of my monitors.

How can this be? Why do sounders usually miss big sharks and bottom-feeding snapper? The answer is surprisingly simple. Remember those sound waves that the transducer sends out? Well, they won't bounce back unless they hit something with a density different from water's.

A shark has no air bladder, so it's like a big, floating water balloon. There's no difference between the density of the shark and the density of the water around it, so the sound waves travel right through the shark and keep on going. Tuna, which have very small air bladders inside a big body, are much the same; very few of the sound waves strike the air bladder, and just about none of them make it back to the transducer. To a sounder, a big tuna looks just like a small mackerel!

Bottom fish like snapper have large air bladders. When they're in midwater, the sound waves bounce off those air-filled bags like crazy. This creates a well-defined image on your sounder screen, one that's hard to miss. What happens if the same snapper is sitting on the bottom? Nothing changes. The sound waves still bounce off its air bladder, and they still come back to the transducer; but because the snapper is right near the bottom, all the sound waves bouncing off the ocean floor come back to the transducer along with the echoes from the fish's air bladder. Because the echoes travel the same distance, the transducer usually can't tell them apart. The snapper's echoes blend in with the other, surrounding echoes to become part of the bottom profile. The result is that you see nothing on the monitor. If you're planning to buy a sounder to spot isolated bottom fish, don't bother. Spend your money on some new jigs; they'll be more useful.

What You Need in a Sounder

You want a sounder to help you track bottom configurations and to spot schools of fish in midwater. Some sounders will do these things better than others. So now you need to know which features make these machines more useful and which features make them only more expensive.

With advances in technology, these complex instruments have become more user-friendly, but their price tags are still high enough to make an angler feel guilty just for wanting one. If you've overcome the guilt barrier, read on. Perhaps I can help you sort out the technical morass of the sounder market by describing some key features.

First of all, you don't want to buy a flasher or a digital depthsounder. Both of these instruments will tell you the depth of water under the boat but not much else. If you study them as you move along, and if you have a great memory, you can construct a bottom contour in your head; but I have no memory and lots of better things to do than stare at an instrument while I'm trying to fish. It's true that flashers are less than half the price of a good sounder, but so what? You'd be better off buying a pizza than a flasher. At least you can eat it if you don't catch any fish.

With these limitations in mind, lets review the qualities that can make a sounder especially useful.

Paper, Video, or LCD

The monitor component of a sounder can take three forms. The underwater image picked up by the transducer can be transmitted onto a moving roll of paper, a video screen (like a TV), or a liquid crystal diode display (LCD). Paper is most useful if you require a permanent record (although some video and LCD monitors can record the image on tape for playback). Obviously the paper must be shielded from adverse weather conditions, so it's suitable only for boats with closed cabins. Video is a little more rugged, produces a fine image pattern, and is much more accurate than LCD screens; but it's bulky, and it's suitable only for boats with closed cabins.

These restrictions make your decision easy. You have no choice but to buy a sounder equipped with an LCD. LCDs are quite compact and very tough. Wind and water don't interfere with their function at all. However, you need a little more skill to interpret the picture because they don't produce as fine an image as paper recorders or video monitors. The quality of liquid crystal displays varies significantly. Since the LCD monitor is half the total cost of a sounder, a unit with a top-quality screen is going to cost big bucks. But those bucks are well spent; here's why.

Pixels

A liquid crystal display screen consists of a layer of liquid crystal sandwiched between two transparent sheets. Each screen is divided into thousands of parts, or *pixels.* A pixel turns black when an electrical current from the transducer darkens the liquid in that tiny part of the screen. When enough of the pixels turn black, an image is produced.

EAGLE

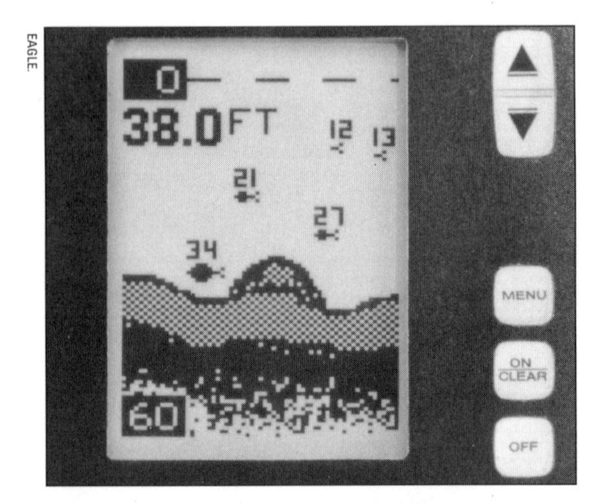

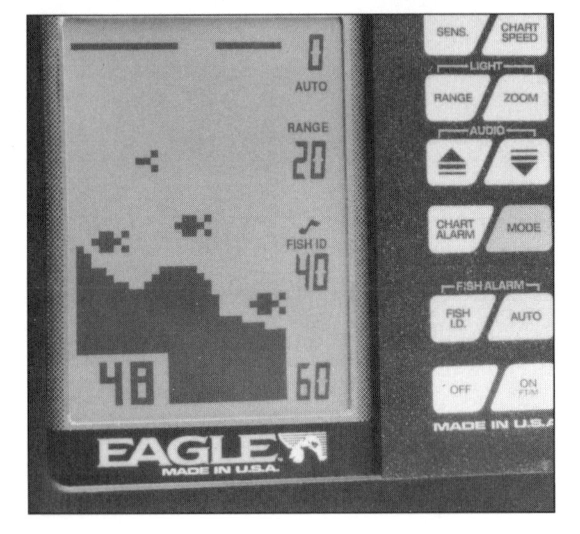

Small pixels (top) on an LCD screen produce a finer image than large pixels (bottom) but are much harder to see in bright light.

If each pixel is small, you get a fine image that's easy to interpret. Videos and paper monitors have many more pixels than LCDs. Most LCDs vary from 350 to 1,340 pixels per square inch (psi), and some of the newest screens have more than 3,800 pixels psi. The greater the density of pixels, the more expensive the screen. For that expense you get a finer image. But unless the screen is of really top quality, the smaller pixels will be harder to see in bright sunlight. This is where the trade-off comes in: small pixels produce the illusion of less contrast, so larger pixels can actually be *easier* to see in bright sunlight.

Manufacturers have coped with this problem by improving the contrast between the pixel and the background color of the screen. These improvements have led to the backlit, Supertwist Nematic LCD screen, and that's what you want to buy. In a few years even better contrast will become available with Double Supertwist and Triple Supertwist Nematic screens. They should provide the ultimate in contrast—black on white. After that will come affordable color LCDs that will substitute color for shades of contrast.

Screen Size and Orientation

Screens vary widely in size. With a larger screen you get a larger picture, which means more information on the screen at any one time. Most LCDs have screens smaller than 24 square inches (155 sq. cm), but the larger screens are easier to use. If you have a poor memory, then select a screen that's wider than it is high; the wider screen preserves the image of what you've passed over for a longer time. If your top priority is a more detailed, real-time image, then select a screen that's higher than it is wide; the vertical format will provide more information about what's under the boat at the moment. Large screens (24 inches) are more costly and can be slightly more cumbersome, but they are well worth it. If you will be fishing ultralight most of the time, you'll be staying in shallow water, where detail is usually good enough anyway, so stick with a screen that's wider than it is high.

Frequency

The transmitter component of the transducer projects sound waves into the water. Sound waves have different frequencies. In deep water the best results are obtained with lower frequencies. Most deepwater sounders use 50 kHz, and most shallow-water sounders use 200 kHz. Since "shallow water" can be as deep as 120 feet, most ultralight anglers will find higher-frequency transmitters more useful. Look for a unit that transmits sound in the range of 200 kHz. You can also buy transducers with dual-frequency transmitters that can switch between 50 and 200 kHz, but that's an extra expense the ultralight angler does not really need.

A screen that's wider than it is high is the best choice for the ultralight angler. This well-used sounder sits on top of a wooden battery box that houses a small automobile battery. Notice how the bright light dims the refined image of a screen with small pixels.

Cone Angle

The best way to understand *cone angle* is to imagine that you are in a dark, smoky room. You turn on a flashlight and shine it against a wall. You see a cone of light leaving the flashlight and forming a bright circle on the wall. Some of the light bounces off the smoke in the air, but far more bounces off the reflective wall. The smoke in the air is like the fish in the water, and the wall is like the sea bottom.

The transmitter in the transducer sends the sound waves out from a point source just as the flashlight shines light on a wall. As the waves travel through the water, they diverge to form a cone. The greater the angle of the cone, the greater the area of bottom surveyed. As you can see from the illustration, a narrow cone is desirable in deep water, but a wider cone is better in shallow water. Most transmitters produce cone angles in the range of

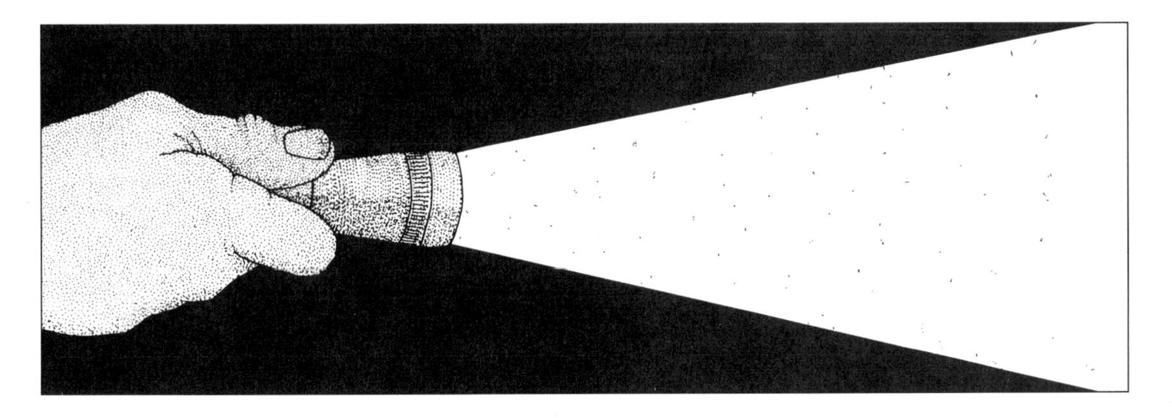

Light waves in a smoky room bounce off the dust particles in the air to produce an image. Your sounder does the same thing with sound waves.

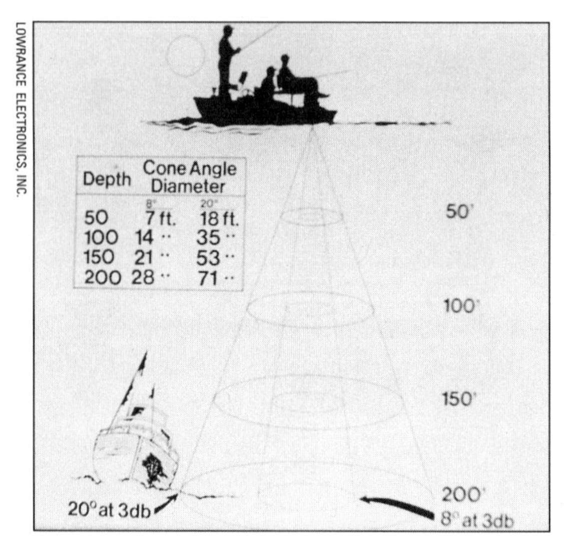

Top: The ultralight angler is better off with a wide-cone-angle transmitter because it surveys more of the bottom in shallow water.

Bottom: The two transducers on the left are mounted at the wrong angle, producing turbulence that disrupts the sound waves with air bubbles. The transducer on the right is mounted at the correct angle to minimize turbulence.

9 to 20 degrees. Some sounders come equipped with two different beam angles so you can switch from one to the other at will. Since ultralight lines are no fun in waters over 50 feet (15 meters) deep, a wide cone angle (20 degrees or more) is the best choice.

Transducer Mounts

The transducer can be placed inside or outside the boat. It's more sensitive outside but also more vulnerable if you strike floating objects or beach the boat. Bubbles and turbulence from the engine also affect the transducer when the boat is moving at speed, and this turbulence is generally worse with aluminum hulls. It's a serious problem if you want to examine large areas of the sea floor while moving faster than 5 to 10 knots.

If you place your transducer on the outside of the boat for improved sensitivity, either mount it flush with the hull at the transom or buy a "kick-up" transducer mount that will swing up if struck. This mount lets you place the transducer a little deeper into the water and farther away from your prop, which may mean better reception when your prop is producing turbulence.

To avoid possible damage to the transducer, you may want to buy a through-the-hull model with your sounder. Through-the-hull transmissions don't work well in aluminum boats, though, because the dense aluminum reflects enough of the transducer's energy output to reduce the energy return from the water. The best way to get good signal reception when you want the transducer inside an aluminum boat is to cut a hole

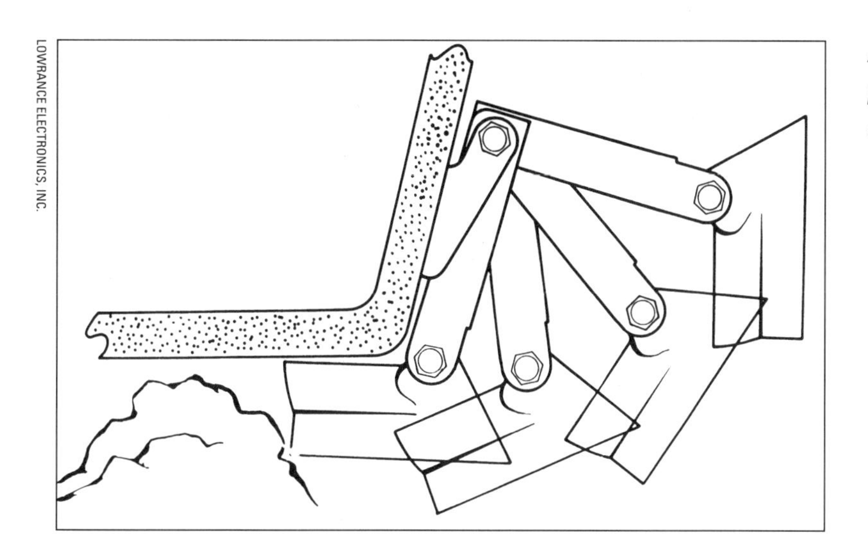

LOWRANCE ELECTRONICS, INC.

A "kick-up" mount that will protect your transducer in shallow water.

in the lowest portion of the hull and weld in a sealed mounting that holds the transducer. This takes time, but it will give you good reception even at speeds over 10 knots.

Since I fish a lot in shallow waters and often beach my aluminum boat, I've mounted my transducer inside. I wasn't too keen on cutting up my boat, so I placed the transducer in the stern in a pool of silicone glue. This provides acceptable sensitivity if you turn off the auto-range and turn up the gain.

If you leave the sounder on auto-range, the reflections from the aluminum will confuse the sounder because the auto-range function works effectively only if there's nothing under the transducer but water. All you'll see on the screen is a single, black horizontal line. To compensate for turning off "auto-range," you'll have to set the range manually, which is no big deal. And to compensate for the energy reflected by the aluminum hull, you'll need to increase the gain. This amplifies the energy that does get through. Again, this is no problem in a quality sounder because you'll be in shallow water, where energy output is not critical.

Sounder or Sonar? 2D or 3D?

Both sounders and side-scan sonar work by projecting sound waves into the water through a transducer. These sound waves travel at about 5,000 feet per second. When they strike something with a different density than water, the waves bounce back to the transducer and are then transmitted electronically onto a screen to form an image.

Most sounders project their sound waves directly below the boat. They produce a two-dimensional image from a three-dimensional cone of sound.

But if you add side-scan sonar to a sounder, you can direct sound waves in any direction. This enables you to read what is happening in the water for several hundred feet anywhere around the boat. (Sonar is designed primarily to detect objects in the water. Sounders are designed primarily to detect bottom configurations.) This combination is more versatile than a simple sounder, but it's also more expensive and complex to operate. Variations on the theme include units with multiple transducers or transducers that project beams in multiple directions. You can switch between beams and see to either side and in front of or behind the boat, or you can use the multiple beams to construct a 3-D image of the bottom.

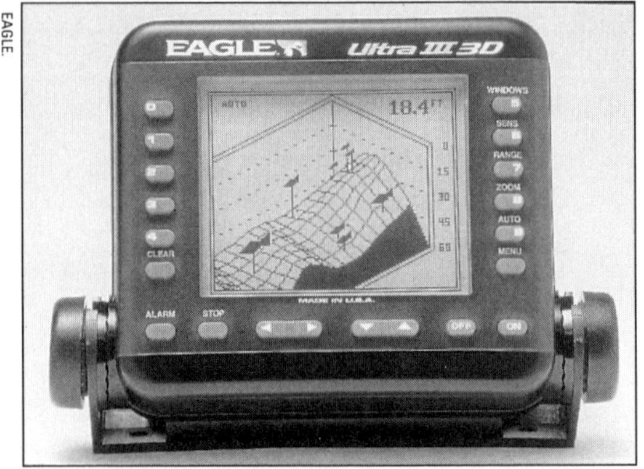

EAGLE.

A three-dimensional image on a two-dimensional screen can be useful if you can cope with the technology.

The technology here overwhelms me. If you can cope with all the options and still enjoy fishing, then a 3-D sounder might be for you. I've just got to keep it simple. I'm going to stick with two dimensions.

Gray Line and Color

When the liquid crystal in the screen receives an electric charge, it darkens. It's all or nothing—the pixel either turns dark or it doesn't. But now *gray line* (also called *gray scale* or *white line*) is available. Its purpose is to make it easier to see bottom fish. Basically, the sounder automatically filters out a certain percentage of weaker bottom echoes in an attempt to highlight the stronger echo from the air bladder of a fish. Because only a limited number of pixels turn black, an illusion of gray is produced. On a hard bottom, where all the returning echoes are strong, the system is virtually useless. On a soft bottom, it *should* help to bring out bottom-dwelling fish. But my experience has taught me *not* to depend on sounders—whether or not they're equipped with a gray-line option—to find isolated bottom fish.

You can also use the sounder to determine the type of bottom you're over. A soft, mud bottom will appear thick on the LCD display because the energy from the transducer goes deep into it before bouncing back to the surface. A hard bottom reflects most, or all, of the energy immediately, so the screen shows a narrow band. The gray-line option will highlight this a little, but it will not really add to your knowledge once you've had some experience on the water.

Another variation of this concept is the multicolor LCD screen. Here the strength of the echo determines the color of the image. A strong echo is red, and a weak echo is green. That's nice too; but it's hard to see in sunlight, and it won't improve your fishing either. Some manufacturers claim you can tell the species of fish by the color of the echo. That's true, but only with severe restrictions. You would have to know the color for each fish in your area at each depth and in each size range. It makes more sense to understand the nature of the fish you're after and look for the conditions they live in and the pattern of the schools they form. At this stage of development, color LCD screens are more likely to confuse than help you.

Other Features

In addition to the those basics, the various sounders offer hundreds of other features that will come with your sounder whether you want them or not; you can decide for yourself if they are useful. I just want to warn you about the "Fish ID" option—it gives you a cute picture of a fish on the screen each time the sounder "sees" a fish under the water. In my opinion this is just a lot of hocus-pocus.

The sounder responds to the intensity of the echo it receives. A loud echo creates a big fish on the screen, and a faint echo creates a small fish. But the strength of the echo actually depends on the size of the fish's air bladder and its distance from the center of the cone of sound. That intensity is further affected by microscopic debris and temperature variation in the water. Furthermore, the echo might not come from a fish at all; it might be from a piece of wood, a ball of weed, a thermocline, or a plankton shoal.

And "Fish ID" is an all-or-nothing proposition. It doesn't give you images that you can learn to interpret with time and experience as, say, a log or a pelagic or a tight school of fish. You get a fish on screen, or you get nothing. "Fish ID" will more likely confuse than help you, so my advice is to ignore it and learn to interpret your own images. You'll be a lot better off.

I hope this information will be of some help as you struggle with the number and variety of sounders available. When you finally buy one, read the operation manual carefully; you'll find it surprisingly helpful. You'll also find that sounders are a lot easier to use than they are to buy.

Chapter Ten

Gadgets

There is no shortage of gadgetry to spend your money on these days, but many of the bits and pieces we buy just lie around taking up precious storage space without ever earning their keep. I'd like to tell you about a few accessories that are actually useful; they make fishing more productive, safer, and more fun. Many of them can be made at home.

Extended Rod Handles

The photo on page 109 shows a series of rod handles handmade by Robert Pope, an American fisherman and rodmaker. Although all the rods are ultralight or light in their action, they have either long handles or handle extensions. Extended handles let you tuck the end of the rod under your forearm or elbow (or push it into your abdomen) for considerably more wrist support during the one to three hours it can take to land a world-record fish.

Of the many factory-made long-handle rods, only a few are in the ultralight class. But any skilled rodmaker can add an extension to your favorite rod.

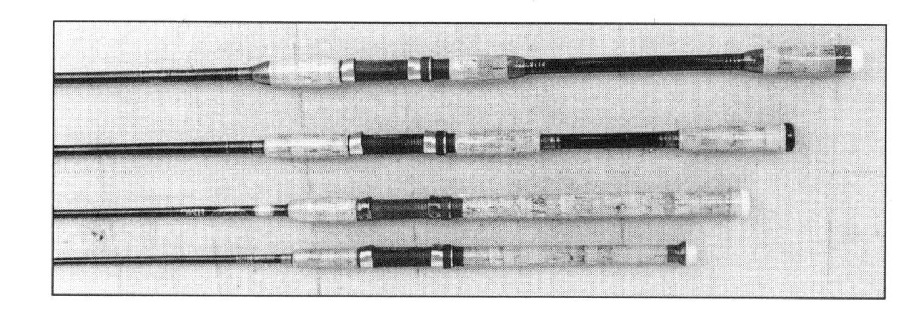

Extra-long rod handles like these make it easier to catch world-record fish with ultra-light tackle.

Line Remover

The next photo shows a device that will help you empty used spools of line from your reel. It is simply a piece of PVC pipe attached to an electric drill with a wood block. When you want to empty a line spool, just pull the line off the reel and tie it to the PVC pipe. Then hold the spool facing upward and start the drill. A few seconds later the spool will be empty, and you'll be ready to refill it. It beats the hell out of pulling the line off the spool by hand.

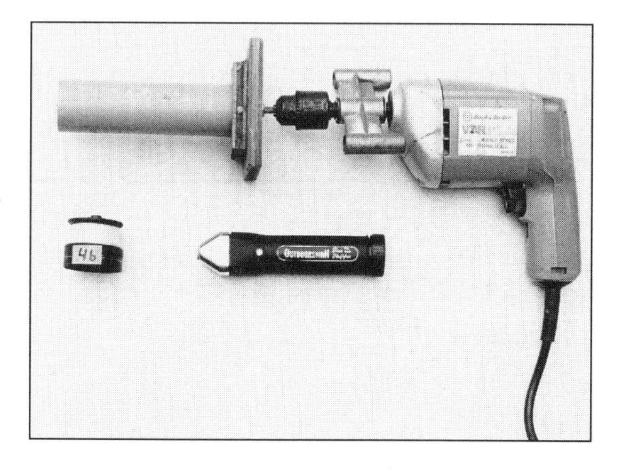

Either of these gadgets will empty a spool of line a lot faster than you can do it by hand. The line stripper on the bottom is made by Berkley.

You can buy battery-powered devices that do the job almost as fast—if you don't mind buying batteries. Berkley makes one that's convenient and economical to run but considerably slower than the homemade model.

Rod Holders

It's always useful to have a rod holder on each side of the stern to hold your rods if you're trolling or still-baiting. They can easily be made from a piece of PVC pipe. Make sure they're mounted at a slight angle, with the upper end leaning slightly toward the stern. At the top of each piece of PVC, cut out a notch large enough to hold the leg of your spinning reels (see the drawing on page 110). The notch will lock your reels in position so the rods cannot be thrown free by an unexpected wave or a strike while you're trolling. If you don't have an extra-long rod handle and don't bother to set the spinning-reel leg into the notch, there's a good chance the rod will end up overboard; one of mine did.

A tremendous assortment of rod holders is available commercially. They're made of high-impact plastic, aluminum, teak, or stainless steel and can do all sorts of tricks like sound alarms, rotate, enable quick release, and even set the hook. They're all fascinating, but I think a piece of PVC pipe does the job just as well.

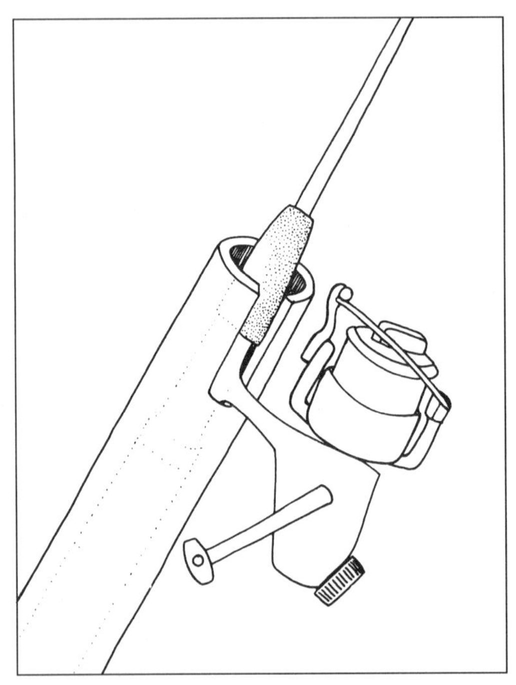

Top: Make sure your PVC rod holder has a slot cut in it so the leg of a spinning reel will slide down far enough to be secure in rough weather.

Bottom: A live-bait box must fit the contours of the boat but still sit as far as possible from the engine.

Live-Bait Box

Have a look at the photo of a live-bait box at the stern of a boat. It's a wooden box carefully molded to fit the profile of the stern; unless you build it with precision, the water pressure will rip it off as you travel. This particular box is 14 by 12 by 14 inches (35 × 30 × 35 cm). It has two notches on top that fit under the aluminum edges of the boat, and it's supported from below by a permanently mounted shelf. A simple locking device on the side of the box makes it easy to attach and remove.

Make sure you paint the inside of the box white, or you won't be able to see the bait in the morning. (It's just about impossible to see a mackerel against the color of wet natural wood in the dim light of dawn.) An aquarium net makes it easier to pull the bait out, and a hinged top is a must. A few holes strategically drilled provide lots of water exchange while your boat is moving or anchored in a tidal flow. Just be careful not to drill any holes in the bottom 3 inches of the box, or the water will be sucked out when your boat is moving at speed. I can keep a dozen mackerel or mullet alive and healthy in this box for 12 hours with no difficulty.

A live-bait box like this makes battery-powered gear like aerators and livewell pumps unnecessary, and it saves boat space for important items like food and drink.

Motor Flushers

If you fish salt water infrequently, your engine's cooling system will clog up unless you give it special attention. A commercial, rubber motor flusher provides an exceedingly easy way to clean the cooling system with fresh water from any garden hose.

If you're fishing salt water daily, flushing isn't necessary since the salt will have no chance to crystallize in the narrow cooling passages of the engine block. But if you'll be off the water for more than a week at a time, your engine may live a very short life unless you clean out the salt.

Motor flushers save you the hassle of maintaining a barrel of fresh water for running the engine at home (the barrel method is ridiculously messy and inefficient anyway), and they're also quite useful when you want to repair or tune your engine without having to launch it. A motor flusher is a "must have" item.

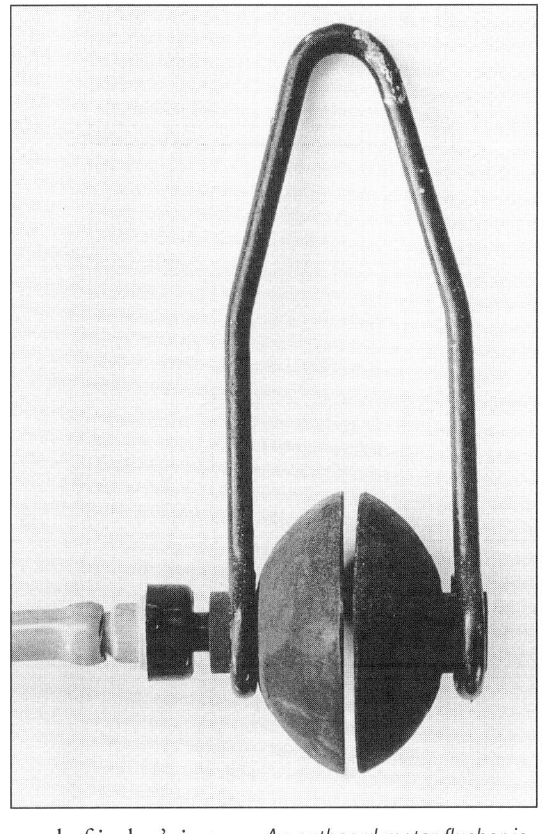

An outboard-motor flusher is a necessity. This one is made by Posi-Flush.

Outboard Extension Bar

Extension bars are made to fit snugly over your outboard-motor handle. Mine consists of a piece of stout bamboo about 4 feet (1.2 meters) long and a small length of radiator hose epoxied to the end of it that's just the right width for a snug fit. A piece of 2-inch (50-mm) PVC pipe glued to the bamboo pole works well too.

If you're away from shore and find yourself in a headwind with no ballast to hold the bow down, an extension could easily save your life:

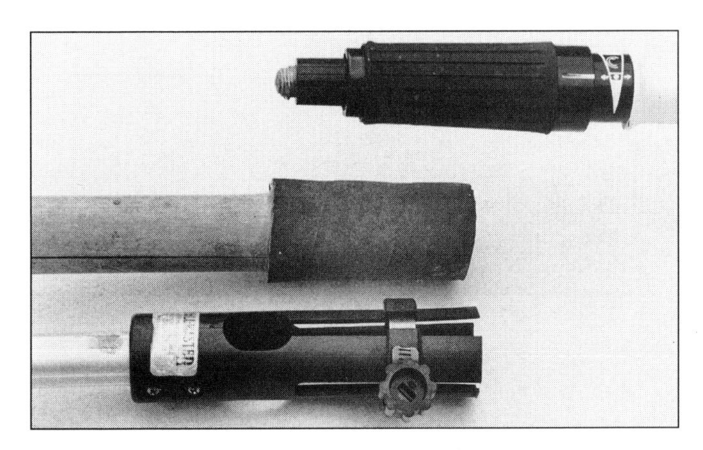

An outboard extension bar can save your life in a headwind. The one on top was made at home with a piece of bamboo and a radiator hose. The one on the bottom is made by Troll-master.

with a 4-foot extension you can sit in the middle seat of a 12-foot (3.6-meter) boat to give it proper trim. An extension also functions as a push pole in shallow water. It's another "must have" item.

Extension bars are manufactured commercially too. They're made of aluminum or stainless steel and clamp onto the engine handle. They feature an adjustable length and a molded plastic handle. They look prettier than the bamboo poles, but I don't think they're as easy to use. The photo illustrates the two options.

Anchor Buoy

Another necessary device is an anchor buoy. Two to four empty plastic detergent bottles tied to the end of your anchor line will enable you to simply drop the anchor overboard when you hook up. Then, once you've landed the fish, you can cruise back and easily recover the anchor. The photo shows my simple setup. Note the nylon strap securing the unused coils of anchor rope so they don't drift all over the ocean while you're away.

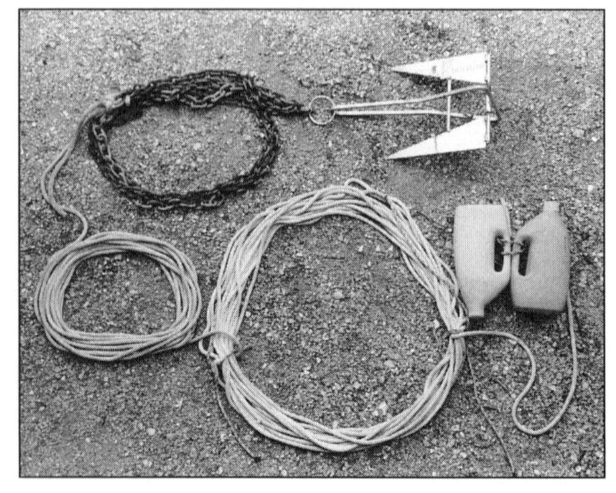

This is what you'll need in order to throw your anchor rope overboard to follow a fish quickly. The coil of rope on the bottom right has a couple of small pieces of cord tied around it so it won't come apart in the water. This anchor will release without a trip line. It's a Waterspike by Carlson Outdoors.

Use enough free anchor line and enough plastic bottles so that strong currents don't drag your buoy down. I've spent several fruitless hours sitting around waiting for the tidal flow to slow so my anchor buoy would pop back up. Don't ever rely on just one plastic bottle either; they have the nastiest habit of springing leaks just when you need them the most. One more hint: don't use white plastic containers—they're too hard to see in a fast-moving current; I use yellow or orange.

Quick Anchor Release

If you like gadgets, you might find a quick anchor release useful once in a while. Called either *jam cleats* or *cam cleats,* they're designed for sailboats and are useful when you want to release your anchor rope without untying it from a standard cleat. They pinch the anchor rope securely, but it can be released by a simple upward tug and dropped into the water to float on the anchor buoy just described. These quick-release cleats are worth having if your boat is longer than 12 feet (3.6 meters). In a smaller boat it's quicker just to reach for the bow cleat.

Knife Sharpeners

I carry two knives in the boat. One is quite heavy, and I use it to cut baits, lines, and rope. The other is thin and flexible and is most useful for filleting fish. Both are made of soft steel so they can be easily sharpened. In my tackle box I carry a small ceramic knife sharpener called a Zip-Zap.

Ceramic sharpeners are quite popular now, and there are many brands available. I stole my first Zip-Zap from my wife's kitchen and was astounded by its effectiveness. This remarkable device is less than 6 inches (15 cm) long, fits easily into any tackle box, and will keep your knives sharp for years. You can usually find one at a kitchen specialty shop. It's a terrific gadget.

Hook Sharpeners

Every angler knows how important it is to have sharp hooks, yet I am continually surprised at how few anglers actually do anything to keep those hooks sharp. Much of the time I hear statements like "It's a stainless steel hook; it doesn't need to be sharpened" or "It's a new hook; it was sharpened at the factory."

These beliefs are clearly off the mark; but when someone tells me something like that, I just change the subject. Fishing is supposed to be fun, and sharpening hooks is not fun. People have a right not to be compulsive about their sport.

Occasionally anglers will turn to me and say how they tried this or that tool to sharpen hooks and it failed, so they gave up. Here for your review is a sampling of tools that have failed and why:

- Sharpening stones: Take too long to use. They break if you drop them. They cost too much.
- Diamond dust sharpeners: Too expensive. Too small. They wear out too fast.
- Files: They rust to death because of the salt. Too big for the tackle box.
- Electric hook sharpeners: Forget it, I'll just buy my fish.

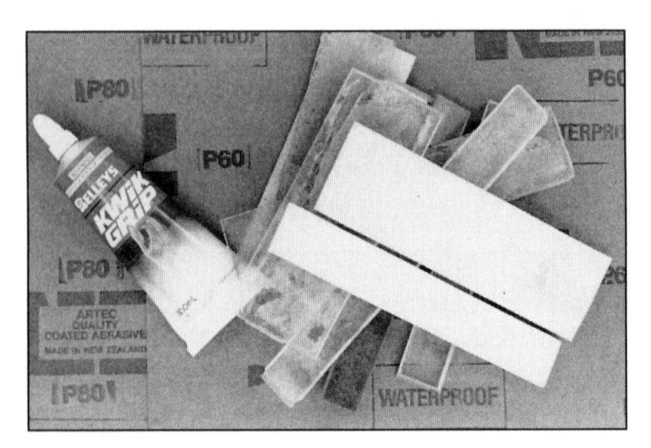

All you need to make double-sided hook sharpeners: some silicon carbide sandpaper, a few pieces of plastic, and contact cement.

I believe all those statements are more-or-less correct, but there is another method that's cheap, works great, and involves a tool that will not rust or take up a lot of room in your tackle box. The only drawback is that *you* have to make these little gadgets; but you can easily make 20 or more in an hour, so it's well worth your while.

Here's how it's done: Go out and buy several sheets of waterproof silicon-carbide sandpaper and some contact cement. Get various grits of sandpaper so you can determine which grit works best for you. Try 60-grit on one side and 80-grit on the other for starters. Then all you'll need is about 20 narrow pieces of 1- by 6-inch (2.5 × 15-cm) wood or plastic—just the right size to fit in your tackle box.

Lay out the sandpaper on a bench with the sandy side down. Take the precut wood or plastic pieces and figure out how many you can fit on the sandpaper. Then coat the sandpaper and one side of the pieces with contact cement and glue the pieces to the sandpaper. When the glue is set, separate all the pieces with a razor knife.

Next, take another piece of sandpaper—the same size but a different grit—and lay that down on the bench. Coat it and the unglued side of your separated wood or plastic pieces with contact cement. Then glue the pieces to the sandpaper and let them set. Once the contact cement is dry, just cut the pieces apart with a razor knife and—presto, you've got 20 two-sided hook sharpeners.

These sharpeners wear out fairly quickly; but they're easy to make, easy to use, rust-free, and highly disposable. The plastic or wood cores can even be reused if you peel off the worn sandpaper. One more hint: don't buy stainless steel hooks; they are so hard that they're difficult to sharpen. It's better to use a softer hook, such as the bronzed or nickel-plated varieties I've already told you about.

Hot-Water-Pipe Insulation

Life on an aluminum dinghy can be pretty unpleasant. The hard seats, salt spray, blistering sun, and exposed conditions can take a lot of the joy out of fishing. Any time I pick up a new idea to make "tinnies" more livable, I like to pass it on.

This is a hint I picked up from an angler fishing the estuaries by the Outer Banks in North Carolina. He was using pipe insulation to pad the gunwales of his dinghy. Pipe insulation is closed-cell foam cut in the shape of a pipe and slit down the side so it can be slipped over a pipe to keep it from freezing in winter and to keep water from cooling on its way from the hot-water heater to the tap.

Why would anyone want pipe insulation on an aluminum dinghy? If you glue it on over the gunwales the entire length of the boat, it does three things for you:

- It provides a bumper for the boat. This means you can tie up alongside other vessels without clanging into them and scratching up their paint jobs.
- It's a nice soft cushion to rest your feet on when you want to lie across the seat and have a little snooze.
- It makes a great place to store mackerel flies and lures that are in daily use. The closed-cell polyethylene foam neither soaks up water nor allows air to circulate. So your hooks do not corrode while they're stuck in the foam; they stay sharp and strong. Have a look at the photo to see how it works.

The closed-cell foam used for household pipe insulation makes a great place to hang your lures. This foam has been on the boat for two years and is just about ready for replacement.

With some insulation on your gunwales, you don't have to worry about getting stuck by loose mackerel flies, and you can leave your lures rigged up to a leader so they're available immediately when the pelagics start rising around your boat.

I've had the pipe insulation on my boat for two years now, and it's a real winner. The biggest problem I had was getting it to stay in place. Silicone glues and epoxy weren't very effective, but contact cement worked great. The polyethylene is pretty soft and can tear easily; but whenever that happens, I just whip out the contact cement and glue the bits right back together.

For most dinghies the ⅜-inch-thick insulation made to fit ½-inch copper pipe is the best size. The stuff is mostly air so it costs only $5 for 12 feet (4 meters), and you can find it at any building-supply center. (Just be sure *not* to buy open-cell foam.)

Wrapping the Warp

My anchor and warp have been a pain in the ass for years. Every time I wanted to do something in the bow, my feet got tangled up in coils of rope. And after each trip the anchor and warp would always deposit a charming collection of old shells, weed, and grit on the floor of the boat. I never realized that there was a way to avoid all this hassle until one day, while vacuuming the house, I had an idea.

I noticed how the electric cord was wound around the handle: it went around two posts that splayed outward so the cord wouldn't slip off. To release the cord, all you had to do was rotate one of the posts to splay inward instead of outward, and the cord would slide right off into your hands. I stared at the vacuum and wondered, "Why can't I put this arrangement on the bow of my dinghy?"

The basic plans for the anchor-warp holder on my boat. The spring under the foredeck (surrounding the middle bolt) is what makes it all work.

I went down to the garage for a quick experiment. It looked like it could be done, so I went off to see Tony Goodman, a local boatbuilder and good friend. He also thought it was doable, and a few days later he had it designed and built. He made mine from four pieces of hardwood, six bolts, and two springs. As you can see from the illustration, the springs and

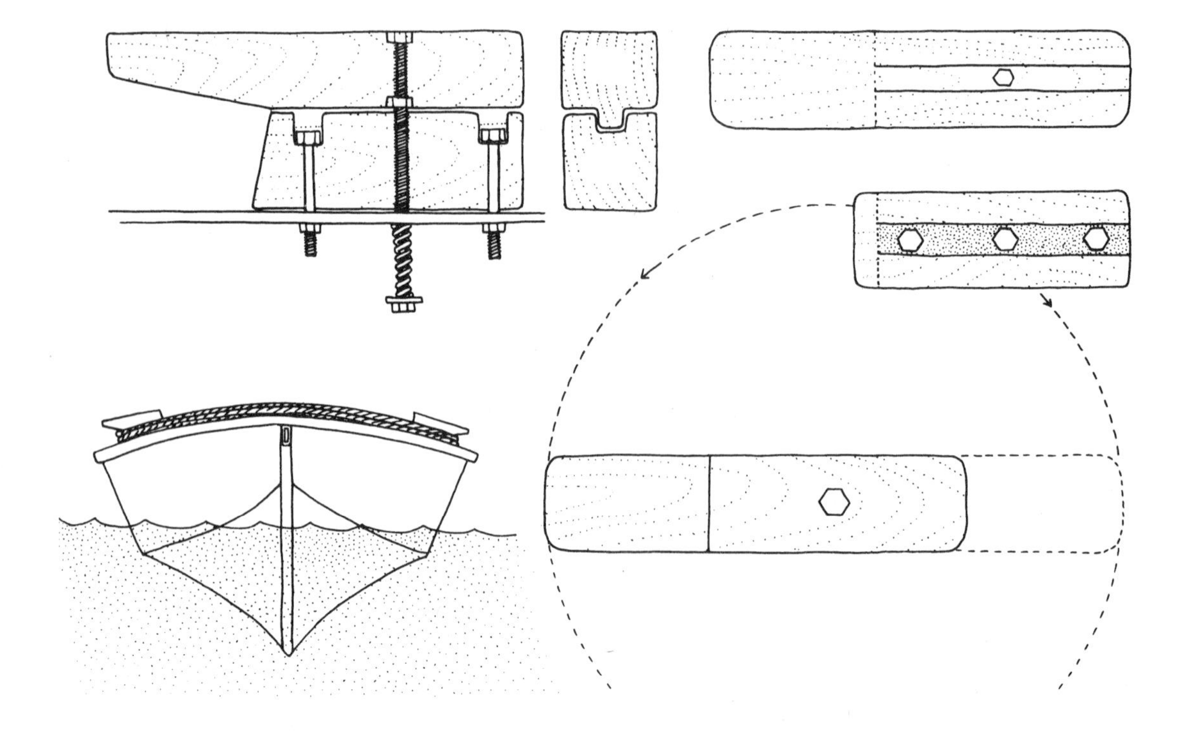

nuts all sit well under the foredeck, where they're protected from most salt spray.

When it's time to drop anchor, I just pick up the top pieces of hardwood that splay outward. Since the device is spring-loaded, there's some resistance. That means when the post is rotated 180 degrees and released, it locks right into the groove on the lower piece. Then all I have to do is pick the anchor rope off the posts.

When it's time to haul the anchor in, the top pieces need to be rotated 180 degrees again, and the rope wrapped around the posts as I haul away. The rope doesn't get tangled, and it never drops a load of garbage inside the boat.

The system has another advantage for ultralight anglers, who often find it necessary to pursue fish after the hookup and have to quickly drop the anchor and warp overboard. With this system of posts on the bow, all you have to do is lift up the coil of rope and heave it overboard. If you're anchored in shallow water, just tie a short nylon ribbon around the unused anchor warp as it sits on the posts. Then, when you return to pick up the anchor, the rope will pop right onto the posts; you won't have to hassle with winding it back on.

I've been so happy with the system that I asked Tony Goodman to draw up the plans shown here. Give it a go.

An Anchor Release

One of the biggest problems with fishing reefs is a stuck anchor. Once the flukes are locked under a large rock or piece of coral, they're just about impossible to free. That is, impossible unless you have a quick-release setup. To prepare this little gem, attach your anchor chain to the crown of the anchor instead of to the shank. Then use some 30-kg monofilament nylon to tie the shank of the anchor to the chain. If you

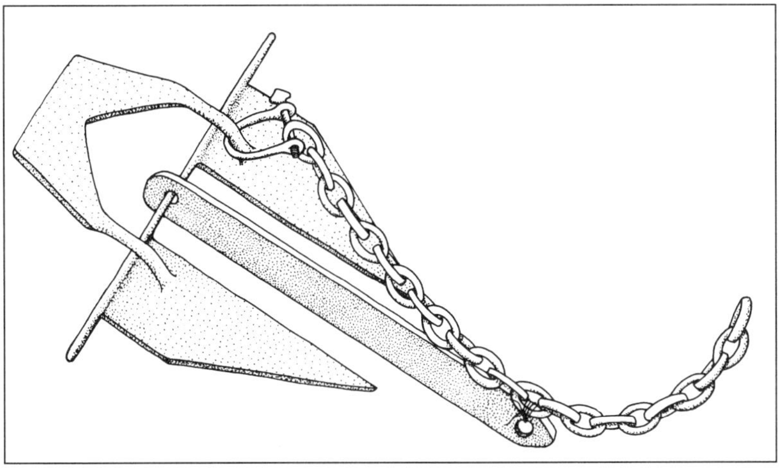

A quick-release trip line can be built into just about any anchor with some 30-kg monofilament and a shackle.

ever get stuck, just give the chain a hard jerk; the monofilament will break, and the anchor will be pulled out of its trap upside down.

Another choice is a Waterspike anchor like the one shown in the photo of my anchor-buoy arrangement. These Waterspikes are designed to break away without a trip line.

Some Other Tidbits

Either beg a pair of surgical forceps from a nurse or buy a pair at your local tackle shop. They're amazingly useful for removing hooks from struggling fish about to be released. The 6-inch (15-cm) size is the best.

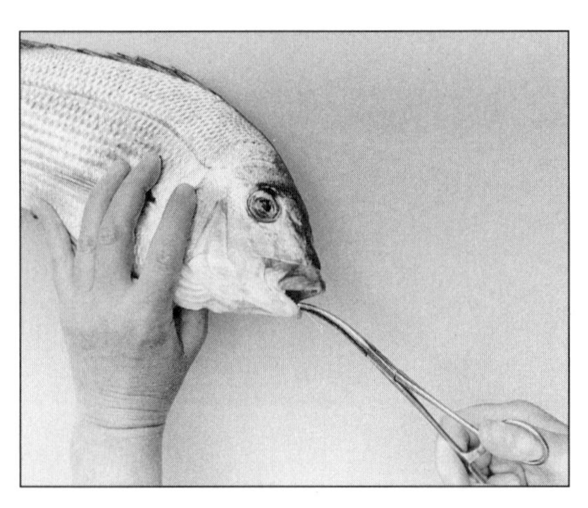

Forceps are a very handy item for fish-hook removal; be sure they have a long handle.

Keep a large sponge in the boat. Don't buy one at the store; it won't be the right size. Cut one from an old foam mattress. The best size is 14 by 9 by 1 inches (35 × 22 × 2.5 cm). The most important dimension is the 1-inch thickness. Anything bulkier is awkward to use and soaks up water too slowly.

Use an anchor chain; it will help your anchor lie flat on the bottom so it can dig in. I've found that a 4.5-pound (2-kg) anchor coupled to a 6-foot (2-meter), 11-pound (5-kg) chain will hold my 12-foot (3.6-meter) boat pretty well.

Electronics

Resist the temptation to crowd your boat with electronic instruments. In no time you can have electrical thermometers, pH meters, light meters, lure selectors, etc. filling your boat and driving you crazy.

There's not much room in a small boat; any item included on board has to be very useful. The only electronic instrument that I think is worth the space is a sounder with a liquid crystal display, and you know all about that.

CHAPTER ELEVEN

Making It All Work

LIFE ON THE WATER CAN BE TOUGH on you and your gear. In this chapter we'll review how to take good care of your tackle and yourself. Then we'll move on to the essential techniques of ultralight fishing, the tricks that will enable you to catch big fish on light line.

Equipment Maintenance

There's no doubt that ultralight gear provides great sport and can turn a mediocre fishing day into a suspenseful and challenging one. But there is a price to be paid in maintenance. No ultralight angler can afford to have a stuttering drag or a nicked rod guide. If you take good care of your gear, it will last a very long time and always perform to your expectations. Anything less will mean lost fish and aggravation at sea.

Spinning Reels

A top-quality spinning reel will last 10 years or more, even with heavy use. Contrary to popular wisdom, it is not necessarily a good idea to rinse your reels in fresh water when you get home. If you're not very careful—if you misdirect the water spray or turn the pressure up too high—you can easily drive salt water into the gear housing or behind the spool.

If you don't fish often, it's better just to lightly rinse the ball hinges, bail-roller, handle, and rear drag adjustment after a day's fishing. After rins-

If you apply waterproof grease around the lip of the reel body, water will never get in.

ing, shake the reel and spin the handle to dry it. Then put some lightweight oil on the areas you rinsed, and you're ready for the next fishing trip. When I'm fishing every day, I don't bother to wash the reels at all. I just oil them up, rub the oil around with a rag, release the drag, and stick them in the rack. Oil is wonderful stuff; you can go for years without washing the reel if you keep the exposed surfaces well lubricated.

After about 10 to 15 hours of fighting time, you should check the drag washers for wear. If they're worn or distorted, they must be replaced. Then, when you close up the reel body again, be sure to add a heavy grease seal around the casing before screwing it down (see the photo) to keep out salt water until your next washer check. Worn washers lead to drag stutter under stress and, eventually, to worn metal parts and an early death for your reel.

The longer a reel lasts, the more success you'll have with it. One of the keys to satisfaction with ultralight fishing is knowing your gear as you know your own body. If you have to buy a new reel every six months, it will always feel alien in your hands.

Check the bail-roller for wear after 20 to 40 hours of fighting time. At the same time, break the reel down completely, clean it with an organic solvent, dry it, and regrease it. If you don't like to do any maintenance until the last minute, you can wait until the reel drag starts to stutter or the bail doesn't snap across as smartly as it should; but if you wait that long, there is an increased risk of damage to the metal parts, parts that shouldn't really be wearing much at all.

Try to keep a stock of parts so you don't have to depend on the dealer every time you need something. My solution is to own three identical reels. I also have a bag of 30 soft drag washers, a few bail-rollers, metal drag washers, bail springs, and ratchet springs. If you buy all that and a few other goodies when you purchase your reels, they won't die an early death from lack of functioning body parts. Turnover in the industry is very rapid now, and fishing reels are like high-fashion clothes: new (new, but not necessarily better) models appear every year.

When you finish cleaning your reel and are ready to lubricate it, be

ABU GARCIA INC.

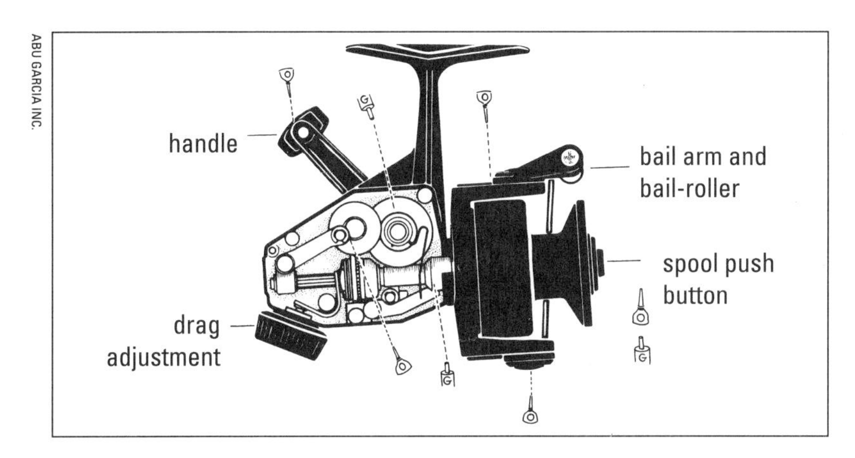

Some parts of a reel require grease; and some, oil. Follow the manufacturer's recommendations; they usually know what they're talking about. The bits that are labeled should be lubricated after each fishing trip.

careful to follow the manufacturer's directions. This is especially important with the drag washers. Some washers (e.g., Teflon) work best if they're not lubricated. Grease can make some synthetic washers impossible to adjust smoothly, resulting in a stuttering spool and broken lines on the water. You may need to experiment to determine what's best for your reel. Do your experimenting in the garage, not on the water. It's a bummer to discover the drag's not working when there's a fish stripping line off at 10 yards (10 meters) a second.

Loading line onto the spool of your spinning reel has to be done correctly, or you'll end up with a twisted line before the reel ever gets near a fish. The first thing you'll need is the right amount of backing on the spool. If you'll be fishing 2-kg line, 100 to 120 yards (about 100 meters) of line is all you'll want. For 1-kg line, 80 to 100 yards (about 80 meters) is usually adequate. I know it doesn't sound like much; you'll find out why it's enough later in this chapter.

Since the spool needs to be filled to capacity to improve castability and reduce line set, the backing has to take up all the remaining space. You have to put on the right amount, and you have to distribute it correctly. Since the spool sizes I recommended in Chapter Three are larger than usual for ultralight, you'll probably have to pile the backing up a little higher in the middle of the spool than on the edges. As you might recall, the only way to determine the best pattern and correct amount of backing is by trial and error. Once you've figured it out, put the same amount of backing on the other reel spools you have, and you'll be set for years.

To avoid line twist while putting monofilament on, you'll need to lay the newly purchased line spool flat on the floor so the line comes off in a

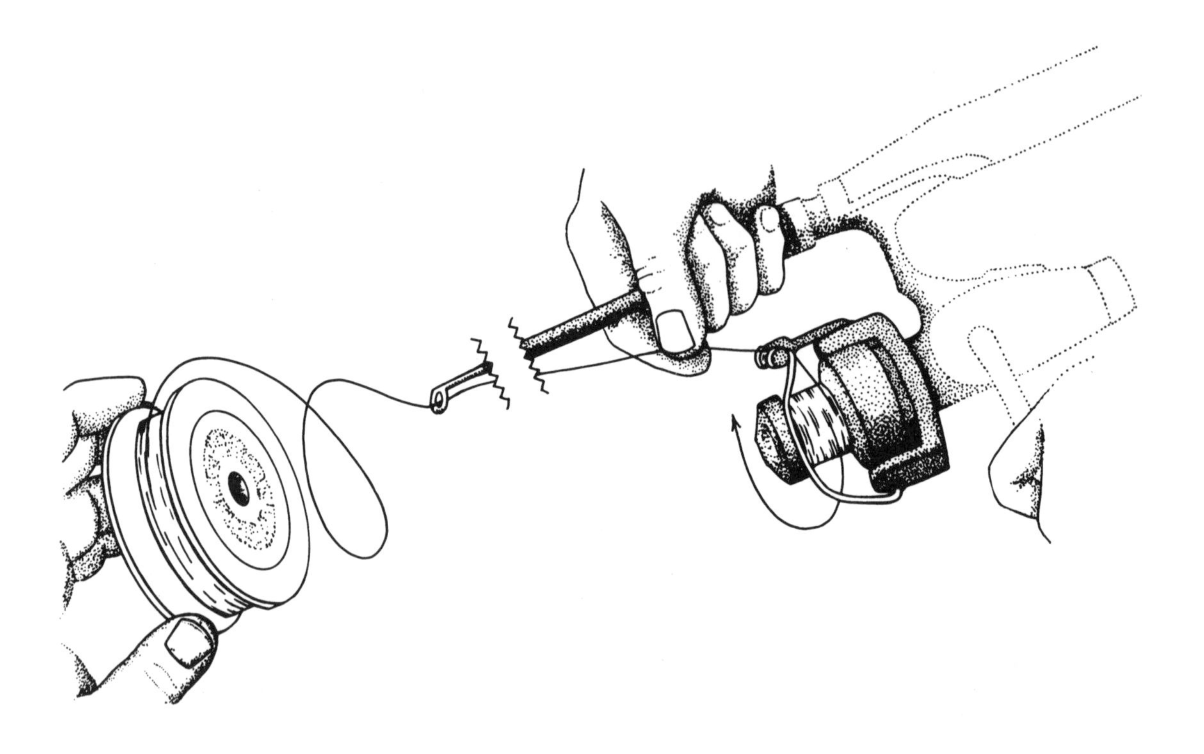

This is a way to load monofilament onto a spinning reel without producing excessive line twist.

counterclockwise pattern as you look down on it. This is because the line goes on most reel spools in a clockwise direction as you look at the reel from the front of the spool. With this method of line loading, the mono flows in a continuous loop from spool to spool with no twist.

If you have one of the few reels that wind line in a counterclockwise direction as you look at the front of the reel spool, lay the line on the floor so it comes off clockwise as you look down on it.

If you're totally confused by all this jabberwocky, look at the drawing. It's worth a thousand words.

Bait-Casting Reels

If you use a bait-caster, the same basic rules apply. If you rinse it off with fresh water, be very careful that no salt gets driven behind the spool. Before going out on the water, lightly grease the spool collar to help keep the salt out and oil any moving parts or levers on the body. This will achieve far more than careless washing. Drag washers in bait-casters usually have a greater surface area than those in spinning reels, so they have to be replaced less often. Nevertheless, occasional checks are necessary if you want to avoid hassles. When you use bait-casters with ultralight lines, you may want to remove the level wind to prevent undue line wear. Be sure to keep any resulting holes plugged with heavy grease or silicone glue to keep salt water out of the reel body.

Loading the line onto a bait-caster is easy. Slip a pencil through the new spool of line and have someone hold both sides of the pencil so that the spool is vertical. If no one's around, jam both ends of the pencil against your knees to hold the spool vertically. The line will go from spool to spool with no line twist and no difficulties.

There's just one trick to loading a bait-caster: be sure the reel is not tilted to one side or the other. If the reel is tilted and you load lots of line, the monofilament will bunch up on the side of the reel that's tilted down. Have a look at the photo to see how to load line by yourself.

Rods

A top-quality rod requires very little care. The reel seat might need to be oiled to keep the nuts moving freely, and you might want to wax the ferrules (with a chunk of rod wax) every few weeks to keep them tight-fitting. The only really important chore is checking the guides.

The guides need to be inspected whenever you think of it. Generally the tiptop wears first. With the sun at your back, hold the guides against the sky to look for irregularities or nicks; and immediately replace any guide that looks worn. A nicked guide is like sandpaper to fishing line. Another way to check guides for wear is to run a cotton swab or nylon stocking around the inside. If the cotton or nylon snags, you know the guide needs replacing.

Today's guides are very hard; if they're not defective and if they haven't been abused, they seldom wear out. But sometimes the whole center of the guide will loosen up. If you don't detect this early, the center will fall out of the metal ring while you're fishing and ride up and down the line like a bead on a string.

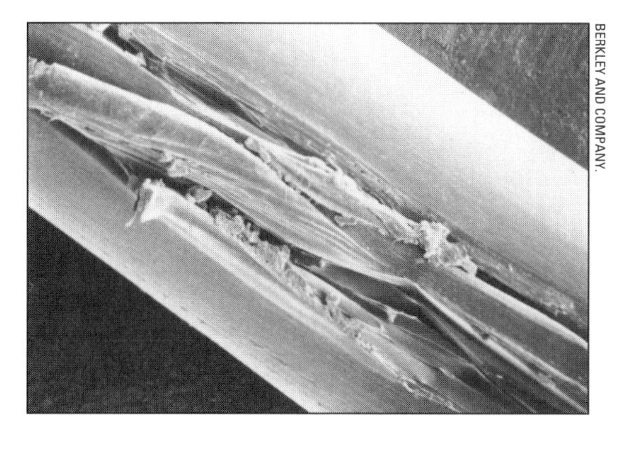

Top: An easy way to load a bait-caster with line if you have nobody to hold the spool.

Bottom: A cracked rod guide can do this to your fishing line.

BERKLEY AND COMPANY.

Replacing rod guides does not require a lot of expensive equipment.

Personal Care

Your body is your single most important piece of equipment. Let's talk about how to protect it from the dangers you'll encounter on the water.

Your Eyes

The sun is a mean machine. Hidden within the warmth it sends us are invisible ultraviolet (UV) rays that act like a slow cooker on the human eye: they inflict gradual but steady damage. And the damage can be very serious.

Our eyes have evolved over time to protect themselves from the sun. When sunlight is intense, the pupils constrict to block out most of it. But the human eye did not evolve on the open sea. It is not designed to cope with the intense ultraviolet radiation that bounces off the water's surface and the sides of an aluminum boat.

To deal with that, our eyes need some help. The best sort of help is sunglasses with a UV filter built into the lenses. These filters are very effective and eliminate almost all the damaging rays. In fact, if you wear sunglasses without a UV filter, you'll actually do your eyes double damage! Because the sunglasses block much of the *visible* light, your pupils will relax and dilate, letting in more of the *ultraviolet* light than you'd get without the sunglasses!

In addition to a UV filter, it's also helpful to have a polarizing filter built into your lenses. Polarized lenses help to filter glare. Only light waves that vibrate in one plane can penetrate polarized lenses; that eliminates the blinding reflections bouncing back from the surface, so you can see *into* the water.

Got all that? Just remember you want polarized lenses with a built-in UV filter. But make sure you don't buy the wire-rim style with minuscule lenses that was so popular in the late '60s. You'll need a pair of glasses with large lenses to block as much of the UV as possible.

Your Skin

The sun can damage human skin much faster than it can the eye. In many areas of the world, unprotected skin will burn in less than 15 minutes. Whether or not you have a tan, that means any sun exposure is too much. When I'm out fishing during the summer in New Zealand, long sleeves and long pants are the daily uniform, no matter how hot it is. In addition, I wear a broad-brimmed hat with a flap on the back to protect my neck.

Most people are not happy with the idea of being completely covered in the summer. If you select the right clothes, though, they will not only protect your skin but actually help to keep you cool. The most effective fabric for blocking the sun is plain old cotton. A tightly woven, orange cotton shirt will block ultraviolet light better than many layers of the finest sunscreen. Even with a loose weave, all the fibers that project from the main thread do an excellent job of absorbing and reflecting UV light. Your clothes should be loose-fitting and flowing so you'll get a cooling air flow around your body every time you move.

Of course, there are some areas of your body that you can't cover with fabric. For your face and hands, I'd suggest a water-resistant sunblock with a sun-protection factor (SPF) of 15, meaning that it will take your bare skin 15 times longer to burn with the sunblock on than without it. Some sunblocks have SPF values well above 15, but they're really no better. The important thing is to apply the sunblock a half hour before sun exposure so it has a chance to bind to the skin. Sunblocks wear and wash off; you must be sure to reapply sunblocks often. If you do that, an SPF of 15 will be more than adequate.

Your lips also take a beating under the sun. Zinc oxide and other ointments containing metallic particles are the most effective sunblocks and are especially good for the lips and nose. Unfortunately they are terribly messy and wear off too easily. An SPF-15 lip balm, applied every half hour or so, works better. Just keep it in the top shelf of your tackle box so you're reminded to use it every time you lift the lid.

One last tip: on an overcast day there is almost as much ultraviolet radiation coming through the clouds as on a sunny day, so take the same precautions, even if it looks like you won't see the sun all day.

Hand Protection

If you go fishing only once in a while, a little bit of water's not going to be a problem for your hands. But if you're on the water a few days a week, it won't be long before the skin starts to dry and crack. To cope with this problem I have a "wet hand" and a "dry hand."

Since my left hand is the one that I use to apply pressure to the spool when there's a fish on, that hand needs to be ultrasensitive. The right hand doesn't need to be so precise, so I use that as the "wet hand"—it holds the bait, lifts fish out of the water, and handles the chum. I put a rubber examination glove on that hand to protect it from cracking and drying. The left hand I leave bare. You can buy a box of 100 examination gloves for $10 at any drugstore. They last a long time.

Seasickness

This is a real problem. It is true that some people can adjust to wave motion; but a tendency toward seasickness is inherited, and there's not a whole lot you can do about it. All of the many drugs advertised to prevent motion sickness have the same drawback: they're very sedating.

Dimenhydrinate, an over-the-counter antihistamine, is as effective as any other drug for motion sickness. It's sold under a number of trade names—Dramamine and Triptone are probably the best known—and is quite sedating. If you use it, you may end up so stoned that the day becomes a washout anyway. I would suggest that you buy a liquid preparation and regulate the dose so that you get some protection from motion sickness without lapsing into unconsciousness. The dosage for the average-size adult is between 25 and 75 milligrams.

If you go to a doctor, you can get a prescription for a scopolamine patch; the brand name is Transderm-Scop. You place the patch behind your ear, where the skin is thin. The scopolamine, a very potent drug, then migrates through the skin and is absorbed into the blood. It's the best drug for motion sickness; but it, too, is very sedating. By using only half a patch (just cut them up), you can get reasonable protection from seasickness and still stay awake.

There are two big problems with scopolamine patches: one is that they need to be put on six to eight hours before you go fishing; the other is that you have to be very careful not to touch your eyes after handling the patch. Scopolamine will make it impossible to focus if it gets in your eyes; you'll essentially be blind for hours if you're not careful to wash your hands after touching the patch.

This is the way I usually deal with seasickness: if there's a big swell on, I just don't go out into the open sea; instead, I fish in the harbors and estuaries, where most of the fish are anyway.

Fish Hooks

Hooks are nasty items. If you get one in your hand it's a real downer, especially if you haven't taken the barb off. A lot has been written about how to remove fish hooks, but most of the methods don't usually work. If the barb is under your skin, you basically have two choices: you can try to work the barb out the same way it went in, or you can drive the hook all the way through so the point and barb emerge and can then be cut off.

Working the barb out the same way it went in is tricky if the skin is thick. Barbs tend to hang up under thick skin, so the only way to get it through is to nick the skin with a scalpel blade or sharp knife and then try to pull the hook out. This method can be so painful as to be impossible to do.

Driving a fish hook all the way through and out is no picnic either. For this method to work, the hook must be strong enough not to bend or break off as you try to force it through, and it also has to be in the right place at the right angle. Have a look at the drawing to see how it's done.

The least painful way to get the job done is to go to a doctor and let him numb the area before he takes the hook out. Of course, this can be expensive and time-consuming. The best way to deal with the problem is to prevent it—if you use barbless hooks, you'll have no problem taking them out; and you'll still catch plenty of fish.

This is one way to get a fish hook out of your skin. It's quite painful, but so are all the other methods!

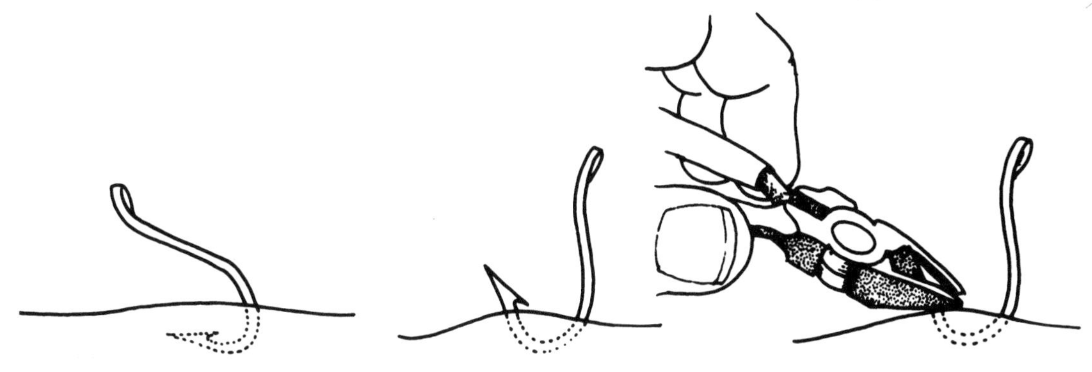

Using Your Tackle

Fishing from a fixed location, like a wharf or anchored boat, sharply limits the options of an ultralight angler. There's no shoreline to scramble along after the fish and no boat to follow it across open water. The tackle in your hands is your only means of control over a fish that could easily break your line in a direct confrontation.

But I'd like to tell you a tale that illustrates the tricks you can use to help even the odds, even from a fixed location.

A Corporate-Style Fishing Trip

The six-lane highway lay ahead of us like an enormous ribbon, weaving its way through the forests of western Maryland. The V-8 van purred quietly as we climbed the hills at the speed limit. This was the quintessentially American outing—big road, Chevy van, and beer in the back seat. Our group was headed for the Chesapeake Bay, one of the world's largest estuaries and the site of some of the best spring bluefish runs in the United States.

Bluefish are aggressive, schooling carnivores. They are found worldwide (though sporadically) and are well known for their sharp teeth and voracious appetites. They have a nasty habit of charging again and again through schools of smaller fish until there are few left alive. For this reason the blues are often followed by hordes of anglers and birds, hovering about and picking up the leftovers.

Each spring, as the waters warm, the blues come north into Chesapeake Bay, the biggest fish usually arriving in the first schools. In the 1970's, 18- to 20-pounders (9 kg) were common, and even some 30-pounders (14 kg) were caught. Like many pelagics, bluefish have great power and endurance. But they're much easier to land on ultralight gear than fish like the yellowtail or trevally because they tend to be surface fighters, and not particularly clever ones.

Each year a company managed by some friends of mine organizes a fishing trip for its employees. The entire staff meets on a Friday at a motel on the shores of the Chesapeake. From their arrival until the wee hours of the next morning, the group proceeds to eat and drink themselves into oblivion. The tables are piled high with steamed crabs from the bay (a real aid in helping the beer go down). By late evening no one is sober, and a few people are comatose. It is no surprise that some of the staff are difficult to rouse at 7 A.M. the next day for the fishing trip. Nevertheless, on Saturday we are all on board the 40-foot launch by 8:30.

One year, our departure was delayed by the grim realization that the beer supply had been sadly depleted. A backup keg had to be obtained on an emergency basis. As you might surmise, few people on board were intent on the fishing. Most were primarily interested in the food and beer, abundantly supplied once again to ease the agony of withdrawal from the night before.

The captain pretended to ignore the debacle and quietly took the boat a few miles up the bay to an enormous barge anchored near an enormous fish trap. In the middle of the barge a lone man with a long-handled shovel stood upon a massive pile of menhaden (a mid-Atlantic herring), slowly filling basket after basket with the corpses. His assistants then passed the baskets on to the waiting fishing boats. Needless to say, the stench was overwhelming; but no one laughed because rumor had it that the man standing atop that reeking pile of fish was making a cool quarter million a year. Corporate America respects money.

After we picked up our bait, the boat took off at full speed for the fishing grounds while the anglers proceeded to get smashed again (for medicinal purposes only). After a 40-minute ride we anchored, and the first mate immediately began tossing menhaden into an electric grinder that spewed its output into the tidal flow behind the boat. Not 20 minutes later the first blues began to show up in the spreading, oily chum slick. The mate had been foolish enough to drop a baited line behind the boat and leave the rod in a holder without loosening the drag. We knew the fish had arrived when, with a loud "crack," the rod and reel rocketed out of the holder and followed a precise parabolic path into the Bay. The last time we saw the rod, it was skimming along the surface like a torpedo, as an angry blue dragged it to a watery grave.

The sight of the runaway rod caught the attention of all but the most inebriated among us, and soon there were grunting anglers and bent rods all around the deck. The standard gear on the boat was a stout, 5-foot, solid-glass rod loaded with 40-pound (20-kg) line on an aged bait-caster. With that sort of weaponry, even the biggest blue had little chance; and soon the fish box was full of 12- to 16-pounders (5 to 7 kg) winched in by the group.

Two-Kg Line

Ultralight anglers are a lonely breed. We are not popular with large fishing parties because it takes us a long time to land our fish, and in the process our lines get tangled around everyone else's. So I had to wait until the others were bored with fishing and had resumed their gastronomic orgy. When their enthusiasm started to wane (drunks have little stamina) I dropped some bait over, using a 2-kg line and an ultralight spinning outfit. The bait was secured on a very sharp 3/0 hook. The leader was 6 feet (2 meters) long and made of 60-pound (30-kg) mono. I don't like using wire leaders and figured the fight on 2-kg line wouldn't last long enough to wear through the heavy monofilament.

I fed the line slowly into the current while pinching it lightly between my thumb and forefinger to control the depth of the bait. The bail on the spinning reel was open so the fish could run freely when it struck. Thirty seconds later I felt the telltale tug of a big blue as it grabbed the bait and ran. Like other aggressive, large-toothed species, the bluefish holds its prey with needle-sharp teeth until it stops struggling and then swallows it whole.

To accommodate the blue's habits I released the line when he picked up the bait, and slowly counted to five. At that point I flipped the bail shut, allowed the line to tighten up, and then set the hook. Since the drag was fixed at the "strike drag" position, there was no danger of breaking the 2-kg line with the sudden force of the hook being set.

Because the drag was set correctly, the fish was able to pull line from the reel without coming close to stretching the mono. That's okay initially, but blues tend to take a long first run and can strip a reel of line if they're not pressured effectively. To slow his run I elevated the rod tip until the rod handle was at a 90-degree angle to the deck. The increased bend of the rod raised the resistance against the fish and slowed him down a bit. By pressing my fingers against the rapidly revolving spool, I was able to add enough additional pressure to bring the line to the maximum stress it would tolerate without producing line stretch. The bluefish was a big one, and the first surface run took out almost 75 yards (70 meters) of line.

The only way to bring back a fish like that with ultralight gear from an anchored boat is with this slow, methodical process: elevate the rod tip to pull the fish closer, and then reel the line in as you bring the rod tip back down. The reel is not a winch—it's necessary to use the rod to pull the fish toward you and then use the reel to gather in the line. To maintain pressure on the fish while you're reeling in, you must keep some bend in the rod as you bring the tip down for the line-gathering process. If you allow the rod to straighten, slack will develop in the line and you can easily lose the fish—the hook falls out or the twisted line balls up into a knot.

With big fish, like this blue, it's usually necessary to apply some finger pressure to the spool while you're pulling the rod tip up. Without that extra bit of pressure, the loosely set drag may let line go out as the rod tip rises. There's always the option to increase the drag setting, but that can mean disaster later on, when the fish is close to the boat and the line is short. In the "moment of passion," when a big fish is alongside, it's too easy to forget about the tight drag. It's usually wise to keep the drag at the "strike drag" position and use finger pressure to provide any fine-tuning that's needed.

This blue was a surface fighter and spent a lot of time leaping frantically out of the water. When he was jumping far from the boat I would lower the rod tip and let the line loosen slightly so that, if he came back down onto the line, it would be less likely to break. As I brought the fish closer to the boat and the line grew shorter, I elevated the rod to "follow" him up as he jumped, keeping the line above him when he leapt so the blue couldn't possibly land on it.

After a half hour of continuous activity, I finally brought the blue alongside. At that point I kept the rod high in the air. Elevating the rod when the fish is close does two things for the ultralight angler: it causes the tired fish to glide near enough that you can grab the leader, and it provides some insurance in case the fish takes off again. Should the fish start another run, all you need to do is lower the rod tip, and the short line will be protected by the developing bend in the rod.

This blue was beaten and made no attempt to move as the mate gaffed it and brought it aboard. It weighed 12 pounds (5.5 kg), which wasn't bad on 2-kg line. Just about everybody else was still drinking, so I thought it was time to try 1-kg line.

If you have a half hour or so, it's no problem to land bluefish like this with 2-kg line from an anchored boat.

One-Kg Line

The year was 1982, and today's world record of 17 pounds (7.7 kg) on 1-kg line hadn't yet been set. All that was necessary in those days to score a record was to land a fish over 10 pounds. Since all the blues were that big anyway, the hardest part (finding the right-size fish) was over. It would be a piece of cake to get this record, or so I thought.

I crimped a 6-foot (2-meter) wire leader to a very sharp 1/0 hook and tied the leader to the 1-kg line. I had to use wire this time because a fight on 1-kg line could go on for hours, and a 60-pound (30-kg) mono leader wouldn't last that long against the blues' sharp teeth. The smaller hook was necessary because it's impossible to set a larger hook with such light line.

A few seconds after I dropped the bait into the chum slick, a blue picked it up and ran. I waited a while, closed the bail, and set the hook. With 1-kg line, that means just elevating the rod tip while the fish keeps moving and praying he sets the hook himself. There's no way to sink a 1/0 hook with the limited force you can muster using 1-kg gear.

Luckily, the bluefish did set the hook himself, and he took off like a bullet, across the surface of the water. The drag screamed, and I applied all the fingertip pressure I dared to the reel spool. The fish just kept going. I watched in dismay as more and more line flew off the reel. More than 50 yards (45 meters) was out now; with just a quick turn, the bluefish could put a long bow in the line, and the water pressure alone would break it like a wet noodle. But he didn't turn; he just kept on going. Finally, with 75 yards (70 meters) of line out, the big blue started to jump and rage around on the surface, using up his strength with acrobatics. I was delighted with the antics. The longer the fish thrashed around, the better my chance of getting some line back. Ten minutes later line began to reappear on the spool as the bluefish responded to the unrelenting pressure and slowly came toward the boat.

Within an hour there was only 20 yards (20 meters) of line out. I hadn't reckoned on how difficult it was to retrieve line from an anchored boat. If I could have followed that bluefish in a dinghy, he would have been a lot easier to deal with, but there was no dinghy, so I just hung in there and hoped the blue wouldn't dive. That hope was dashed as soon as the fish came close. The instant he saw the boat, the blue went right for the bottom. With over an hour's worth of stress on the line already, I knew it wouldn't tolerate much more than another hour's worth of abuse. It's a difficult and time-consuming process to drag a fish off the bottom with

1-kg line, and there was little chance of success. So I applied more pressure than was prudent. The results were predictable. Ten minutes later the line parted and the fish was free. I was a little tired, but the bluefish were still in the chum slick (and most of the drunks were asleep); another try was in order.

In 10 minutes I had a new spool of 1-kg line on the reel and a new wire leader with a very sharp hook. Within seconds of hitting the water I was again hooked up; and the sequence was repeated, with the blue taking off on a long, straight run. For the first hour it was a matter of hanging on while the fish streaked about on the surface and jumped all over the place. Every five minutes or so I dipped the rod into the water to lubricate the guides and try to reduce line wear. If the surface of the bail-roller dried out, I applied a little saliva to keep it slick and salt-free. Otherwise I spent most of the time keeping a tight line and retrieving mono whenever possible.

A stiff tide was running. Normally that would make things more difficult for me, but this bluefish was exceptionally stupid—he chose to stay upstream, so I could use the current to my advantage. After an hour and a half I noticed the boat was very quiet. Those people still sober enough to stand were all watching as I played the blue to within a few yards of the hull. No one spoke as the tension mounted. Even the radio was quiet since boats all around were listening in to hear what was happening. If I could bring the fish just a little closer, the mate would be able to grab the leader; and I'd have another world record.

Things looked promising as the blue rolled belly up. Ever so slowly I elevated the rod and dragged the fish closer to the boat. Then, as the mate moved to grab the leader, the blue righted himself and gave a flick of his powerful tail. In the "moment of passion" I had failed to watch my rod tip and didn't realize that the line had slackened a bit near the top of the rod.

Because of all the long runs the bluefish had taken, the line had twisted upon itself hundreds of times during the fight. The instant the line was allowed to go slack, it balled up around my nearly vertical rod tip and stayed there. I watched in dismay as the big blue moved off and the weakened line parted. We looked on in silence while the bluefish swam slowly out of sight. There was a collective groan from the folks on board as I slumped down to rest my aching arms. I wasn't sure how I felt. I wanted that record; but, then again, it had been a good fight, and the fish had won fair and square. Such is the way of life.

The ride back to port was surprisingly subdued. The party was over at last, and lots of people had headaches—the perfect ending to a corporate-style fishing trip.

The Basic Lessons

Here's a list of the key moves necessary to land big fish on light line.

- Protect yourself from those "moments of passion," when grace is overcome by anger or fatigue. Leave your reel set at the "strike drag" while fighting a fish, and there will be less chance that you'll stress the line by accident.
- Use an elevated rod tip and finger pressure on the spool to increase the drag. This is the key to setting world records with spinning gear. Never rely on the mechanical drag; trust your hand instead.
- Try to avoid stretching your mono. Once the line is stretched beyond its elastic limit, it will be permanently weakened. Even in moments of desperation, it is usually a bad move to stretch your line. The only exception is when certain doom is approaching (like your fish heading straight for a coral reef, where your line will be cut instantly).
- Use your rod to pull the fish toward you; then use the reel to gather in the line. The reel is not a winch.
- Always keep some bend in the rod. If your line is not tight, it's much easier for the line to ball up or for the hook to fall out. Even a well-set barbed hook can fall out during the second hour of a fight. The longer the fight, the greater the chance the hook will work loose; keeping a tight line is even more important toward the end of a fight than at the beginning.
- Keep the rod guides and bail-roller moist to reduce line wear during long fights. Wet guides and a wet bail-roller cool and lubricate the monofilament line as it rubs against these hard surfaces.

- Beware the jumping fish. The fish can break a tight line if it lands on the mono. If the fish jumps far from your position, put the rod tip down and let the line lie on the water. There's no way you can keep a tight line 50 yards (45 meters) from an airborne fish, so letting the line slacken a bit is the only correct response. If the fish jumps nearby, raise the rod with the fish so the line stays tight and above the fish as it leaves the water.
- If a fish sounds and you don't have the power to force him up, you have three choices: continue to apply pressure from one direction and hope the fish will eventually tire; move in a circle around the fish, constantly varying your position, and hope the fish responds by getting angry and coming up before the hook falls out; or put the maximum pressure on the line and "move it or lose it."

If the fish is close when it jumps, tighten the line so it rides up out of the water with the fish. If the fish is far away when it jumps, protect your line by laying it down on the water's surface.

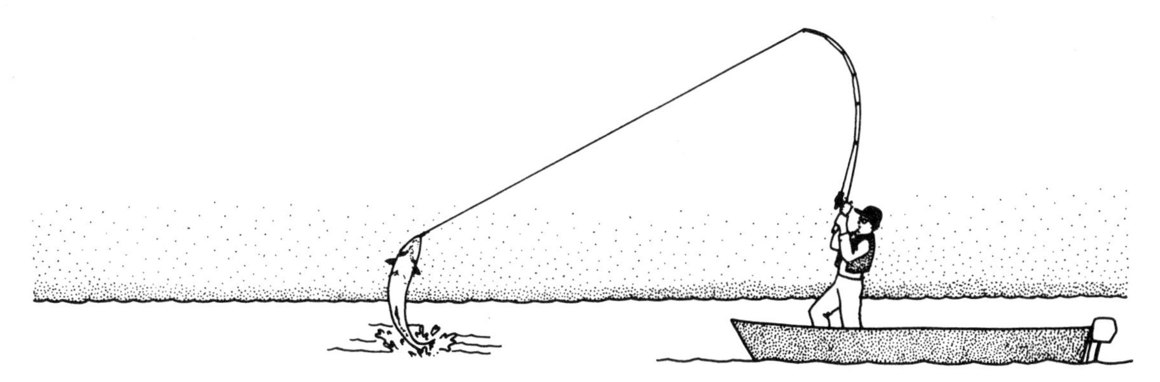

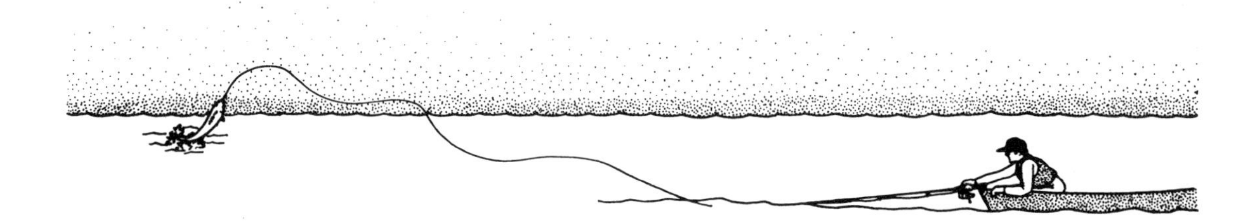

- If the fish dives and you feel the line vibrating as it rubs over an underwater object, you are in big trouble. Your only chance for success is to drop the rod tip and open the bail arm. The fish might spontaneously free the line, if you're very lucky.

The big lesson from my story is that it's tough to set world records from a fixed position. If you want to catch big fish with ultralight gear, you must be able to follow them. To do that you'll need a boat, and we'll talk about that next.

Following

In the spirit of teaching by example, I'd like to tell you about another adventure of mine. Then we can go over the major elements of playing big fish on ultralight lines from a moving boat.

Ten to One on Ultralight

We're all entitled to a perfect day once in a while; a day when it all comes together—the fish are there, the sea is calm, and you can do no wrong.

It was the spring of 1984. The place was Mangonui, a sleepy harbor in the Far North of New Zealand. The winter rains had passed, and it was a magnificent morning. The fog hung heavily over the harbor, dimming the sun as it rose over the surrounding hills. Just under the calm surface of the water, thousands of young mullet and mackerel swam lazily in the gathering tidal flow. A more peaceful scene would have been hard to imagine, but it was not to last.

Suddenly, without warning, columns of mullet sprung from the water, struggling to escape the marauders below. Within seconds the mirror-like surface shattered into a thousand fragments as dozens of kahawai hurtled through the schools of baitfish, gorging themselves.

My 12-foot dinghy lay quietly at anchor, right in the middle of the carnage. The livewell was full of free-swimming mackerel. A pair of identical ultralight spinning outfits—each rigged with 2-kg line, 20-kg leaders, and 5/0 Aberdeen hooks—were ready to be used at a moment's notice. The delicate carbon-fiber rods lay in the boat. While the kahawai ravaged the mullet around me, I just waited. The kingfish would come next. They always did.

The kingfish, or yellowtail, is distributed along most of the west coast of North and South America, in Australia and New Zealand, among the South Pacific Islands, and in Asia. The world's largest yellowtail kingfish live in New Zealand, and that's why I was there.

The kingfish is a fabulous gamefish by any definition. It is powerful and fast. It's capable of great endurance and exceeding cleverness. It seems to understand the dynamics of fishing line and will try to wrap it around any object it can find in order to break off. Landing a kingfish is never easy, especially on ultralight. Since yellowtail favor areas with obstructions and reefs, the angler must have a detailed knowledge of the bottom configuration in order to outwit this formidable foe. I did, and I continued to wait.

After the kahawai had moved on to hunt elsewhere, the surface of the water calmed again. The mullet resumed their lackadaisical movements in the current. When the surface had been quiet for five minutes, I put a live mackerel on the hook and lowered it into the water on an unweighted line. After a few surface runs, the baitfish headed to the bottom.

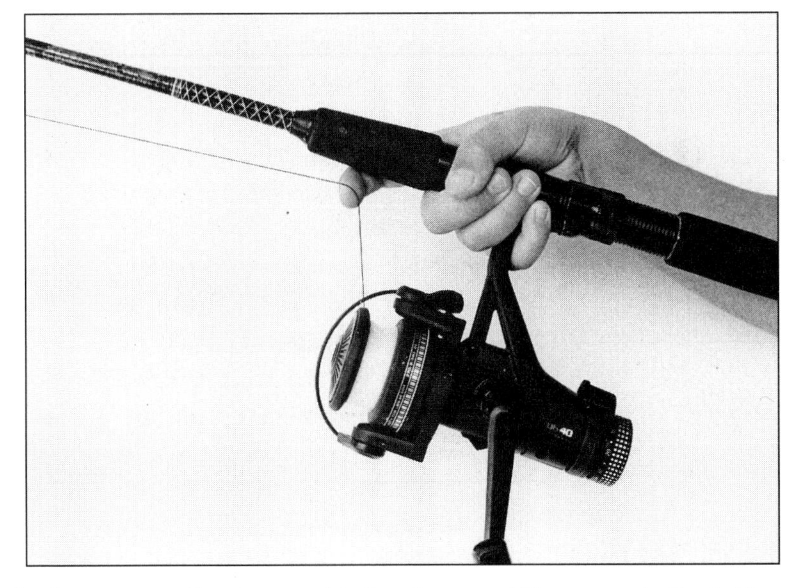

Whenever you're live-baiting, let the line rest on your index finger while the bait swims freely; when a predator strikes, just move your finger to drop the monofilament.

As the mackerel struggled against the line, his movements transmitted panic throughout the waters around him. The sound of fear carries far underwater, and it wasn't long before a group of kingfish came to check it out. The thump, thump, thump so characteristic of a kingi's attack was telegraphed up the 2-kg line, and I knew my turn had come.

Most fish are lost within the first minute of hookup, and I often fumble around then like everyone else. But this day was different. I had responded to the tranquillity around me; I was relaxed and ready. The bail of the spinning reel was open, and the line lay across my index finger. When the kingi struck, my index finger moved away, and the line began to flow off the spool as the big fish took the mackerel and ran.

I let the kingi run with the bait for several seconds. Then I closed the bail and set the hook with as much force as the ultralight line could muster. The fish took off like a rocket for the center of the harbor. By then I'd released the anchor line to float on its buoy and was able to use the engine to follow my rapidly disappearing line, hoping it would lead me to the kingfish somewhere ahead.

It was apparent that the fish was both unusually powerful and unfamiliar with the harbor. Kingfish that fed frequently in the harbor knew the locations of all the snags and made quick work of fishing lines. This fish made no attempt to cut me off. He headed straight for the channel and stayed there. That meant I probably knew more than he did about the local waters and had a chance of landing him. Opportunities like this were rare indeed.

For the first 30 minutes the kingi stayed deep in the channel and made one rush after another. Each time he started on a run, he changed direction in an attempt to rid himself of the irritating fish hook. I matched every move he made with quiet precision. By keeping the boat within 20 yards (20 meters) of the fish, I could easily tell when he was about to change speed or direction. No matter where the kingfish ran, I tried to keep the dinghy downstream of him; he had to continuously fight the tidal flow, while I used it to my advantage.

After a half hour his sudden bursts of activity ceased, and we settled down to a slow, methodical battle. My boat matched each run the fish took; I followed every move the kingi made. The pressure on him, though light, was constant and unrelenting. I stayed downstream and to one side of the fish so he always had to fight the line from the same direction.

It was a dance of death: the fish led and the boat followed. When the kingi would panic and run, I would pursue him at a constant distance, using the boat to keep the fish from taking too much line. When he calmed, I would slowly draw him ever closer to the ominous dinghy. To overcome the aching in my arms, I moved the rod from hand to hand and maneuvered the boat with the tired arm.

After the first hour, we'd reached the harbor entrance and the treacherous rocks that surround it. But he kept to the main channel and headed toward the open waters of the bay in search of relief from the constant pressure of the 2-kg line. I couldn't believe my luck—only clear water and a sandy bottom ahead.

In the deeper water he tried dive after dive, but the line always followed him and the pressure never ceased. When he panicked, I let him go with only minimal resistance. When he calmed, I applied as much pressure as I dared with gentle upsweeps of the rod tip to slowly draw him upward again. When the rod was as high as it would go, I allowed it to sink back down so I could gather line onto the reel spool. We repeated this process over and over again as we moved out of the bay and into the open sea.

By the end of the second hour, we had traveled more than 5 miles, and the kingi was beginning to tire. No longer able to hold his depth against the line, he tried some surface runs; but it was too late. His strength was gone, and we both knew it. His runs were short, never faster than 20 knots. An hour later he rolled, belly up, on the surface. I leaned over and lifted him into the boat like a baby. The kingfish was exhausted and did not resist at all.

After three hours and 8 miles of travel, this world-record yellowtail finally gave up.

Back at the wharf he weighed in at an amazing 34 pounds (15.5 kg), 9 pounds (4 kg) larger than my previous world record for kingfish in the 2-kg category. Several months later, after the IGFA had tested the line, they announced the catch was eligible for a world record and the 10:1 Award. The line had worn badly during the battle and tested out at under 1,500 grams, so the weight of the fish was 10 times greater than the strength of the line.

Luck had been with me.

The Essential Moves

Catching world records always requires some luck, but there are a lot of "tricks" that can increase your chances of success. Let's go over some of the techniques you'll need to use if you're going to land record fish on ultralight line.

- Stay close to the fish. Fishing line is subject to great stress from the friction of water passing over it. It's surprisingly easy to break your line just by towing it through the water in a straight line with absolutely nothing on the end. The two factors that determine its breaking point are the speed it travels through the water and the amount of line that's under the surface.

For example, if you're traveling along at 10 knots and slowly release 1-kg line behind the boat (with no terminal tackle at all), it will break about the time you get 100 yards (90 meters) into the water. You can see that there's not much line strength left to work with if the angler allows the fish to get too far from the boat. So the first trick in ultralight fishing is to stay close to the fish.

Do not steer directly for the fish. As soon as the fish feels the hook, he will begin his first run. By the time you start your engine and drop anchor, the fish can be 60 yards (55 meters) or more from the boat. But fish seldom travel in straight lines; it's entirely possible that there will be 60 yards (50 meters) of line forming a loop in the water when you see the fish surface only 30 yards (27 meters) away.

If you steer directly toward the fish, a giant loop of line will form in the water. Instead of recovering your line, you will drag the loop through the water at high speed; and the friction of the water passing over the line will break it off. Because most of the pressure on the loop is near the fish, the line can break before the drag ever engages. You're left with no fish, a broken line, and no clue to explain your predicament.

Follow the line, not the fish!

The solution to the problem is simple: Follow your line through

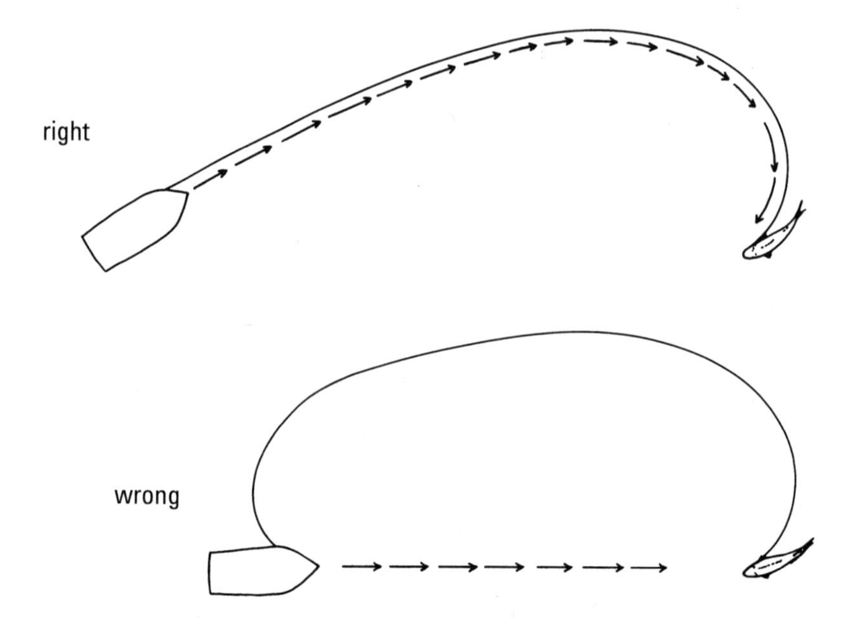

the water. Do not follow the fish. If you travel the same path the fish did, no loop will form and the stress will be more uniform over the length of the line.

- Stay to one side of the fish. Following directly behind the fish usually leads to disaster because the leader is constantly rubbing against his dorsal fin. If you're lucky enough to avoid getting it wrapped around his body, then you'll probably end up with a broken leader from all the wear imposed on the mono. If you're after a shark, the chances of landing him when you follow directly behind are just about zero. The shark's hide is so rough and his movements so circuitous that the leader is bound to die an early death by entanglement.

  As long as you'll be following the fish toward the side, try to stay on one side or the other. This will force him to fight you with the same muscles all the time, and it will increase the chance that he'll tire out before you do.
- Pay attention to your line. Always watch the point where the line enters the water. Subtle changes in its angle to the boat are the first indication that the fish has changed direction or speed and that you must do the same. If the fish has changed direction and you are unaware of it, you will overshoot him. Overshooting produces loops of line under the water and loops produce excess friction; that means no fish for dinner.
- Keep the automatic drag loose. A skilled ultralight angler does not depend on the reel drag. To determine the proper drag setting for your line, simply tie the end of the line to a heavy object on the ground. Then whip your rod upward as fast as you can. If the line breaks, it's much too tight. If the line stretches, it's still too tight. If the pole bends through a 180-degree arc before the drag releases, it's still too tight. If the drag releases as the rod is being pulled upward, it's just about right. That setting is called the "strike drag," and that's pretty much where the drag should always be set.

  Remember that loops of line always form when fish pick up the bait, so the strike drag must be set loose to compensate for the stress these loops will put on the line. When you're close to the fish and the fish is running free, it's easy enough to use your fingers to apply pressure on the reel spool to increase the drag. There's no mechanical drag made that comes close to the reliability and sensitivity of the human hand.

- Use the boat as a drag. Line twist is a major problem whenever you use a spinning reel; it weakens the line and can cause horrendous tangles. It is to your advantage to reduce line twist by using the reel drag as little as possible; use the boat as a brake instead.

  You can minimize drag operation by using precise engine handling to maintain a constant distance between you and the fish. The best indicator of changing distance is the pressure on the line. Line pressure can be gauged by fluctuations in the arc of the rod. So watch the rod; if it begins to straighten, slow down the boat and reel in the developing slack. If the rod's arc is increasing and getting close to the stress needed to operate the drag, just speed up or alter the boat's direction toward the fish. If you use the boat, you'll keep the fish under maximum pressure while he's moving; but the spool will not rotate and the line will not twist.

  It might seem that operating a boat with such finesse must be difficult, but you'll be surprised how easy it is in the right-size dinghy on a windless day. In a stiff wind or heavy chop you'd be better off fishing for small bottom fish in some pleasant, sheltered cove. At least you'd be able to take home a meal.
- Use the tide. When a fish runs with the tide, he gains a free ride. To find out for yourself, anchor your boat in a tidal flow and attach a 1-kg (2-pound) dead fish to the end of a 2-kg line. Throw it in the water and let out 25 yards (23 meters) of line. Now try to retrieve the fish. You'll be lucky if the line doesn't break.

  It's embarrassing to be beaten by a dead fish. So to avoid the "dead fish follies," always stay slightly downstream from the fish you're fighting. Since most fish run with the tidal flow, you'll actually be leading the fish, not following it. During these periods it's imperative to stay very close to the fish so that your line is almost vertical in the water, forcing the fish to exert constant effort to stay deep and resist your line pressure.

  That's the secret to success with ultralight: constant, unrelenting pressure that gives neither the fish nor the angler a chance to rest.

CHAPTER TWELVE

Finding Fish

ONE OF THE BEST WAYS TO FIND FISH is to look for them—sounds easy, but it can actually be very difficult to see fish that are even just a few yards away. They're most easily spotted in clear streams, on tropical sand flats, and in shallow estuaries; but even in those places they're also easily missed. The surface of the water is like a mirror that reflects distorted images and glare. To spot fish you have to learn how to look past these surface reflections into the water below. It takes practice.

It's most difficult on sunny or windy days, and almost impossible with a combination of bright sunlight and a disturbed surface. To help yourself out, try to keep the sun behind you so it highlights the fish below instead of bouncing back into your eyes. And wear sunglasses with polarized lenses. They make it easy to look beneath the surface because they filter out most of the glare that is so distracting, dramatically improving your vision. A broad-brimmed hat can also help by cutting down on the light striking your eyes from above.

While you are looking for fish, remember that they are looking for you too. When you're fishing a stream bank or lakeshore, walk softly and slowly. Most of the fish are hiding in overhangs and holes right under your feet and can easily be frightened away. Many freshwater fish are territorial—the biggest fish take the best feeding and resting places. In streams, those places are the holes formed by curves in the riverbed, rocky irregularities, or fallen trees in the water. And that's where you'll find bass, carp, trout, grayling, pike, and steelhead. These holes are often right next to the riverbank and are easily approached.

If you know an area well, some of the best freshwater fishing can be had by fishing these holes "blind." Stoop down or crawl the last 10 yards to the edge of the stream and drop the bait or lure into the hole without standing up or being able to see the water. The fish will not have seen, heard, or felt your presence and will not be suspicious. It can make a big difference, big enough to get on your hands and knees for.

The same idea applies when you're fishing from a boat; let the boat drift with wind and tide, or pole the boat quietly and stay low to reduce your image size. If you're on an estuary or sand flat, it's usually better to follow the incoming tide along the channel edges. Fish congregate in these gullies to wait until enough water covers the flats so that they can feed. Large predators like sharks also follow the channels as they hunt among the waiting fish for suitable prey. On a windless day the tidal flow will carry the boat naturally along these waterways, and you can keep the engine off for extended periods while you look for the fish you want.

When the tide's flowing onto the flats, the fish are relatively bold because they know the water will be around for a while. Once the tide begins to go out, the fish become anxious and less likely to take your bait as they head for deeper water. During the two hours around low tide, the fish gather in the deepest channels and holes at the headwaters of the shallows. They're hard to see in these deeper areas, so a sounder can be helpful if the waters are unfamiliar. There are lots of exceptions to these rules, though, so seek local advice or hire a guide if you're fishing alien territory.

When you cast to a fish you've found by sight, try to do it soundlessly. Use as small a bait as possible—and no sinker at all—to minimize the splash as your line hits the water. Don't hit the fish on the head with your offering. Cast a few yards ahead of the fish and then create a little disturbance on the bottom; the swirling mud will attract the fish's attention toward your bait and away from you.

As the fish goes for your bait, open the bail on your reel (so the fish will be able to run). When it picks up the bait, drop the rod tip, let the fish run for a few yards, and close the bail. Then wait for the line to straighten out. When the line tightens up, set the hook and stay alert. Fish fight hardest in shallow water, where they feel insecure because they're exposed. With no water below them, they will dash at high speed in all directions. Keep your rod tip high so the line doesn't scrape on the bottom, and stay within 20 yards (20 meters) of the fish if you can. On a fast-flowing stream it's imperative that you stay right with the quarry or there will be no chance of landing it. This is the most exciting form of fishing. Whether you're after permit on the tropical flats, carp on an American stream, or trevally on a South Pacific estuary, fishing by sight can't be beat for its challenge and excitement. Here's a short tale of just how good it can be.

An Exciting Time with a Dull Fish

My favorite form of fishing is targeting large carp in the clear streams of central Pennsylvania. Most people fish these small rivers for trout, smallmouth bass, and other popular species. The much larger and wiser carp are seldom pursued because of the American's prejudice against them. That's fine with me since I agree with the Europeans that carp are a superior fish, well worth hooking in cool waters where they can fight hard and use their weight to advantage.

Carp are quite civilized; they prefer to wait until midmorning to move out of the ponds and feed in the clear streams. As they head upstream, they comb the river bottom cautiously for food. They have grown large because they're old and careful. They have a lot of experience with anglers and aren't about to be fooled by anyone they can see or feel crashing around the riverbank.

To entice these carp I use a 1-kg spinning outfit with two size-10, barbless Carlisle hooks. Each hook is baited with 4 or 5 kernels of corn on its long shank. The kernels weigh just enough so that I can cast the ultralight line, but not enough to create a splash when they hit the water. There's nothing else on the mono to frighten these sophisticated fish.

Because of their large size, carp are relatively easy to see in the shallow water. I usually wait, very still, in the reeds along the edge of the stream with the morning sun behind me. As the sun warms the spring air, activity of all sorts bursts forth around the reeds. The red-winged blackbirds dart back and forth feeding their young, turtles crawl up on fallen logs to sun themselves, ducks paddle along while feeding on the lush water plants, and an occasional muskrat blunders by looking for its next meal.

It's all very welcome entertainment because I may have to wait and watch for 20 to 30 minutes before a large enough carp comes by. When the carp comes near enough, it's time to cast the bait 2 or 3 yards (2 to 3 meters) upstream from the fish. Once the bait strikes bottom, a twitch of the rod tip creates a little dust cloud to attract the carp. If I'm lucky, the fish will pick up the corn and swim slowly upstream, holding it in his mouth to examine it carefully. To calm its suspicious nature I leave the bail open on the reel and feed the carp line as it swims. Once I'm sure the fish isn't going to drop the bait, I let the line tighten up and give it a short tug to set the needle-sharp hook.

Then all hell breaks loose. The morning calm is shattered as the carp takes off upstream like a bullet while I jump out of the reeds and try to keep up. The 1-kg line doesn't make much of an impression at first, so I have to move quickly or the line will drag along the bottom and I'll lose the fish. While following the carp along the riverbank, I must keep the rod tip high and keep maximum pressure on the fish, or it will never tire. It's an absorbing and challenging battle, and—win or lose—I have a great time.

Usually it takes about a half hour to land the carp. By that time every living thing around has been frightened away by all the noise, and the other fish have fled back to the deeper waters of the pond. Then it's time to return to my hiding place in the reeds, put a new spool of line on the reel, and bait up again. After that, it's a matter of waiting patiently as life comes back to the river, and the wise old carp finally come upstream to feed again.

Using Birds

The easiest way to find fish at sea is to know how to identify and interpret the actions of seabirds. The high-flying birds have a tremendous advantage over the surface-bound angler. Because of their altitude, not only can they see for great distances, they can also look into the depths of the sea and spot schools of fish that would never be visible to a person in a boat.

Left: Black-back gulls like this are more solitary than other gulls and are seldom of any help in finding fish.

Right: Red-billed gulls are very social animals. When you see lots of them at sea, you can be sure there's some sort of food around.

Each species of bird occupies a slightly different niche in the food chain and gets its food in a different way. Some birds specialize in swimming after small fish, others pluck them from the surface of the sea, a few species dive deep into the water, and some are quite versatile in their methods. Because most birds have specialized feeding behaviors, it's important to be able to recognize them by species so you can predict which fish are around. I'll review some of the more common seabirds and tell you what their activities have come to mean to me.

Gulls are the birds most frequently seen, but their eating habits are so diverse that they're not much help in identifying what sort of fish are around. Their greatest value is as a directional signal. If all the gulls around you are flying in one direction, you know something's going on over there. It may be a commercial fisherman cleaning his hooks or a cook throwing leftovers into the sea, but it could also be something much more interesting. You'll need to look for other species that provide more specific information.

From a distance the next most easily spotted birds are the gannets and boobies. These magnificent creatures circle high above the water and then dive down to capture mackerel, mullet, herring, or other small fish within 10 feet (3 meters) of the surface. But these skilled hunters are capable of diving deeply and quickly enough to catch their food without the help of gamefish attacking the same quarry from below. When you see gannets diving, you know there are baitfish around, but—quite possibly—there's little else.

An efficient hunter, the gannet needs no help from fish or other birds.

Terns can also be seen from a moderate distance. Delicate birds but superb flyers, they circle and hover over the feeding schools of gamefish. When hunting fish force smaller prey to the surface, the terns swoop down and grab them. If you see terns, you're probably in luck. They're seldom around unless there are big fish feeding below.

If the terns are moving rapidly in one direction as they swoop down to feed, you can be sure the gamefish are moving too. Following a quickly moving school in a small boat is usually a waste of time. All the noise made by the prop as you pursue the school just makes the fish avoid you all the more. If there are still a lot of baitfish in the area, it's likely the gamefish will be back to try again. For this reason it's usually best to stop and reassess the situation before heading anywhere new. Why chase fish around all day when you can just wait and let them come to you?

Shearwaters (muttonbirds) and petrels are attractive little birds that usually sit like ducks on the water's surface. When they feed, they poke their heads underwater to look around and then grab any tiny baitfish forced up by the gamefish below. When the baitfish are not close enough to the surface, the shearwaters will dive down and "fly" under the water in pursuit.

If you see shearwaters sitting around with their heads in the water, you know that they are feeding; and there's an excellent chance hunting pelagics are under them. But don't ignore these birds when they're just sitting there, apparently doing nothing. They *are* doing something—they're waiting. The birds are pretty certain that food is going to come their way soon.

Terns usually hunt anchovy and other small fish at the surface when the baitfish are forced up by hunting pelagics.

The shearwater is also very helpful as a directional signal. If you're on the water in the morning and spot a group of them flying a few inches above the surface (virtually through the troughs of the waves) in one direction, you can be quite sure they're

Left: Cormorants usually gather in colonies to breed. A colony like this is a good sign that schools of small fish congregate nearby.

Right: If a bird takes your bait, treat the bird like a fish: play it and bring it aboard the boat to remove the hook. If you just cut the line, the bird will fly off and get tangled up, enduring a prolonged and painful death.

heading toward a feeding area. But beware; the shearwater might not appear to be a good flyer, but it is. It is entirely possible it will be traveling many miles to feed, much farther than you might want to go in your boat.

Cormorants, or shags, like gannets, do not need gamefish to feed. Shags swim about on the surface, dive down amidst the schools of bait-fish, and catch their meals in vise-like bills. They are poor flyers and don't like to travel great distances, nor will they follow fast-moving schools.

If you see shags swimming around among feeding shearwaters and circling terns, you know it's your lucky day. There's bound to be a well-established school of gamefish lurking in the water underneath all the feeding birds. Because the gamefish have been there a while, there's usually an extra, added bonus waiting for you, the result of bad table manners.

Surface-feeding pelagics are not very neat eaters. When the hunting is good, pieces of fish drop from their mouths and fall to the bottom undetected. Within an hour or so, bottom fish gather below the pelagics, picking up the tidbits that drop from above. These bottom fish can provide good sport and excellent eating if you tire of the gamefish on the surface. All you need to do is drop down a jig about the same size as the dying

baitfish, and you can expect action within minutes. Your jig has to be right on target to attract those bottom feeders, so just be sure to consider the prevailing currents before you drop it, and remember that a lead lure drops a lot faster than a dying baitfish.

Jigging below and downstream from a school of surface-feeding pelagics will often yield tasty bottom fish for dinner.

Finding Fish without Birds

Sometimes there will be no birds to help you. Very early in the morning there may not be enough light for the birds to hunt. In midday, they may be offshore, where you can't follow in a small boat. In those cases the best way to spot feeding fish is to use a sounder or look for disturbed water.

And birds aren't really a factor in some kinds of fishing: when you're looking for bottom dwellers or midwater species, when you're targeting isolated fish along shorelines or near structure, and when you're searching a river mouth for fish awaiting the turn of the tide.

Worried Water

Obvious splashes on the water's surface can mean nothing more than jumping mullet, or they can indicate actively feeding gamefish. Mullet can be identified by their habit of rocketing out of the water, stiffening their bodies, and then falling back to the surface in a classic "belly flop." Mullet are seldom attracted to a bait, so look elsewhere if you see them jumping about. If the source of the splashes is frightened halfbeaks or rising gamefish, the chances are you can hook up if you're quiet enough.

Another helpful sign is "worried water"—one area of the water's surface that, on calm days, is marked by slight ripples that somehow seem out of place and that, on windy days, is marked by ripples in a pattern different from all the others. Worried water is produced by hundreds of fish feeding just below the surface. Usually they're crustacean-eaters like trevally, mao-mao, or perch; but they can also be small kahawai, dorado, bluefish, or mackerel. It takes a sharp eye to pick up worried water, but it can lead you to excellent fishing.

Using the Sounder

You already know that you can't rely on sounders to "see" isolated bottom fish, nor will they "see" sharks or most tuna. But sounders can help you find all these fish and more if you understand what each species requires in its feeding and resting places.

The main purpose of a sounder is to give the angler a picture of the bottom and any structure that may lie there. "Structure" can be any object—something as massive as a coral reef or sunken freighter, or as subtle as a sunken branch or mass of weed. Small fish like to hang out by structure because the marine life colonizing its surfaces provides them with food; and the structure's nooks and crannies, where little fish can conceal themselves, provide them with shelter.

The best lie around any structure is usually downstream from the prevailing current. That's where the biggest fish will be.

Since big fish eat little fish, the big guys tend to hang out by structure too. Big fish are also looking for protection, but of a different sort: pro-

tection from prevailing currents. Water is seldom stagnant; it's always moving, because of tidal flows, temperature variations, or currents originating elsewhere. Moving water brings food, but swimming against its flow is tiring. Ocean- and lake-dwelling fish, like trout in a stream, seek out shelter from the moving water—places where they can rest from the current but still take advantage of the food it brings.

Because the best lies have such great value, they're usually inhabited by the dominant—usually the biggest—fish. Generally, you can find the biggest fish if you can find the best lies.

And you can do that by using your sounder to detect bottom structure and by dropping down a line with a light lure to determine the direction of the current. With this information you can construct a map in your head of where the fish will be. The two most desirable locations for fish are just downstream and just upstream of the structure. Both areas have relatively quiet water—the downstream position because it's in a current shadow, and the upstream position because a dead space is created by water bouncing off the structure into the face of the oncoming flow.

If the water is deep, both these lies can be hard to fish. It's just too easy for the line to get snagged on the structure as you drift by or if you anchor upstream. One way to avoid line snags is to approach the structure from downstream and advance slowly until the boat is directly over the highest point. Then drop down your line as you begin to drift back. When you follow this strategy, the water will become increasingly deeper under the boat, so there's less chance of getting hung up on the bottom.

Since it is so very easy to get snagged when fishing the best lies, a better move may be to target the secondary lies along the sides of the structure. You may be less likely to get the biggest fish; but you're also less likely to lose your terminal tackle along these edges, and you're much more likely to hook up. All you need to do is motor upstream from the structure, keeping just a few yards to either side. As your boat floats by, the bait will drift along the side of the structure, not into it.

Yet another way to fish structure is to wait for deadwater, the condition that occurs when tidal flows slow and eventually reverse. At deadwater the big fish tend to move away from the structure, either coming up to the surface to look for food or moving out into midwater. Scour the surface with your eyes and use your sounder to look for these marauding fish. This may be your chance to hook that big one far away from the dangerous structure that can break your line.

And that brings us to another problem in fishing structure with ultralight. What happens if the fish picks up your bait and then runs right into the structure, wrapping you up on some loathsome, abrasive outcrop? Well, what happens is that you lose the fish. But there is a way to avoid this disaster that works surprisingly well. It's called "walking the dog."

Walking the dog is just like other aspects of ultralight fishing in that it replaces brute force with technique and stealth. Fish run when they're hooked because they are surprised and frightened. You can prevent this by letting the fish take the bait; and then, very gently, use the boat to move away from the structure. Once the fish realizes how tasty the bait is, he will usually be reluctant to drop it. Instead, he will follow you if you move very slowly and at a steady rate. When you're far enough away from the structure to avoid disaster, it's time to set the hook and play the fish.

River Mouths

A river mouth is a unique and unusually rich habitat. As the tide rolls out, the river dumps enormous amounts of organic material into the sea, attracting the small fish that feed on it. The cloudy appearance of these waters is deceptive. The dirty fresh water is lighter than the denser salt water, so the fresh water pouring out from the river does not mix with but actually flows over the clear salt water beneath it.

Hunting fish most often position themselves at the interface of fresh and salt water. Here they can see their prey in the clear salt water, yet are right next to the freshwater outflows that provide their food. Where in that interface between fresh and salt water will the big fish be lurking? The big guys are going to set up shop near their food supply, and that food supply is usually small fish. So all you have to do is figure out where the small fish are feeding. Here's how you do it.

At the river mouth, fresh water flows over the top of the salt water. Fish will be waiting at the interface of fresh and salt water to feed on whatever flows by.

Since rivers generate great turbulence, the small fish will seek out

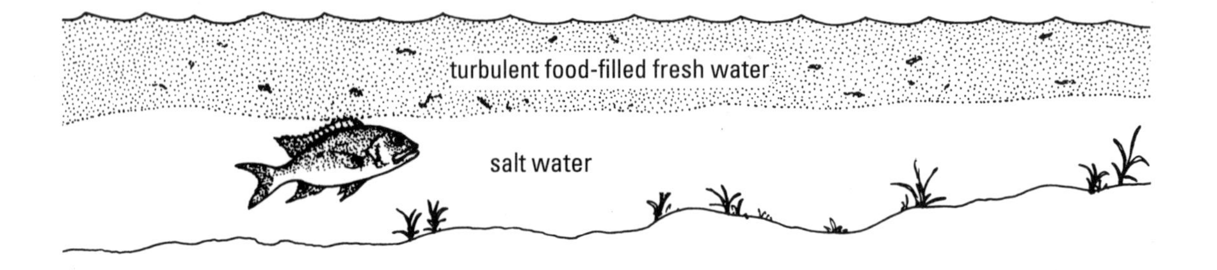

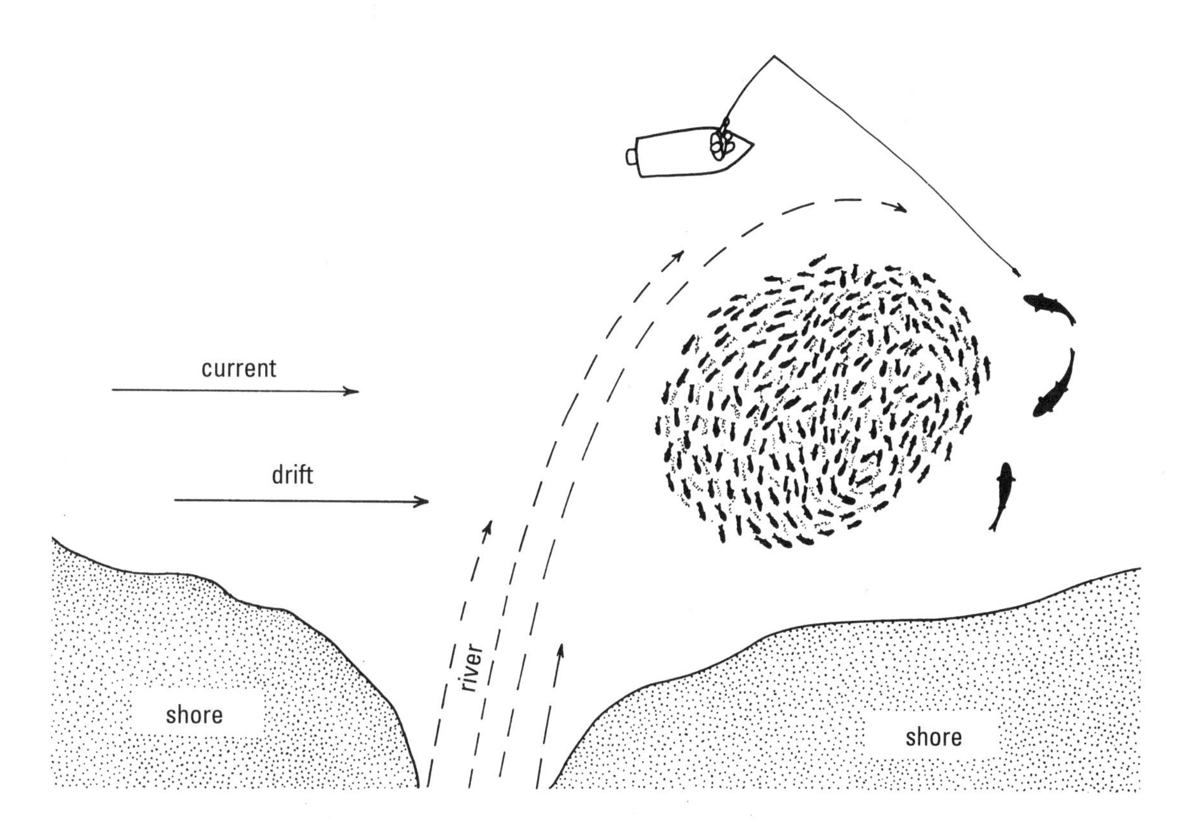

quieter waters where they have more control over their position, usually somewhere down the beach from the river mouth. All beaches have a net current flow in one direction on the outgoing tide, so rivers almost never empty straight out into the sea. The fresh water is instead directed by the prevailing current, forming a giant whirlpool. Inside the whirlpool the water moves relatively slowly, and food accumulates as the water settles. The small fish gather here, waiting to consume the organic debris coming from the estuary. The big fish wait just on the downstream side of the whirlpool, right along the edges of the circling water. That's where they have their best chance of picking off a hapless baitfish caught up in the fast-moving water.

Look for pelagics on the outgoing tide at river mouths. Fish where the whirlpool forms at the downstream side of the prevailing ocean current.

Your best approach to the whirlpool is from the upstream side; drift in and throw the bait ahead, toward the downstream edge of the circling water. Leave the bail open and feed line out so the bait moves naturally with the whirlpool. When you see the pattern of line motion change, close the bail; strike when the line tightens up. With a little bit of luck you'll hook dinner and maybe a trophy as well.

The Estuary

When the tide shifts and the salt water begins to run up into the estuary, the fish follow and so should you. Although the same rules apply here, the structure is different, so the angler has to adapt to the new environment. In the estuary the big fish seek out the quiet lies where they can rest but still be near the rapid currents that will bring them food. These lies will be potholes along the edges of turns in the river, rocks or fallen logs where the disturbed water creates dead spots and holes, or the edges of channels where gamefish may lurk on the bottom and capture baitfish as they pass overhead from the shallows.

Hunting gamefish always face into the current flow, so your bait must approach from that direction. Cast the bait so it will flow naturally into the lie. If your bait lands right on top of the fish, it'll scare the hell out of the fish and you'll lose it, your "great cast" notwithstanding.

Unfortunately, the best lies are often near fallen trees and overhanging branches. Once a fish takes the bait in a situation like this, you'll have no chance with ultralight line unless you've practiced the art of walking the dog. Let the fish take the bait, and ease the fish ever so gently out of the hole. If you can lure the fish out into the main stream, there's a good chance you can land it.

How to Be a Groundbait Gourmet

If you can see the fish or can use birds to find them, you don't need groundbait (also called *chum, berley,* or *rubby-dubby*). If your sounder can find the schools for you or you're absolutely sure where the fish will be at a particular time of the tide, you can also do without it. Otherwise, it is in your interest to know how to make and use chum.

Potatoes, dried bread, chicken feed, oatmeal, meat, and sea lettuce are all useful groundbaits; but the most effective chum is fish livers, fish flesh, fish bones, and other seafood leftovers. The ideal way to collect these delicious ingredients is to save the remains of your catch from the last fishing trip. I accumulate fish entrails, skeletons, and leftover scraps of bait in the freezer. They're kept in a well-sealed container because the odor that escapes from these little treasures, even while frozen, can permeate any other food you store with them. Whenever the stack of fish bits gets high enough, I sneak the grinder out of the kitchen, grind the scraps to the consistency of hamburger meat, place the ground scraps in 1- or 2-quart plastic containers, and freeze them.

I must warn you to be very careful with the average kitchen grinder. Do not, for example, put fish heads or heavy bones through it. Such items will usually stop the motor and otherwise damage these expensive machines. Take your collection of fish bones and heads and mash them up with a hatchet or hammer, pop these juicy tidbits into a thick plastic bag, and freeze them too. They will come in handy when you fish the flats. Be sure you do this work far away from the house in an area where cleaning up is not difficult. The smell and flies that collect around such an operation can be quite amazing.

If the thought of preparing gallons of chum doesn't turn you on, you may want to buy it in the form of ready-to-use, frozen bricks. (Many tackle shops sell it this way.) Once you have the groundbait, it's important to use it effectively—the idea is to attract the fish to the area of your hook, not to feed them. If you're fishing on the surface, you want the chum to float (at least initially). If your bait is on the bottom or near midwater, then the groundbait has to sink relatively quickly.

Since most gamefish are pursued at or near the surface, let's attack that first. If you make and store your own chum as I just described, then floating chum will always be waiting for you in your home freezer. As you walk out the door to go fishing, just take one or two of the containers out of the freezer. Once you're on the fishing grounds there are many ways to distribute the groundbait, but there is only one object: to keep up a continuous stream of chum leading right to your hook. If you're fishing alone, the easiest way is to throw the still-frozen block of groundbait into an onion sack or an old pair of panty hose and toss it over the stern. Tied to the stern, it will ooze oil and bits of flesh for an hour or two. If there are several people on board, you can toss the frozen mass into a water-filled bucket and pour it over a cup at a time. This ensures maximum control over the flow of chum from the boat.

If you're too lazy or busy to make your own floating groundbait, you can buy bottled fish oil and use that. If it's mixed with bread crumbs or oatmeal, it will sink very slowly and perform well. If you use it "straight," it will simply float and attract only those fish that are very near the surface.

When you want to catch bottom-dwelling fish on the sea floor, you need a totally different approach, so that the groundbait will get to the bottom before it disperses. To accomplish this, you can fill an onion sack or an old pair of panty hose with a few rocks and your frozen chunk of fishburger and toss it overboard on a rope, or fill a can or specially made chum basket with groundbait and drop it overboard on a rope. The problem with these methods is that there's an extra rope in the water that could tangle with your line. To avoid the extra rope, you can attach the chum basket to the anchor line when you arrive at the fishing grounds. The drawback to this trick, of course, is that you'll have to retrieve the anchor to refill the chum basket.

A better approach is to let the chum get itself to the bottom. There are several ways to do this. One is to freeze rocks inside the chum block when you prepare it. Another is to put the chum and some rocks in a paper bag and drop the bag overboard on a rope. About the time it hits the bottom, give the rope a hard pull. The bag will break up and release the groundbait, and you can retrieve the rope. You must be careful to melt the chum chunk first, or it will bob up to the surface like a cork. This provides a laugh for your mates but no fish for you.

The best method to groundbait the sea floor in shallow water is to use the mashed-up fish bones and heads that you stored in the freezer. These sink quite well on their own and do a fine job of attracting fish. When I'm fishing for tope in the shallow estuaries of New Zealand, this method proves most productive. The sharks are attracted for miles around as the odor disperses along the mud flats with the flow of the incoming tide. Just be sure you toss the bits far enough upstream so they end up reasonably close to the stern of the boat once they're on the bottom.

Where to Chum

It's possible to waste lots of time and all your chum looking for fish in the wrong places. Although an oily chum slick will travel for miles on a fast-moving tide, it's a lot more fun to get some action quickly. Ideal places to start your chum trail are near reefs, edges of channels, and steep drop-offs. You can find these places by using a sounder to trace the bottom or by studying the shoreline. Look for locations where an irregular, rocky shoreline enters the water suddenly; most likely the rugged configuration will continue underwater. Areas like this provide safety for a variety of sea life and are naturally attractive to many species of gamefish.

Reefs that rise up from a deeper sea floor provide a similar, productive environment. You can locate them by using a sounder or by employing local knowledge. Pinnacles that tower up like skyscrapers from the ocean bottom are among the most productive fishing locations.

The best way to exploit an area like this is to anchor in deeper water nearby so that the chum trail will travel with the tide along the rocky reef

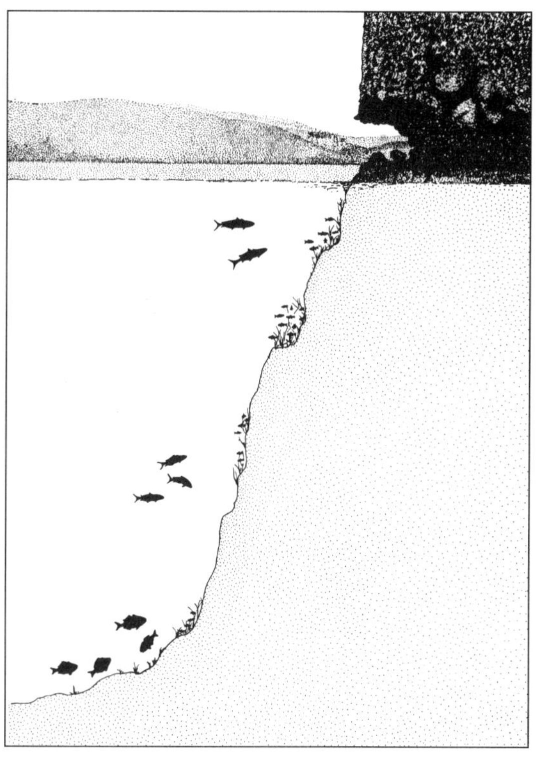

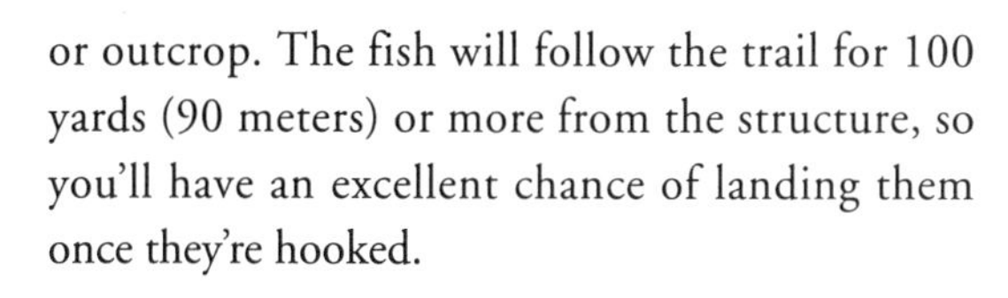

or outcrop. The fish will follow the trail for 100 yards (90 meters) or more from the structure, so you'll have an excellent chance of landing them once they're hooked.

Left: Upstream from a headland like this is an excellent place to lay a chum trail.

Right: A headland like the one at left looks something like this underwater.

Fishing the Slick

Whether the chum slick is on the surface, in midwater, or on the bottom, the idea is to keep the bait right in the middle of the flow of goodies. As the fish follow the trail of lovely aromas up the chum slick, they should bump right into the bait you've put out.

If the target of the day's fishing is on the bottom, then all you have to do is drop the bait on a weighted rig just downstream from the chum bomb planted earlier. When using ultralight lines, you can't place the weight on the main line because it will abrade the surface and weaken the mono. Use a sliding weight—just heavy enough to get the bait where it's needed—on the leader. Keep the main line under tension at all times to prevent the weight from dragging the ultralight line along the bottom when a fish takes the bait.

Things get a bit trickier with a surface slick. When the berley is all on the surface, the bait needs to be there too. That means using a small float or balloon on the line or using an oily bait that will keep the line on top without help.

When there's a rapid current flow, the bait will float up naturally

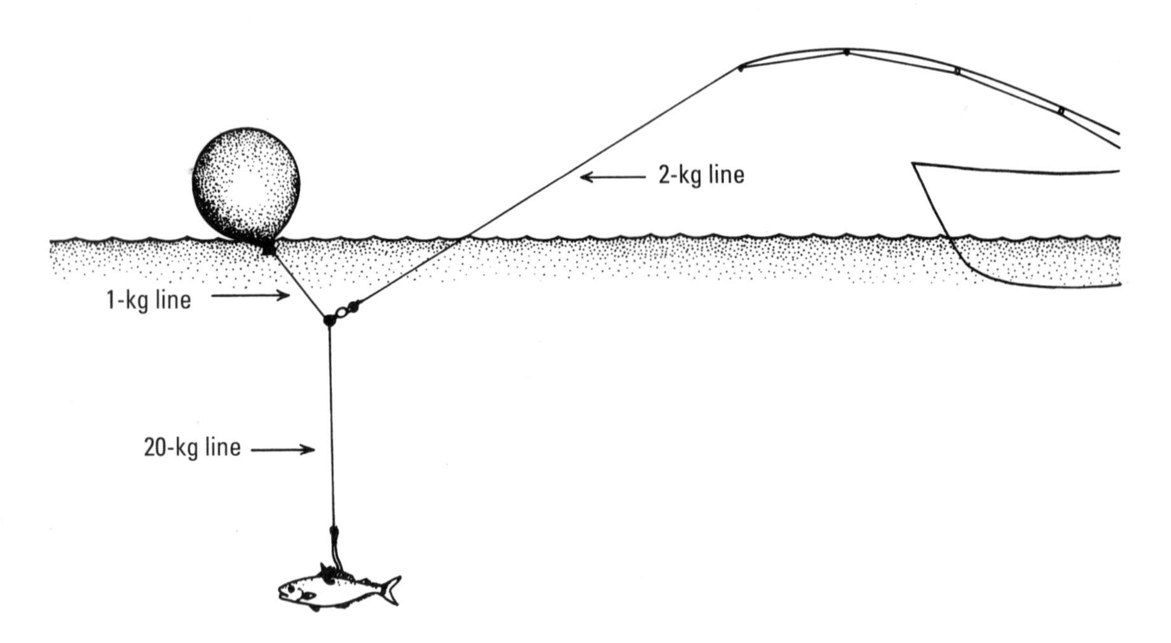

There's a trick to drifting live bait under a balloon: always be sure the line to the balloon is the weakest one in the sequence so it breaks off first.

because the force of the current against the weightless line will keep it from sinking. The only problem is that a suspicious fish will avoid anything that's not moving appropriately with the tide. If educated fish are in your area, the best solution is to drop the bait into the berley trail and let it drift back while you hand-feed the line. When the bait sinks too low, retrieve it slowly and start again.

If you're live-baiting in a surface slick, you'll have to use a balloon or similar float. Attach the balloon to the swivel at the top of the leader. If the line used to attach the balloon to the swivel is light enough (1 kg is best), then the balloon will pop free when the live bait is taken. With this method, any stress to the ultralight line is avoided until the gamefish starts its run.

A slowly sinking chum trail and a surface slick pose similar problems. To keep bait in the trail, the line has to be hand-fed at a slightly faster rate than the current flows so the bait sinks with the slick. This means the line should stay limp as it's fed out. Stay alert; if the line straightens out, it's being released too slowly or a fish has picked up the bait.

Live baits need to be positioned either on the surface near the boat or under a balloon downstream. If you let the balloon drift back just the right distance from the boat, the length of the leader will equal the depth the chum trail has sunk to. This way, the gamefish following the trail will bump right into your live bait, and you'll have an instant hookup.

Fish often get excited by the activity in a chum slick, and you can capitalize on that excitement by using lures instead of bait. Any lure that can be made to resemble a baitfish feeding in the chum will do nicely.

If there are several people in the boat, try to keep a hooked fish on at all times because, when you're playing a fish in the slick, other fish will often follow it around, becoming so aggressive that they're easily hooked—guaranteed action for the next person who wants to hook up.

Sometimes large fish—like cobia, amberjack, yellowtail, or sharks—will attack the fish on your line or follow it to the boat. For these occasions keep a 4-kg rig set up in the boat and extra live bait in the well. When the big follower seems to be most excited, drop the live bait in front of its nose and get all the other rigs out of the water. The action is usually instantaneous.

CHAPTER THIRTEEN

Endgame

THE FISH IS SOUNDLY BEATEN. You've hooked, fought, and followed it. It's lying on its side, exhausted, next to the boat. What's the next move?

Landing Fish

If the fish is meant to be breakfast or dinner, then the goal is to preserve its freshness and condition. If the fish is small and well hooked, it can be lifted into the boat by the 10- to 20-kg leader. Larger fish will have to be gaffed, netted, or brought in by hand.

Fish, even when exhausted, respond to harsh stimuli. If they feel a pair of hands grab and squeeze them abruptly, they will fight anew. To avoid being stabbed in the hand by flailing dorsal or pectoral fins, take the fish out of the water gently by placing your hands underneath it and lifting slowly while supporting the fish from below. Most tired fish will not resist your removing them from the water, and it's quick and easy.

For fish with large teeth and aggressive natures—like bluefish, pike, and barracuda—using a net or gaff will mean fewer lost fingers. If there's room in your boat for an adequate-size landing net, then it's a better choice than a gaff. Once the fish is exhausted, guide it headfirst into the net. When the fish is *totally* within the net, it can be lifted out of the water. If the fish is netted tail-first or is not totally within the net when you lift up, it can easily flip itself out by using the net frame as a fulcrum.

When you have no net or when the fish is large, try to gaff it near the head. This reduces the chances that the fish will flip itself off the gaff and prevents damage to the flesh you want to eat later. Once you've driven the gaff in, swing the fish out of the water and into a clear area of the boat in one, uninterrupted motion. After a two- or three-hour fight, the last thing you want is to battle a 30- to 60-pound (15- to 30-kg) fish struggling on the end of a gaff!

The best way to kill fish is the Japanese method called *Iki Jime*—forcing a steel spike into the brain, causing instant death. The Japanese believe this improves the taste of the fish dramatically; they ought to know—they eat more fish than anybody else.

Many people bleed their fish, but I don't think this makes much difference in the flavor if the fish is properly cared for. If you want to bleed your catch, the easiest way is to cut the gills. Fish should be stored in the shade and iced or covered with a wet cloth to keep them cool and moist. Smaller fish can be placed in the live-bait tank to be kept alive until it's time to head in.

It's worth your while to take good care of the fish that's destined to be your dinner. If it's kept cool and moist, you can have a superb meal instead of something that tastes like mushy, frozen fish sticks.

Boating Sharks

Sharks are notoriously difficult to gaff because of their thick hides and tendency to twist and contort their bodies once impaled. Since sharks are poor eating and almost always contain excessive amounts of mercury, it's wise to release them at the boatside. For this purpose I either use wire cutters to cut the leader or long-handled forceps to remove the hook. When working near a shark's jaws, try to keep your hands behind and under the mouth so your fingers are out of harm's way.

There are occasions when a shark must be boated because it represents a hard-earned record. Unfortunately, gaffing will make the shark bleed and lose weight, which can mean the loss of a record. Since nets are too small for sharks, I've settled on another method: I pick them up by their tails and pectoral fins and then haul them into the boat by hand. This must be done quickly and smoothly to work well. It is *not* a technique I can recommend as safe. It is a dangerous way to do things, and I have been hurt bringing sharks into the boat this way. But I've been unable to develop a safer method. Sharks are unpredictable, and those that seem most docile can suddenly erupt into action when they are touched. You must always

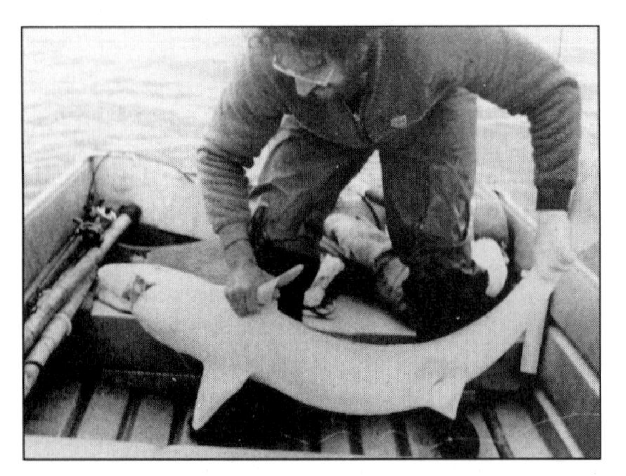

One way to bring a shark into the boat for tagging; it's much safer for the shark than it is for the angler.

be prepared to let go and renew the battle with rod and reel if the shark offers any resistance.

Sharks are even more hazardous than most people think—a few hundred needle-sharp teeth are not the only danger they pose. Their skins are thick and coarse like sandpaper. It takes only a second for a shark's skin to peel the flesh from your arms and deposit hundreds of tiny spicules that will cause irritation for weeks. If the skin doesn't get you, then the tail might. Men have been killed by the powerful tails of thresher sharks. Even if you haven't landed a thresher, watch out for that tail. I've spent several minutes rolling around the bottom of the boat, moaning with pain, after a shark had a go at turning my genitals into pancakes!

Here's a tale of misadventure that highlights how easily things can go wrong.

A Shark Tale

Dawn was still a half hour away as my wife, Liz, and I staggered around our trailered boat like zombies. We were getting ready for our last shark-fishing venture of the season. By the next week the tope would be back out in the open sea, far beyond the reach of our ultralight lines. Today would be our last chance.

Tope are a species of shark found worldwide. In the spring months the females school up and travel into shallow-water areas; no one really knows why, but come they do. In schools of 20 to several hundred, the sharks enter the harbors and take over the waters for a few days at a time.

In an isolated area in the Far North of New Zealand, Liz and I had found a place where the tope still existed in great numbers. It's a harbor called Parengarenga. The only people that live on this massive harbor are the indigenous Maoris, clustered in a tiny village on one of the harbor's five arms. Aside from that, there has been virtually no human impact on Parengarenga. It is stark and untamed, one of the last wilderness harbors left on Earth.

Liz and I had already accumulated a couple of dozen world records between us. We were certainly experienced ultralight anglers, but today was to be a new challenge. Liz was going to try to land a tope on 2-kg line, and I was now going to try to boat one of these sharks on 1-kg (hoping to get my first IGFA 20:1 Award).

As we loaded the delicate ultralight rods into the car, I was overcome by early-morning pessimism—it was absurd to fish for these sharks with such light gear. The idea of going back to bed suddenly seemed very appealing, but Liz jabbed me in the ribs and off we went.

During the drive we worked out our strategy. Knowing full well the odds were against us, we picked our fishing area very carefully. In our years of fishing the harbor, we had acquired a great deal of knowledge about its currents and configurations. Today we would go to a shallow channel about 5 miles (8 kilometers) up one of the harbor's arms. There, at high tide, the tope would gather as they prepared to head back to the sea with the receding tide.

Several things would be in our favor. The smooth, sandy bottom would be free of the obstructions that could easily cut our fragile lines. Far from the harbor mouth, the water moves more slowly and not at all for an hour around the tide change. This would make it possible for us to fish the bottom without any weights that could drag on the harbor floor and break our lines. We had chosen this early hour so we'd be done fishing before the winds came up. Any wind makes it impossible to control the boat precisely. And without perfect control over the boat, it is just too difficult to fight and land a fish 10 to 20 times heavier than the strength of the line.

Just as the sun rose above the horizon, we positioned the boat and started to chum heavily, throwing small chunks of fish frames upstream from the boat. Liz was to fish first with the 2-kg line. It would take me such a long time to land a shark on 1-kg gear that Liz's only chance would be to go before me.

It was only a few minutes after her bonito bait touched bottom that the first tope came along. Since Liz was already a veteran shark fisherwoman, she waited patiently as the tope nibbled and played with the bait. Finally, as the shark moved off steadily, Liz struck.

As you might expect, it is very difficult to set a hook with such light line; yet it is imperative that it be done properly. We had lost many sharks at the boat the past few weeks because the hook had simply fallen out of their mouths when we grabbed the leaders. This time, however, Liz struck too hard—the line snapped like sewing thread in the early-morning haze.

I was not happy but quietly tied on another 10-foot steel trace so Liz could try again. We were right on top of a huge school, and it was only seconds before the next strike. This time she failed to maintain adequate tension as the tope ran with the bait, and the line scraped along the bottom and broke again. After I delivered a brief but coarse lecture on maintaining proper line tension, Liz tried again. A minute later another tope came along, but the line tore on the bottom once more!

I was fit to be tied! After cursing and muttering for the 10 minutes it took me to prepare a new leader and change lines, I told her this was her last chance: If she didn't hook up properly this time, I would fish and she could wait. The tope weren't going to be there much longer. It was no time to get nervous and make mistakes. I didn't mention the fact that I was probably more anxious than she was, but Liz had been living with me a long time and knew my ultimatums and profanities were a sure indication of my apprehension.

Liz's next try was a beauty. She let the line run out so it never touched the bottom, yet did not hold it so tightly that the tope would drop the bait. She set the hook like a master. I dropped the anchor buoy overboard and started the engine as the drag on her spinning reel started singing its song. The hardest part was over. We were hooked up and running free. It was the beginning of another good fight.

As we pursued the shark around the harbor, Liz used her fingers on the reel spool to maintain a constant tension, while I ran the boat to keep us at the right distance and angle. It was only a matter of time until the shark surrendered to the unrelenting pressure; 40 minutes later I grabbed the tope by its fins and hauled it into the boat to give Liz her eleventh world record, a 35.9-pound (16.3-kg) tope on 2-kg line.

Now it was my turn. It was high tide, and the current flow was nil. The harbor surface was mirror-smooth and the anchor was right in the middle of a big school of sharks. Everything was just right. My palms were sweaty, and my mouth was dry. Fishing was supposed to be fun, and here I was—more nervous than a schoolboy on his first date.

Within a few seconds I had a tope on the line, but luck was not with me. Only five minutes after the hookup, a piece of weed touched my line a few feet below the surface and the 1-kg monofilament parted instantly. A few minutes later a new spool was on the spinning reel, and another tope was on the hook. Much to my dismay, yet another piece of weed touched the line in the first few minutes, and a second fish was lost! My curses and invocations could be heard for miles on the still waters. It was even worse when I lost a third tope to another piece of weed. It was unbelievable; I'd never even seen weed in Parengarenga before!

I put my last spool on the reel and threaded the 1-kg line through the guides of the delicate graphite rod. Then I attached the long steel leader and, still fuming, dropped the bonito bait into the still waters. Within minutes the razor-sharp hook was set, and we were off and running.

With the anchor dropped away and the engine roaring, we pursued the fleeing tope, trying desperately to quiet the screaming reel drag and recover line before the water pressure broke it. With my 5:1 reel, I quickly piled line back on the spool. Soon the boat sat less than 10 yards from the shark as it began the long run toward the open sea.

From then on it was simply a matter of accurately maintaining about a pound (450 grams) of pressure on the shark and anticipating its every move. From experience we knew that our best bet was not to let the tope take line at any time because the more the delicate line traveled over the guides and bail-roller, the faster it would wear. It was far wiser to use the boat and rod movements to shadow the shark and maintain maximum line strength. We followed doggedly as the shark twisted and turned in its attempts to be rid of this minor irritation. After about 3 miles (5 kilometers) the tope began to tire and came near enough to the surface for us to see it in the clear waters. Even from a distance, it was obvious the shark was big enough to set another world record, perhaps even 20 times heavier than my line strength.

It was getting hot. The sun was beating down, and the sweat was pouring off me as I worked to stay with the shark. As my excitement grew, my mouth felt drier and drier. We traveled another 4 miles (6 kilometers) in the next hour and a half, and I knew the line couldn't last much longer. Suddenly the 10-foot leader appeared on the surface as the shark rolled right next to the boat.

It was going to be the only chance, and I took it. Grabbing for the leader, I pulled the tired tope to the boatside and reached down and carefully gripped the pectoral fin. Just as my other hand reached for its tail, the shark made a last bid for freedom. Instead of letting go, my arms instinctively lunged over the side, and I grabbed the shark like a baby. We fell backward into the boat, the tope on top. Liz watched in amazement as the tope and I rolled around on the bottom of the boat. Finally *I* got on top and managed to stun the shark with a blow to the head. Once the shark was immobilized, there was enough time to reach for the club and finish the job.

I stood up in the boat, surveyed the carnage, and realized that the blood all over the deck was mine. The skin on my bare arms and legs looked like overcooked lasagna. Within a day my limbs had swollen up like party balloons. In a few seconds of contact, the shark's hide had scraped away a layer of skin on my arms and legs, depositing hordes of tiny spicules that inflamed my skin for a month. For the next few weeks my idea of fun was to sit in a chair with cool compresses around my arms and legs; but I had learned a lesson: The abrasiveness of a shark's skin is not to be ignored!

Left: Liz's 16.3-kg (35-pound, 14-ounce) tope, the 2-kg world record in 1985. The present record is 17.5 kg (38 pounds, 9 ounces).

Right: My 18.5-kg (40-pound, 11-ounce) tope, the 1-kg world record in 1985 and big enough for the IGFA's 20:1 Award. The present record is 22.3 kg (49 pounds, 2 ounces).

The shark tipped the scales at 41 pounds (18.5 kg). Since the line tested at about 750 grams (well below 2 pounds), I had my first 20:1 fish; and, yes, I got another world record. But I also paid for my obsession.

Potential Dangers

It's important that every angler be aware of the dangers of handling and eating fish. More than 2,000 species of sea animals can inflict a venomous bite or are poisonous to eat. Two thousand species are too many to cover in one chapter; instead of trying to do it all, I'll tell you about the most common problems and what you can do to avoid them. When you're away from home it's always wise to seek out local knowledge. If local people tell you not to eat or handle a species, just assume they're right. It's a good way to stay alive.

Punctures

All fish are equipped with sharp, protective spines that also serve as a framework to support fins or feelers. Some fish have evolved special poison glands associated with these spines. The most common are the marine catfishes found worldwide, the European weaverfish, the American scorpionfish, the entire family of puffers (blowfish), the tropical stonefish, the lion or zebrafish, and the well-known stingrays.

All of these species are relatively sedentary; their spines are strictly defensive weapons, to be used only when they are disturbed. Thus the best way to avoid being injured or killed is to leave them alone. Whenever you walk along a coral reef, be sure to wear thick-soled running shoes. Poisonous species of starfish, shellfish, and sea urchins live along these reefs; and the reefs, themselves, are actually poisonous. Their living corals, when disturbed, deposit toxic materials under the skin that can cause irritation and infection for months. It's a lot easier to avoid the injury than to have to deal with it later.

When you walk in shallow water where a stingray might be hiding, be careful where you step; experienced waders move slowly and slide their feel along the bottom. Stingrays have a habit of burying themselves under loose sand or mud. When they are disturbed, they whip their tails up into a defensive posture. If you happen to be in the way, the poison barb located midway along the tail will end up in your leg, and you will not be happy. If you hook a stingray and manage to get it near the boat, just cut it off and let it go. It's crazy to bring a dangerous animal like this into a small boat when it has such a potent weapon on its tail.

The first aid for these punctures is simple. If a spine is embedded in your skin, try to remove it without squeezing too hard or breaking it off. The forceps you have for extracting fish hooks are an excellent tool for removing poison spines. Once the spine and its attached poison sac are removed, soak the area in the hottest water you can tolerate (don't burn yourself) for at least an hour. The heat breaks down most marine poisons rapidly; it can save your life. Even if things go well and the heat relieves the pain, make sure you go to the nearest emergency room; delayed reactions are common and can be fatal.

Bites

The danger of bites from sharks and other fish with sharp teeth is obvious. But bites from certain other marine animals pose an even greater danger that is not obvious at all. Included in this category are the sea snakes and octopi.

Sea snakes are reptiles that live in warm waters throughout the world. Almost all these snakes are poisonous, and some are deadly. If you end up with a sea snake on your line, do not handle it and do not try to remove the hook. Just cut the line and stay out of the way.

Octopi are another story. There are plenty of confirmed tales from Australia of fatal bites from blue-ringed octopi that were allowed to come into contact with human skin. This species has modified salivary glands that secrete poison when the animal uses its beak to bite. Sometimes the fatal bite is painless, either because it's exceedingly shallow or because there are numbing agents in the poison. You'd have to know a lot about octopi to predict which octopus can kill you and which cannot. If you don't have local knowledge of these species, do not handle them, no matter how attractive they look or how tasty you hope they will be.

Tetanus

Tetanus is a nasty disease caused by a minute bacterium called *Clostridium tetani* that lives around decaying material. Once the bacteria get inside your body, they begin to secrete a deadly toxin. The poison circulates rapidly, and pretty soon the toxin causes involuntary muscle contractions. These spasms often begin around the jaw muscles, hence the term "lock-jaw."

You're much more likely to get tetanus from a dirty object, especially around a farm pond or estuary, than from the proverbial rusty nail. If you do get a wound while out fishing and it's been more than five years since your last tetanus shot, go see your doctor. The shot's no fun, but death from tetanus is a real bummer.

Mercury

Elemental mercury, that silver-colored stuff that's in thermometers, is often harmless. But when mercury compounds fall to the bottom of the sea, they are always dangerous. In the bottom silt, bacteria convert the mercury to methyl mercury, a deadly poison. The bacteria that create the poisonous forms of mercury are eaten by tiny, one-celled animals. The one-celled animals are eaten by plankton, and the plankton are eaten by tiny fish and shellfish. Step by step, the mercury is concentrated as it makes its way up the food chain. By the time a good-size snapper comes along and starts chewing on those shellfish, it receives a significant dose of methyl mercury with every bite. After a few years of eating contaminated shellfish, the snapper's flesh builds up toxic levels of mercury too.

When people come along and eat the snapper, they also eat the mercury. Like the fish, we concentrate the mercury in our tissues. Although we can excrete mercury at a slow rate, it tends to build up if we consume it faster than we get rid of it. People who live primarily on fish can accumulate mercury at an alarming rate. Children and fetuses have much more trouble with mercury than adults because mercury poisoning affects growing cells first.

As mercury accumulates, it creates more problems. At first it causes depression and mental slowness. Then numbness and tingling develop in the limbs. After that, people stagger around and become blinded. Finally, coma ensues, and death follows if you're lucky. If you're not lucky, you recover from the coma to spend the rest of your life with profound retardation and bizarre physical disabilities.

The most famous cases of mercury poisoning have occurred in industrial areas around Japan, where huge amounts of industrial mercury were dumped into local harbors. But mercury is also present in pristine waters like those around New Zealand. In those areas natural mercury is leached from the soil by rivers and hydrothermal activity, then dumped into the sea and freshwater lakes.

There are two easy ways to avoid mercury poisoning:

- Be aware of local warnings issued by health authorities. Most industrialized countries regularly test fish and seawater for toxic levels of mercury. They will usually know if things are getting out of hand.
- Don't eat old or large fish like swordfish, stingrays, any sharks, and large sea bass. Big fish have lived a long time and have had many years to accumulate mercury in their flesh. Young fish haven't, and they're tastier anyway. So let the big ones go and keep the little guys. It's good for the sea and good for you too.

PCBs and Dioxin

PCB stands for polychlorinated biphenyl. How's that for a mouthful? Well, it actually gets worse; polychlorinated biphenyls are part of a class of compounds called aromatic halogenated hydrocarbons. Another member of the group is tetrachlorodibenzo-p-dioxin, or dioxin for short. These compounds and others like them are exceedingly toxic to humans. They don't kill you the minute you eat them; their effects are far more subtle and insidious.

None of these compounds are natural. They have been created by humans—either intentionally, for industrial purposes, or unintentionally, as the by-products of chemical reactions. The aromatic halogenated hydrocarbons are virtually indestructible. They simply will not go away. They don't break down in the human body for the same reason they don't break down in the environment: Nothing will eat them. Instead of being altered by the body, they are stored in the fat and excreted in breast milk, where they float along with the fat in the milk.

When blood levels of these poisons get high enough, the first sign of poisoning is a horrendous case of acne called chloracne. The other effects of these everlasting chemicals are still being researched, but we know they cause cancer and suspect they also attack the immune system and the liver.

PCBs and dioxin have the same effects on fish that they have on humans. Fish pick up the stuff in their food and can't get rid of it. So older, larger fish that live near industrialized areas have high concentrations of aromatic halogenated hydrocarbons in their tissues. When you eat those fish, the poisons become part of your body, which is not a desirable state of affairs. The bottom line is the same as for mercury: pay attention to local health warnings, and don't eat old or large fish.

Ciguatera Poisoning

Here's a disease you may never have heard of but ought to know about. It is caused by a naturally occurring poison that accumulates in fish the same way mercury and PCBs do. The poison is produced by a microscopic organism called *Gambierdiscus toxicus* that lives almost exclusively near tropical coral reefs. The poison was discovered by the Spanish when they initially explored the Caribbean Sea. It affected Columbus and his crew and nearly killed Captain Bligh and his men after the mutiny on HMS *Bounty.*

Within a few hours of eating fish that have stored ciguatoxin, a person will experience nausea, vomiting, and profuse diarrhea. These are not unlike the initial effects of a variety of other food poisonings; but then ciguatera distinguishes itself by causing all sorts of nervous symptoms, including burning feet; tingling in the hands, feet, and face; the feeling of loose, painful teeth; dizziness; a staggering walk; hallucinations; the feeling that cold things are hot and vice versa; and, finally, coma and occasionally death. The nervous symptoms often disappear after two weeks but sometimes linger for months.

The poison is stored in the viscera and roe of fish, so don't eat those at any time of year. Fortunately, the organism that causes ciguatera is not present all year round, and the fish do clear the toxin after a period of time. But in some areas the situation is so bad that year-round bans are in effect on some species. For instance, it's illegal to serve barracuda in Southern Florida, and jack tuna over 25 pounds (12 kg) are always thrown back in Hawaii.

To prevent ciguatera, avoid eating all tropical fish during seasons of the year when the toxin is most concentrated. Usually the local people can tell you when to avoid fish completely. Fish that most often cause the disease are barracuda, sea bass, amberjack, snapper, jack tuna, and king mackerel. Just as with other biologically concentrated poisons, you should pay attention to public health warnings and eat only small, young fish. Since alcohol makes ciguatera much worse, avoid drinking alcohol with fish meals that are suspect.

Scromboid Poisoning

Now that I've ruined your taste for fish, I'd like to close this section with a disease you can actually prevent: scromboid poisoning. Scromboid is the result of not keeping dark-fleshed fish on ice. When the dark muscle is allowed to warm up, bacteria in the meat produce histamines that cause typical allergic reactions: flushed skin, diffuse itching, diarrhea, a throbbing headache, a fast heartbeat, and cramps. The longer the fish is in the sun, the more toxic it gets. If you put your fish on ice as soon as it's caught, you'll have no trouble with scromboid. The species you need to be most careful with are dorado (mahi mahi), bluefish, tuna, bonito, and mackerel.

Antihistamines, logically enough, block the effects of histamines from the fish and are a very effective treatment for scromboid. If you get sick, go to the nearest emergency room and tell the doctor what you think you've got.

Please Release Me, Let Me Go

Running rampant through the fishing literature, so that you'll find it virtually anywhere you care to look, is misinformation about the low survival rates for exhausted fish. It is said that fish die far more often when they fight for prolonged periods on light lines than when they are promptly boated and released. Believe what you want, but it just ain't that simple.

In many of the studies on the subject, experimental conditions invalidate the conclusions. The fish were kept in small tanks, had blood drawn, and were handled, held out of water, anaesthetized, and deprived of food. All these factors stress the fish, alter their natural hormone levels, and increase their mortality rates. Yet it is these flawed studies that gave rise to the notion that exhausted fish cannot survive release.

In general, a fish—no matter how tired—has the potential to recover, swim away within minutes, and stay alive. Lactic acidosis (a lack of oxygen), often cited as the cause of death in exhausted fish, is a natural part of any vigorous physical activity. Lactic acid is produced by living cells when they run out of oxygen, as black smoke is produced by a fire starved of air. Marathon runners, sprinters, rugby players, and particularly high-altitude mountaineers all get some degree of lactic acidosis. And lactic acid levels can increase a hundredfold when an athlete is stressed. But even when the acidosis is bad enough to stop a person cold, the muscles can function normally again in a few minutes as oxygen reaches them and the lactic acid burns up.

Fish are the same. They can burn up the lactic acid and recover completely if they can get enough oxygen and if they don't have any other injuries. If you want your fish to survive release, there are lots of things you can do to increase its chances.

How to Handle Fish

If you want to release your fish to fight another day, here are some things you can do to foster its survival:

- Handle the fish with care. Fish are soft-bodied; they are supported by the water around them, so their tissues are tender and unaccustomed to pressure variations. Grabbing them and squeezing tightly causes internal bleeding and organ damage that will kill them hours later.

  If you play a fish until it's exhausted, it will not struggle when you handle it; you can often remove the hook without taking the fish from the water, which is a real plus; and you can release the fish more quickly. This reduces the chances of internal injury.
- Wet your hands. Fish are covered by a layer of mucus that protects their skin from infection. Dry hands or rough handling will remove this protective layer and expose the fish to potentially fatal disease. Use smooth rubber gloves, a wet cloth, or wet hands to handle the fish.
- Use small, barbless hooks. Barbless hooks are much easier to remove from a fish and are far less likely to cause serious internal injury. And a hook with a small point is also less likely to produce lethal damage to a gut- or gill-hooked fish.

  A fish brought to the boatside with a barbless hook in its jaw can usually be released with a single flick of the hook shank—without ever being handled.
- Remove the hook. If the hook can be removed without causing the fish harm, it's worth doing. With forceps, even hooks that are deep down can be removed easily if they're barbless. Contrary to popular myth, hooks rust very slowly underwater, so they irritate the fish for several months if they're left in.

  Stainless steel hooks are the slowest to decompose, but they cause the least irritation. Bronzed hooks seem to kill fish because of toxins within the metal. So ordinary tinned hooks are probably the best compromise.

  For metal to rust, it must be exposed to high concentrations of oxygen. Since water contains relatively little oxygen, months or years can pass before a large hook breaks down. Fish will deposit tissue around the hook to wall it off, but this takes weeks. And if the hook is large and lodged in the gut, the fish may be unable to eat until the hook is encapsulated.

Nevertheless, it's worth the effort to release even gut- or gill-hooked fish because research has shown that many of these fish do survive. Any chance of survival is better than none.

- Resuscitate the fish. If the fish just lies belly up when released, it will need a little help to recover. Hold the fish loosely by the tail and body and move it, headfirst, through the water. The oxygen in the water will run over the fish's gills and revive him within a few minutes. When you feel the fish start to move, let him swim off on his own.
- Don't keep a fish out of the water. All around the gills are tiny filaments that float freely in the water. These filaments are like our lungs—they are the organs that enable a fish to absorb oxygen. When fish are brought out of the water, these filaments collapse into a soggy mess and can no longer take in oxygen.

A fish that's fatigued after a long fight and left on the deck too long will later die from lack of oxygen because its collapsed gill filaments no longer have the capacity to absorb the oxygen its body needs to burn up lactic acid. The trick is to remove the hook while the fish is still in the water. Pulling a fish out of the water after a struggle is like putting a plastic bag over the head of a person who's just run a marathon. It's not the fight that kills the fish; it's the lack of oxygen afterward.

Tagging

Tagging is a scientifically important and internationally respected procedure that benefits us all. Many countries throughout the world sponsor tagging programs through some central agency. In general, an angler tags a fish by sending a card to that agency. The card contains the agency's address and a tag number, and the angler fills in the date and place of capture, the estimated size and species of the fish, any injuries observed, and his or her own name and address.

If the fish is recaptured, the new angler records the tag number and sends a new card to the agency. With this information scientists can deter-

Tagging a small shark. Sharks survive this sort of abuse far better than pelagic fish.

mine how far the fish traveled, how fast it grew, how the tag affected it, and how it survived the trauma of capture.

By comparing the results of many tag returns, scientists can map migratory routes, determine population sizes, and define growth rates for various species. With this sort of information, intelligent decisions can be made on recreational and commercial fishing limits in various locations.

The International Game Fish Association (IGFA) publishes an updated list of tagging agencies in its yearbook every spring. The book also has a complete collection of world fishing records and several articles especially useful to sport anglers. You can get a copy from the IGFA, 1301 East Atlantic Boulevard, Pompano Beach, Florida 33060, USA.

There are many types of tags, and it's best to contact your local agency to find out which type is appropriate for the fish you pursue. Keep your hands wet when handling the fish, lay it on a moist foam pad, cover the eyes with a soft, wet cloth, and follow the proper procedure for inserting the tag. If you exercise care when placing the tag, the fish will survive to help you and your children enjoy better fishing in the future.

What Next?

Forty years ago people thought the resources of this planet were without limit. Anyone who suggested that the oceans could be fished to exhaustion was dismissed as just another prophet of doom. But now the unthinkable is actually happening. Giant purse seiners, pair-trawlers, longliners, factory ships, and—most destructive of all—hundreds of driftnetting vessels are rapidly depleting our oceans. Already the giant bluefin tuna is on the edge of commercial and recreational nonexistence and may be heading for biological extinction as well.

Though the bluefin is the first important gamefish to approach extinction, many others could follow. The twin forces of financial greed and political incompetence have combined to prevent effective management of our global fisheries. Even the world's greatest fishing ground, off the coast of eastern Canada, is now all but dead, a victim of the same mindless greed and incompetent management.

No matter where you travel on this planet—the frozen Antarctic barrens or the lush New Guinea rain forests—you find too many people chasing too few fish. The relentless exploitation of the sea must cease, or yet another resource will be lost to humankind. Without the active intervention of the world's recreational anglers, there is little chance that sport fishing will survive, as we have known it, into the twenty-first century.

Sharp cutbacks in the numbers of fish available to commercial interests will come sooner or later. But if we wait until the commercial fishery collapses, there will be nothing left for the rest of us either. If we act now, our children, and our children's children, may still have the opportunity to experience the joy of fishing.

Do what you can to help.

APPENDIX

Getting Your Name in "The Book"

CATCHING A WORLD RECORD requires a lot of luck and a little work. Part of the work is preparing your world-record claim so you can be in The Book—*World Record Game Fishes,* published each year by the International Game Fish Association (IGFA). The IGFA is the worldwide organization that updates and maintains all the international fishing records. The IGFA has representatives in most countries of the world, but its headquarters are in Florida in the United States.

It's nice to get your name in the record book. All it takes is a little patience and a lot of luck.

If you ever want to apply for a world record, you'll need to fill out the "IGFA World Record & Fishing Contest Application." The application form is in The Book and is also available from the IGFA at 1301 East Atlantic Boulevard, Pompano Beach, Florida 33060, USA.

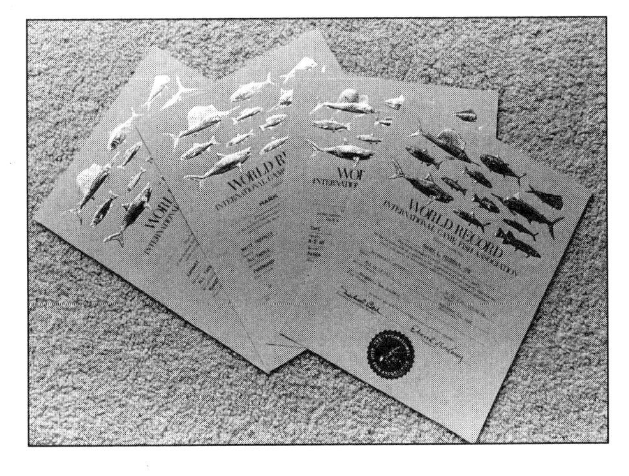

World records are kept for each major species of fish. They are divided into all-tackle records and line-class records. An all-tackle record is the largest fish of a species caught on any line. A line-class record is the largest fish of a species caught on a specific-strength line. The line classes important to ultralight anglers are l-kg, 2-kg, 3-kg, and 4-kg.

Each copy of The Book contains the complete set of rules. It's a smart move to get a copy of the rules before you set out to catch a world record; but if you can't wait, here's some basic information an ultralight angler can get started with.

- Do not attach your spool backing to the main line.
- In salt water a leader can be no longer than 15 feet (4.57 meters). In fresh water the limit is 6 feet (1.82 meters).
- The length of the rod butt may not exceed 27 inches (68.58 cm). (The rod butt runs from the center of the reel to the end of the butt.) The rod tip may not be under 40 inches (101.6 cm). (The rod tip runs from the center of the reel to the end of the tip.)
- No more than two single hooks may be used.
- Do not use swinging hooks. A swinging hook is one that dangles freely some distance from the bait or lure. See the accompanying drawing for details.

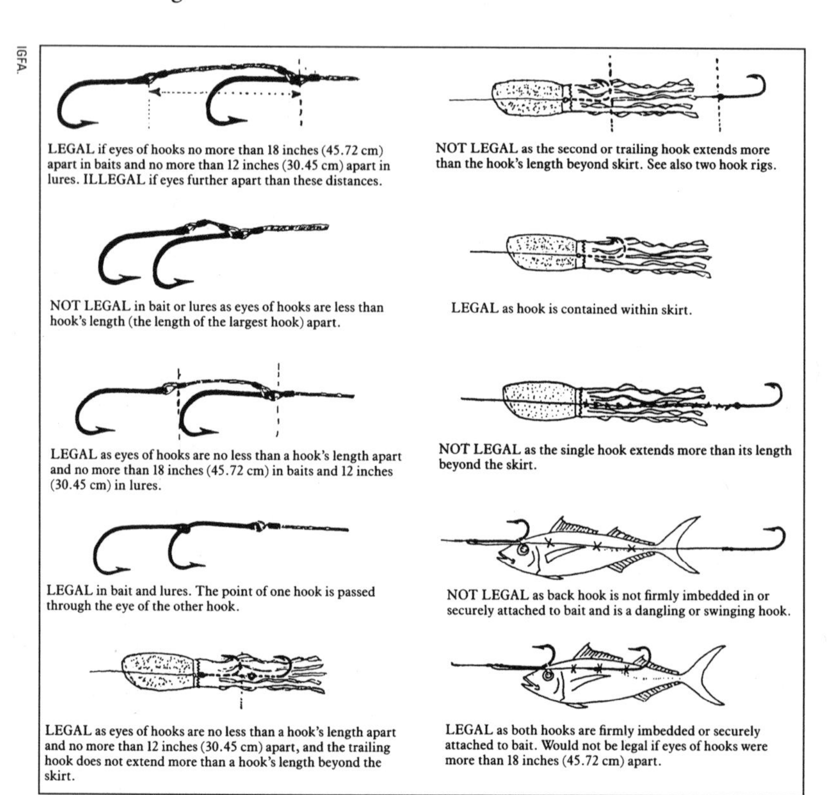

The IGFA single-hook rules.

- If you use a float, it must not hamper the fighting ability of the fish.
- No one may help you land the fish until it's close enough that the leader can be grabbed.
- No one may ever touch your main line until the fish is secured. If a piece of weed gets caught on the main line, someone may cut it free but may not touch the main line in the process.
- Chum or bait made from mammals is prohibited. The only exceptions are pork rind and hair for flies.
- It's always best to have the fish weighed by a disinterested party on a government-approved scale. The IGFA is usually pretty reasonable about this rule; they'll allow shop or wharf scales to be used. It's always best to have a weigh-master, but the IGFA usually accepts the application if the weight is confirmed by the signature of anyone familiar with the scale.
- It's a good idea to have the application signed by a witness to the catch and a witness to the weighing.
- To replace a previous record, a fish under 25 pounds (11.33 kg) must weigh at least 2 ounces (56.69 grams) more than the record weight. If your fish is over 25 pounds, then it must weigh ½ of 1% (.005) more than the record weight.
- For fish caught in the United States, the application must be in the IGFA office within 60 days. For fish caught anywhere else, you have three months.
- Your entire leader and 50 feet (15.24 meters) of the main line must be sent to the IGFA for testing. Wind the line and leader around something large to avoid tangles. I use pieces of corrugated cardboard about 8 inches (20 cm) long and 6 inches (15 cm) wide.
- You'll need photos of the fish hanging and lying flat next to a ruler. For sharks you'll also need a photo of the teeth and a view of the back taken from above. Also required are photos of the scale, and the rod and reel used to make the catch. You can meet most of the requirements with one photo of you with the rod and reel, standing next to the scale, while the fish hangs broadside from the scale.

Hope to see you in The Book!

Index

Note: Numbers in **boldface type** refer to illustrations that fall far from the text reference.

C

D

M

N

O

P

Q

R

S

Y

Z